LOVE OF GOD AND SOCIAL DUTY

IN THE RĀMCARITMĀNAS

Love of God and Social Duty in the Rāmcaritmānas

EDMOUR J. BABINEAU

MOTILAL BANARSIDASS
Delhi :: Varanasi :: Patna

Indological Publishers and Booksellers
Head Office : BUNGALOW ROAD, JAWAHAR NAGAR, DELHI-7
Branches : 1. CHOWK, VARANASI-1 (U.P.)
2. ASHOK RAJPATH, PATNA-4 (BIHAR)

ISBN 0-89684-050-6

First Edition : *Delhi*, 1979

Printed in India
BY SHANTILAL JAIN, AT SHRI JAINENDRA PRESS, A-45, PHASE-1, INDUSTRIAL AREA, NARAINA, NEW DELHI-28 AND PUBLISHED BY NARENDRA PRAKASH JAIN FOR MOTILAL BANARSIDASS, BUNGALOW ROAD, JAWAHAR NAGAR, DELHI-7

DEDICATED

To

THE TEACHING STAFF AND STUDENT-COLLEAGUES

Of The Department Of Religious Studies,

McMaster University, Hamilton, Ontario.

CONTENTS

ACKNOWLEDGEMENTS

I would like to express my gratitude to all those who contributed in any way to the success of this study. Among those, my thanks go first and foremost to Professor David Kinsley my chief advisor, whose promptitude in offering the needed help and guidance enabled me to work at a steady pace. I also want to thank Professors Paul Younger and John Hitchcock, whose interest in the subject of my thesis prompted them to offer stimulating suggestions and numerous criticisms, and to Professor Krishna Sivaraman, who was particularly helpful during the initial stages of my research.

To Mr. Braj Sinha and Mr. Kapil Nath Tiwari, fellow-students at McMaster University, my heartfelt appreciation for their assistance in translating Sanskrit texts. I also want to thank Professors Yvonne Chiasson and Charles Soong, for reading the first draft of this work and suggesting improvements in style and expression.

ABBREVIATIONS

V.R.	=	*Vālmiki Rāmāyaṇa*
A.R.	=	*Adhyātma Rāmāyaṇa*
H.L.A.R.	=	*Holy Lake of the Acts of Rāma* (*Rāmcaritmānas*)
B.P.	=	*Bhāgavata Purāṇa*

Introduction

THE *Rāmcaritmānas* is the most popular religious text of North India, and its excellence is generally acknowledged among Hindus of the whole sub-continent. In order to read it in proper perspective, it is important to bear in mind that it was meant to be a *rifacimento* of the *Vālmiki Rāmāyaṇa*, written approximately twenty centuries earlier. That is, in rewriting the story of Rāma, Tulsī Dās felt free to make a number of alterations allowing him to present his own religious views and inclinations.

The most consequential change that Tulsī Dās introduced in his new version of the *Rāmāyaṇa* is the importance given to the interaction of love of God and social duty. It will be argued in this study that the attempt to relate these two competing claims is shown in the *Rāmcaritmānas* to result in a state of tension in the sense that the intensity of the devotee's love of God causes a dilemma *vis-à-vis* his obligation to perform his normal social duties: whether to endure physical separation from the Lord in order to fulfill his obligation, or to abandon his duties in order to follow the Lord more closely.

Rather than using the *Rāmcaritmānas* as an illustration of any particular theory on social causality, this study will attempt to attain a clearer insight into the problem of relating love of God and social duty as it arose from Tulsī Dās' own consciousness. In order to do so, an effort will be made in Part I to present the available information on his life and work, thus highlighting his importance in the history of medieval North India.

In the historical section, which forms the second part of this book, we shall attempt to understand how Tulsī Dās might have sought to situate his position in terms of the Hindu tradition, to which he repeatedly claims his own indebtedness throughout the *Rāmacaritmānas*. It will be argued that as he looked back, he could discern, on the question of the tension between love of God and social duty, at least three main alternatives expressed with various emphases at different periods. A first alternative gave priority to the claims and salvific rôle of social duty to the point of either totally subordinating or denying the rôle of love of God. Another alternative stressed the priority of love of God while neglecting the value of social duty. A third alternative, which for the sake of convenience will be referred to as the "middle position", held that love of God was not inconsistent with the performance of social duty. Tulsī Dās' understanding of these alternatives led him to choose the third in his attempt to formulate a solution which would emphasize love of God while at the same time insisting as much as he could that social duties were important.

The present work then studies to what extent Tulsī Dās' perception of this problem might have been affected by his environment. It will be shown that the immediate context could be viewed as a challenge to Tulsī Dās, that his *magnum opus* may be considered as a response to this challenge, and that his response revived the "middle" alternative. This section is not meant to establish that Tulsī Dās was socially conditioned in his response, nor to show that the impact of his views followed any particular sociological pattern. Rather, it is meant to explain how he chose to meet the challenge of his day on the basis of his own religious inclinations, and in what sense his response could have fulfilled the expectations of his immediate hearers.

The final section of the book is devoted to exegesis of the *Rāmcaritmānas*, aimed at illustrating Tulsī Dās' understanding of love of God and social duty. In the final chapter, it will be held that in dealing with the tension between love of God and social duty Tulsī Dās formulated a balance which was new in the Rāmāyaṇic tradition of North India, and which is one of the most important solutions to this perennial problem of religious mysticism.

The English phrases "love of God" and "social duty" will be used throughout this study in preference to Sanskrit equivalents such as *bhakti* and *dharma*, partly because the latter are frequently used with differing connotations and partly because the *Rāmcaritmānas*, along with other sources, uses a variety of terms to designate these concepts. The expression "love of God" is taken here in a broad sense so that it may include the various forms of affectionate attachment to the Divine, which Tulsī Dās describes using such terms as *bhakti*, *prema*, *saneha*, *prīti*, *bhāva*, and *rati*.[1] The expression "social duty" is used here to designate the obligations associated with the status of the householder, and transmitted by the oral or the written tradition. Social duty is usually referred to in the *Rāmcaritmānas* as *dharma*, *nīti* or *karma*.[2]

1. Thus, Bharata, who is shown affectionately clasping Rāma's feet is described as "overpowered by love (*prema*)" and promises Rāma he will serve him "with sincere devotion (*saneha*)". At the sight of such a touching scene, Rāma and the assembly of saints and sages praise his "greatness of devotion (*bhagati*)". (*Rāmcaritmānas*, II. Caupāī 301—Chanda 12, pp. 283—284. The quotations from the *Rāmcaritmānas* are taken from W.D.P. Hill's translation: *Holy Lake of the Acts of Rāma*. Henceforward, this translation will be referred to as *H.L.A.R.* Likewise, *caupāīs* will be referred to as C.; *chandas*, as Ch.; *dohās*, as D.; *sorațhās*, as S.; and *ślokas* as Ś). Likewise, after describing Bharata placing on his eyes the dust of Rāma's footprints, Tulsī Dās praises such "exceeding love (*prītī*) which no tongue can tell." (*Ibid.*, II. D. 198, p. 241.) In the same vein, the sage Bharadvāja's love (*bhāva*) and devotion (*bhakti*) fills Rāma with joy. (*Ibid.*, II. C. 108, p. 205). Finally, the sage Vālmīki praises those who "demand but one reward, devotion (*rati*) to the feet of Rāma". (*Ibid.*, II. D. 129, p. 214.)

2. Thus, Rāma's mother declares that if she keeps her son from going to the forest "(I) shall not have done (my) duty (*dharma*)". (*Ibid.*, II. C. 55, p. 184.) Likewise, Rāma orders Lakṣmaṇa to stay at Ayodhyā "and regard this as your duty (*nīti*)". (*Ibid.*, II. C. 71, p. 190.) Finally, Rāma instructs Lakṣmaṇa about "careful attention to one's own special duty (*karma*)", as a method of faith. (*Ibid.*, III. C. 15, p. 305.)

Part One
Life and Work of Tulsi Das

Part One

Life and Works of [illegible]

Chapter I

Life of Tulsi Das

THE biographical sources for a life of Tulsī Dās are abundant, although much of the available material is not considered reliable. First, we shall examine the autobiographical indications generally considered authentic. Then, we shall examine the early biographical accounts of Tulsī Dās, particularly the *Gautamacandrikā* and the *Bhakta Mālā*. Finally, we shall try to ascertain, from both the legendary material and the research of modern scholars, the central events of Tulsī Dās' life.

1. *Autobiographical indications*

Although Tulsī Dās frequently refers to his personal life, particularly in the *Vinaya-patrikā*, such disclosures are meant to confess his sinful condition, to proclaim his utter dependence on Rāma, or to deplore his physical ailments. When he does make allusions to particular events in his life, their meaning is not always clear.

In a section of *Kavitāvali*, which he wrote in his later years, Tulsī Dās writes this concerning his earlier childhood :

> His father and mother brought him into the world and abandoned him,
> Destiny has written nothing good upon his forehead,
> He was low, a vessel for disrespect, a coward who was glad to get even the scraps thrown out for dogs.[1]

The interpretation generally given of this passage is that the poet was born on an inauspicious day, and as a result his parents felt obliged to disown their new born baby as an impure and untouchable child. Such an interpretation is corroborated by another statement found in *Vinaya-patrikā* :

---

1. *Kavitāvalī*, VII. 57. (The passages quoted from the Kavitāvalī are taken from F. R. Allchin's translation: Allchin, F. R. *Kavitāvalī*.

And as the wretched snake casts off its
slough, so did my father and mother
abandon me...
They feared even to touch my shadow
such was my misfortune.[2]

According to the current interpretation of those passages,[3] the child was born at the ill-omened conjunction of two asterisms where astrological indications recommended that he be abandoned. If this explanation is correct it may account for the "anguish and remorse" of his parents alluded to in *Kavitāvalī* VII. 73 :

I was born in a family of beggars,
when the band played in celebration,
My father and mother hearing felt
anguish and remorse.

About his childhood, Tulsī Dās makes only one reference indicating that he was rescued by *sants*, i.e. believers of Rāma :

I told my poverty at every door,
I gnashed my teeth and fell at feet,
till some holy men (sants) saw my
misery and said:
Sorrow no more, Rāma is the refuge
of wretches.[4]

On the basis of a passage in the opening lines of the *Rāmcaritmānas*, it is usually thought that Tulsī Dās was adopted by a *Rāmānandī guru*[5] named Narahari :

---

2. *Vinaya-patrikā*, 275. (The passages quoted from the *Vinaya patrikā* are taken from Allchin's translation: Allchin, F. R. *The Petition to Ram.*

3. This interpretation, shared by such scholars as W. D. P. Hill and F.R. Allchin, is based on the *Gautamacandrikā*, which claims A.D. 1624 as its date of composition.

4. *Vinaya-patrikā*, 275; see also 277.2.

5. Hill, W. D. P. *op. cit.* There are several saints mentioned in the *Bhakta Mālā* bearing the name Narahari. The *Rāmānandī* referred to above could be the disciple of either Ananta Deva or of his disciple Śrī Raṅga, who are both spiritual descendants of Rāmānanda. But there are other possibilities. See Allchin, F. R. *Kavitāvalī*, pp. 34-35.

I do homage to the lotus-feet of my guru,
Ocean of grace, Nara-rūpa Hari.[6]

It is probably from his *guru* that he received the name Tulsī Dās, since in *Kavitāvali* VII.100 he claims that his name is Rāma Bolā. No indications are given, however, as to Tulsī Dās' age when this change of name might have occurred.

According to the *Gautamacandrikā*,[7] whose author, Kṛṣṇa Datta, was a contemporary of Tulsī Dās, Narahari Dās lived on the banks of the river Narmadā and at Śūkarakheta. This is confirmed by the information given in the *Rāmcaritmānas* that, as a child, Tulsī Dās heard from his *guru* at Śūkarakheṭa[8] the story of Rāma, which because of his tender age he was at first unable to understand. He may also have been initiated early to the other works which he admits using as sources of the *Rāmcaritmānas*, such as the *Purāṇas*, particularly the *Bhāgavata Purāṇa*, and other sources which I shall try to identify in a later section of this dissertation.[9] Additional information may be obtained on this point from another work which has been recently established as one of Tulsī Dās' earlier works, namely the *Jñānadipikā*.[10] The colophons of this text give either direct or indirect references to the *Mahābhārata*, the *Bhāgavata Purāṇa*, and the *Yoga Vāsiṣṭha*, with which we may assume Tulsī Dās was familiar from a rather early age.

Tulsī Dās makes a few allusions to what may have been either his marriage or some love adventure. The following is typical :

In childhood, my mind went straight to Rāma
And taking Rāma's name I begged and ate the scraps;
but then I fell into the ways of the world.[11]

Of the middle years of his life, Tulsī Dās says next to nothing. His earliest clearly dated poem is the *Rāmājñāpraśna*, composed in *Saṃvat* 1621 (A.D. 1564). The poem also mentions the name

6. *H. L. A. R.*, I, śloka 1, p. 2. (Henceforward, *ślokas* will be referred to as S.)

7. For more information on the *Gautamacandrikā*, see infra, pp. 10 ff.

8. *H. L. A. R.*, I, D. 30a, p. 20.

9. See infra.

10. See Allchin, F. R. *Kavitāvalī*, introduction.

11. *Hanumān Bāhuka*, 40, quoted by Allchin, F. R. *Kavitāvali*, p. 35.

of Gangā Rām who was, according to the *Gautamacandrikā*, a resident of Benares and a personal friend of Tulsī Dās.[12] According to a recently discovered manuscript of the *Jñānadīpikā*, the latter was also composed in *Saṁavat* 1621.[13]

Tulsī Dās is very specific in revealing the date when he began to write his most famous work, the *Rāmcaritmānas*, at Ayodhyā:

> In the Samvat year of sixteen hundred
> and thirty-one (A.D. 1574), I lay my head
> on Hari's feet and write the story; on
> Tuesday, the ninth day of the month of
> Caita, in the city of Avadh, I begin
> the story of his acts.[14]

The next date considered reliable is the date of a short poem written by Tulsī Dās the *Pārvati Maṅgala*, written in *Saṁvat* 1643 (A.D. 1586).

Finally, frequent allusions are made in *Vinaya-Patrikā* and *Kavitāvalī* to his broken health and to a calamity, and these are generally associated with the pestilence that raged in Banāras in A.D. 1616:

> Home of the Goddess and the God, the Ganges,
> dwelling-place of saints and excellent sagas,
> Wiping away at a glance the ill-fates
> written on the foreheads of the evil.
> Tulsī makes lamentation, O compassionate Rām,
> Such is the sad condition of Kāśī
> brought about by the terrible Dark Age.[15]

2. *Biographical Notes from the Gautamacandrikā*

The information just gleaned from Tulsī Dās' own works is probably the most reliable biographical material that is available.

Among the contemporary or near-contemporary sources, perhaps the most useful and the closest to Tulsī Dās' time, since

12. See Allchin, F. R. *Kavitāvalī*, p. 37.
13. *Ibid.*
14. *H. L. A. R.*, I, caupāi 34, p. 22. (Hence-forward caupāis will be refered to as C.)
15. *Kavitāvalī*, 182.

it claims *Saṁvat* 1681 (A.D. 1624) as the year of its composition, is the *Gautamacandrikā*, written by one Kṛṣṇa Datta, already mentioned above.

The latter supports the views that Tulsī Dās was born in *Saṁvat* 1600 (A.D. 1543), that he was born at the ill-omened conjunction of two asterisms, at an hour when parents were advised to abandon their child, and that the poet's *guru* was, as already pointed out, Narahari Dās, of the *Śāṇḍilya gotra*, who resided on the banks of the river Narmadā and at Sūkarakheṭa.

The *Gautamacandrikā* also relates that its author, Kṛṣṇa Datta, met Tulsī Dās for the first time while he was paying a visit to his own *guru* at Banāras. On that occasion, we are told that Tulsī Dās related in tears how he had come from Ayodhyā and had stayed on the banks of the Jamunā, where he had been struck by "the arrow of the love god".

The *Gautamacandrikā* also indicates that upon the invitation of Kṛṣṇa Datta's *guru*, Tulsī Dās sang a new hymn to Viṣṇu in front of an audience of enraptured *sādhus* gathered at the *guru*'s house. The work also describes Gangā Rāma, already referred to, as a *parama satsaṅgi*, a member of a pious group which probably included Tulsi Das as well. It also mentions one Toḍar Mal who knew Tulsī Dās, and for whose family, according to a document of A.D. 1612, the latter is known to have acted as arbitrator. What is significant here is that the same Toḍar Mal is mentioned in a list of some twenty persons, which would give support to the view that the latter may have been the company of saints so frequently mentioned by Tulsī Dās. The verification of such a hypothesis would be particularly revealing of Tulsī Dās' practical attitude towards the lower-class devotees as, according to indications given in the same document, the group is composed of a majority of low-castes, even outcastes, and one Muslim named "Mīr, the Muslim minstrel."

The *Gautamacandrikā* informs us that when Tulsī Dās was twenty years old, he went with other members of his group on a pilgrimage which lasted over ten years and which took him to the very places where many of the incidents related in the *Rāmāyaṇa* are said to have occurred. According to this account, Tulsī Dās interrupted his pilgrimage when he was thirty years old, in order to spend time writing the *Rāmcaritmānas* at Ayodhyā.

He continued writing most of the following year while pursuing his pilgrimage, which finally ended in Banāras.

The *Gautamacandrikā* goes on to describe the enthusiasm which was aroused by Tulsī Dās' masterpiece, which attracted pilgrims from all directions, and prompted admirers to compare its author to Mount Sumeru. Kṛṣṇa Datta also speaks of Nābhā who wrote the *Bhakta Mālā*, which would imply that the latter, who speaks of Tulsī Dās in Chapter 129 of his poem, was also his contemporary.

Of Tulsī Dās' final years, the *Gautamacandrikā* speaks of the effect produced on him by Toḍar's death, and the quarrel which arose among the latter's heirs and which Tulsī Dās was called upon to arbitrate. It also speaks about Tulsī Dās' failing health, restored through the intercession of Hanumān, and about the great pestilence which ravaged Benares in 1616. Finally, it gives the year Saṁvat 1680 (A.D. 1623) as the year of Tulsī Dās' death, adding that the poet's ashes were deposited in the Gaṅgā. Because of the early date of the *Gautamacandrikā* and the way in which most of its information fits in with the impression one could gather from Tulsī Dās' works, we may consider this source to be generally reliable.

3. *Biographical Notes from other Sources*

a) The *Bhakta Mālā*

Although the *Bhakta Mālā* is often considered unreliable, its author Nābhā Dās, seems to have been a contemporary of Tulsī Dās and there may be some foundation for the information he offers us.

We have already seen that the identification of Tulsī Dās' *guru* has been made difficult by the fact that in the *Bhakta Mālā* several saints are referred to by the name Narahari.

The verse in Chapter 129 already referred to above, which proclaims Tulsī Dās' fame, is corroborated by a statement in the *Kavitāvali*,[16] where it is said that the world likens the author of the *Rāmcaritmānas* to Vālmīki, and by a passage of the *Vinaya-patrikā*,[17] where Tulsī Dās admits that before becoming pre-

16. *Ibid.*, VII, 72.
17. *Vinaya-patrikā*, 35.

sumptuous he had been respected. Here is what Nābhā Dās writes concerning Tulsī Dās :

> For the salvation of being in this perverse Dark Age Vālmīki has become Tulsī;
> In the former Tretā age he made the thousand million verses of the *Rāmāyaṇa*
> Of which but one letter can redeem even a man who has slain a Brāhmaṇ.
> Now he has again published abroad God's many wonders as a comfort for all devotees,
> And intoxicated with the love of Rāma's feet he repeats his Name both night and day according to his vow.
> Thus he has secured an easily accessible boat for crossing the boundless ocean of existence;
> For the salvation of beings in this perverse Dark Age Vālmīki has become Tulsī.[18]

As this dissertation progresses, it will be our duty to verify the truth of the refrain repeated by Nābhā Dās in the poem just quoted : "Vālmīki has become Tulsī."

b) *The Commentary on Bhakta Mālā*

Many popular legends are also contained in Priyā Dās' commentary on the *Bhakta Mālā*, which is dated A.D. 1722, but these are now generally considered unreliable.[19]

c) *Rāmū Dvivedī's Commentary on the Rāmcaritmānas*

Sometime before Saṁvat 1662 (A.D. 1606), a disciple of Tulsī Dās, named Rāmū Dvivedī wrote a commentary on the *Rāmcaritmānas* which contains an interesting verse considered descriptive of his master :

> He is fair skinned, when he hears even the syllable "Rā" his flesh thrills and his hair stands on end; on his breast is a necklace of Tulsī beads; he wears a loin-

18. Quoted by F. R. Allchin, *Kavitāvalī*, p. 40.
19. W. D. P. Hill gives examples of such legends in his introduction to the translation of the *Rāmcaritmānas*, pp. xi-xiii.

cloth and time on time in a deep voice he repeats the line "Then Bharat stood".[20]

The above material reveals very little concerning the date and place of Tulsī Dās' birth, his parentage, and his marriage. In the absence of solid information on these facets of Tulsī Dās' life, a number of legends have developed. Modern scholars have sorted through these legends and ventured a certain number of opinions on these questions, of which the most important will now be presented.

4. *The Date of Tulsī Dās' Birth*

Modern scholars are far from having reached a consensus on this question. Atkins has suggested 1523 or 1527;[21] scholars Hill and Vaudeville have accepted Grierson's suggested date of 1532;[22] while Allchin has accepted Wilson's and Blumhardt's date of 1543.[23] This last date seems most probable, as it is confirmed by the *Gautamacandrikā* referred to previously.

5. *The Place of Tulsī Dās' Birth*

According to a popular tradition, Tulsī Dās was born at Rājapūr in the Banda district.[24] However, others have suggested either Hājīpūr, near Citrakūṭa, Tārī in the Doab, Śūkarakheṭa or Ayodhyā in the Faizabad district, or Soron in the Etah district.[25] The arguments for these other alternatives are largely conjectural and there seems to be no major reason to doubt the popular tradition.

6. *Tulsī Dās' Parentage*

Popular tradition again holds that Tulsī Dās was a Dūbe of the *Parāśara gotra* of the *Sarayūpāriṇa Brāhmans.* According to

20. Allchin, F. R. *Kavitāvalī*, p. 41.
21. *The Rāmāyaṇa of Tulsī Dās*, Trans. A. G. Atkins. introductory notes.
22. Grierson, G. "Notes on Tulsi Dās", *Indian Antiquary* XXII, 1893, pp. 264-74.
23. Allchin, F. R. *Kavitāvalī*, p. 33.
24. Hill, W. D. P. *op. cit.*, p. ix.
25. For a closer look at these views, see Gupta, M. *Gosvami Tulsī Dās*, pp. 108-111; see also Growse's introductory notes to his translation of the *Rāmcaritmānas*: *The Rāmāyaṇa of Tulsī Dās*, Trans. F. S. Growse.

the *Bhakt-Sindhu*, a modern poem,[26] his father, Ātmā Rāma Dūbe, is said to have been the headman of a village on the Jumna River in the Bandā district. The poem adds that his mother's name was Hulasī.

7. *Tulsi Dās' Marriage*

According to a widespread tradition, much of which is based on the *Bhakta Mālā*,[27] Tulsī Dās was married to the daughter of Dīnabandhu Pāṭhak called Ratnāvalī, and the couple's only son, Tāraka, died in infancy.

The story goes that one day, Ratnāvalī decided to visit her father. Unable to bear the pain of separation, Tulsī Dās hurriedly caught up with her, only to hear her disapproving words to the effect that no one but Rāma deserved such devotion and attachment:

> Are you not ashamed of following me here?
> A curse on such love!
> What can I say to you, my husband?
> My body is nothing but bone and skin;
> and if such love you have for it
> had been devoted to the Lord Rāma,
> you would have no reason to dread rebirth.[28]

The reprimand had such a profound effect on the poet that he abandoned his family ties shortly after, and returned to Banāras, where he became an ascetic votary to Rāma.

It seems clear that the author of the *Rāmcaritmānas* was reared from childhood in the cult of Rāma, whose glory he sang until his death. It also seems clear that his *rifacimento* of the *Rāmāyaṇa* won him immediate recognition, thus prompting Tulsī Dās' admirers to liken him during his lifetime to Vālmīki himself.

26. According to Growse the *Bhakt-Sindhu* is a poem of no great authority; see introductory notes to his translation of the *Rāmcaritmānas*.

27. See F.S. Growse's introduction to his translation of the *Rāmcaritmānas*.

28. Quoted by Hill, W. D. P. *op. cit.*, p. x.

Chapter II

Works of Tulsi Das

THE study of the works of Tulsī Dās presents two special difficulties: one, the fact that many poems traditionally attributed to him are no longer considered as authentic, and the other that most of his works cannot be dated.

The first important discussion of Tulsī Dās' works in Western literature was done at the end of the last century by Sir George Grierson in a long article entitled "Notes on Tulsī Dās," published in 1893 in *Indian Antiquary*. Most of Grierson's views were accepted by W. Douglas P. Hill, who in 1952 reexamined his list in the introduction to his translation of the *Rāmcaritmānas*. Additional light was also thrown on this question in 1964 by Professor F. R. Allchin who, in the introduction to his translation of the *Kavitāvalī*, offered a critical analysis of all Tulsī Dās' works. I have found no grounds for disagreement with Allchin's conclusions.

There can be no doubt that Tulsī Dās' *magnum opus* is the *Rāmcaritmānas*, whose date is clearly given by the author himself as *Saṁvat* 1621 (A.D. 1574). We have good reason to believe that it was completed the following year, on the basis of the information given by the *Gautamacandrikā*, referred to in the preceding chapter.

Next in importance rank the *Vinaya-patrikā* and the *Kavitāvalī*. Although both are undated, frequent references to the poet's broken health and to the pestilence of A.D. 1616 suggest that the poems were written in the last twenty years of his life. These two long-poems reveal in a striking manner the aging poet's ever-increasing love for Rāma.

The next work whose authenticity is undisputed and which is clearly dated is the *Pārvatī Maṅgala*. Written in *Saṁvat* 1643 (A.D. 1586), this poem deals with the marriage of Śiva and Pārvatī.

On the basis of a manuscript recently come to light, we may now consider the poem *Jñānadīpikā* as authentic and accept the date *Saṁvat* 1621 (A.D. 1564) given in the manuscript as reliable. We have already seen that the colophons of this text supply important informations concerning the author's religious education.

Although Grierson gives Sunday, 4 June 1598 A.D. as the date of composition of the *Rāmājñāpraśna,* Allchin affirms that the date given is in reality *Saṁvat* 1621 (A.D. 1564). The seven chapters of this work, whose authenticity has not been questioned, give a summary of the corresponding seven books of the *Rāmāyaṇa,* and contain *dohās* meant to serve in the prediction of omens.

On the basis of its immaturity of style, the undated short poem *Rāmalalā Nahchū,* which deals with Rāma's investiture with the sacred thread, is considered to be one of the earliest, if not the very earliest of Tulsī Dās' poems. Likewise, because the undated *Vairāgya Sandipinī,* another short poem dealing with the nature of the real *sant,* reveals less poetical talent than the *Rāmcaritmānas,* it is considered chronologically earlier than the latter.

The undated *Gitāvalī,* which Tulsī Dās is believed to have written after a meeting with Sūr Dās, contains sonnets dealing with the story of Rāma. Allchin places it around the end of the sixteenth century.

The *Jānakī Maṅgala,* which describes the celebration of the marriage of Sītā and Rāma and which betrays the influence of the *Adhyātma Rāmāyaṇa* is considered earlier than the *Rāmcaritmānas,* although no precise date has been suggested.

Professor Allchin also includes in the list of works attributable to Tulsī Dās four other undated poems whose authenticity has been questioned by earlier scholarship.

The first poem, *Kṛṣṇa Gitāvalī,* is dated prior to A.D. 1605, on the basis of a reference to it in the *Prema Rāmāyaṇa* of Rāmu Dvivedī, written in that year. As the title indicates, this poem deals with Kṛṣṇa rather than Rāma. This factor, coupled with a difference of style, arouses suspicion concerning its authenticity.

The second poem, *Satsai* is belived by certain scholars like Grierson to be partly attributable to a later Tulsī Dās; contrary to the other works of the author of the *Rāmcartimānas,* it gives a systematic account of its author's religious belief. According to Allchin, the poem is dated *Saṁvat* 1642 (A.D. 1585).

Finally, the third and fourth poems, the *Hanumān Bāhuka* and the *Dohāvalī*, both discarded by Hill, are accepted by Allchin as authentic and placed among Tulsī Dās' latest works on the basis of frequent references in both to the author's failing health and to the pestilence of A.D. 1616.

By way of summary, the following list of the fourteen works accepted as authentic by Allchin will now be given in the chronological order suggested by the same scholar:

1. *Rāmalalā Nahchū*, undated but shows immaturities of style and of content.
2. *Rāmājñā-praśna*, dated Samvat 1621 (A.D. 1564).
3. *Jñānadīpikā*, dated Samvat 1621 (A.D. 1564) in a new manuscript recently come to light.
4. *Vairāgya Sandīpinī*, undated, but reveals less talent than the *Rāmcaritmānas*.
5. *Jānakī Maṅgala*, undated, shows influence of the *Adhyātma Rāmāyaṇa*.
6. *Rāmcaritmānas*, dated Samvat 1631 (A.D. 1574).
7. *Satsai*, dated Samvat 1642 (A.D. 1585).
8. *Pārvatī Maṅgala*, dated Samvat 1643 (A.D. 1586).
9. *Gītāvalī* (also known as *Padāvalī Rāmāyaṇa*), undated.
10. *Kṛṣṇa Gītāvalī*, undated, but written before A.D. 1605, for Rāmū Dvivedī refers to it in his *Prema Rāmāyaṇa*, which was written in that year; a collection of songs on Kṛṣṇa.
11. *Vinaya-patrikā*
12. *Kavitāvalī*
13. *Hanumān Bāhuka*
14. *Dohāvalī*

} undated, but frequent references to Tulsī Dās' broken health and to the pestilence of A.D. 1616 suggest the last twenty years of his life.

The list given by W. D. P. Hill, in his introduction to the translation of the *Rāmcaritmānas* corresponds roughly to the above, with the addition of the undated *Baravai Rāmāyaṇa*, which he claims is accepted by most scholars, and with the omission of the *Jñāna-dīpikā* and the *Dohāvalī*.

He furthermore gives a list of nine works, including the

Hanumān-bāhuka, which are given by the *Śivasiṁhasaroja*, but which he considers as probably spurious.

Apart from the *Rāmcaritmānas*, the *Vinaya-patrikā* and the *Kavitāvali*, it is unfortunate that most of the works attributed to Tulsī Dās still remain to be translated in modern European languages. We may also deplore the fact that modern scholarship, both Eastern and Western, has given too little attention to the works of Tulsī Dās, including the *Rāmcaritmānas*, the *Vinaya-patrikā*, and *Kavitāvali*.

It is hoped that the study made in Part two of this book dealing with the immediate context which Tulsī Dās lived in, will throw additional light on both the man and his work.

Part Two
The Tradition

Chapter III

The Historical Background

THE currents of Indian thought have altered from age to age, from community to community. Because of the ease with which Hinduism has absorbed throughout the ages the beliefs and rituals of peoples with whom it came into contact, it is difficult to find distinctive features capable of binding together its different forms. As one looks for common denominators one is confronted by the difficulty of blending, for instance, the Vedic and the non-Vedic, or the literary and the non-literary traditions. As the total tradition developed, however, there seem to emerge general emphases which by medieval times had worked themselves into distinct streams. Even though these streams do not form an established set of patterns used to characterize the tradition's self-understanding, they are nevertheless helpful in situating Tulsī Dās' position regarding the relation between love of God and social duty.

One of these streams might be defined as "Vedic Orthodoxy", which gives a low place to love of God and relies heavily on traditional regulations to define behaviour in terms of duty. A second stream might be seen as "Antinomian Theism", which considers love of God as an end in itself to the point of dismissing traditional regulations. Between these two conflicting currents stands "Orthodox Theism" in which there is a conscious attempt to integrate love of God and social duty in such a way that social and domestic life is maintained.

1. *Vedic Orthodoxy*

Vedic orthodoxy, as it is viewed here, is that model of religious behaviour which gives a preeminent place to traditional regulations, rather than to love of God, as the guiding principle of man's behaviour. In many aspects of the Hindu tradition, to be a Hindu is essentially to undertake faithfully one's individual duty (*sva-dharma*) and thereby to contribute to the ordering of the world (*loka-saṅgraha*). Chaos impinges on society precisely when caste duties and family obligations are not fulfilled. Such insistence on the fundamental necessity for social and domestic order is persistent throughout the history of the tradition.

Perhaps the best place to look for an early systematized presentation of this tendency is the *Mīmāṁsā* school, classified among the six philosophical systems known as *darśanas.* Regarded as the direct continuation of the Vedic culture, the *Mīmāṁsā* came to be acknowledged by most Hindus of the intellectual class as the orthodox position *par excellence.* As the *Mīmāṁsā* school variedly emphasized two distinct aspects of the Vedic tradition, namely the ritualistic and the speculative, it is customary to distinguish between the *Pūrva-Mīmāṁsā*, which emphasizes the ritualistic aspect, and the *Uttara-Mīmāṁsā*, which emphasizes the speculative aspect. The more usual names of the latter two being *Mīmāṁsā* and *Vedānta* respectively, the common usage will be followed here.

The earliest authoritative source of the *Mīmāṁsā* system is Jaimini's *Mīmāṁsā-sūtra* usually assigned to a date earlier than that of the other *darśanas*, not later than 200 A.D. although its tradition is much older.[1] The earliest extant commentary of the *Mīmāṁsā-sūtra* is the *Bhāṣya* of Śabara, written probably about 100 B.C. Śabara's *Bhāṣya* was in turn given two important commentaries, one by Prabhākara (A.D. 650) and the other by Kumārila Bhaṭṭa (A.D. 700) whose influence will be discussed in the next chapter.[2]

For the *Mīmāṁsā* school, the Vedic texts supply the criterion of what is right and what is wrong. In its anxiety to secure supremacy for the *Vedas*, this system does not admit the existence of a God whose authority would exceed, or be equal to, that of the *Vedas*. A good life is therefore one which is led in conformity with the injunctions of the *Vedas*, and not with the personal will of a divine creator. Although the Vedic hymns show that a cult was addressed to specific deities, the *Mīmāṁsā* insists that rituals should be performed because the *Vedas* prescribe them as injunctions, the deities serving merely to indicate that in

1. S. Dasgupta dates it back to 400 B.C.: *History of Indian Philosophy*, Vol. I, p. 370.

2. *Ibid.*

whose name an oblation is to be offered at a sacrifice.[3] Doubts have been raised as to whether the *Mimāṁsā* could be called atheistic without qualification:[4] the fact remains that we are dealing with a system where "ethics reaches, through ritualism, the highest point of its glory, namely the conception of duty for duty's sake."[5]

True, the *Mimāṁsā* deals with sacrificial rather than social and domestic duties as such. However, its principles stand in close relation with the social dimension of Hindu life. Skill in the *Mimāṁsā* is considered, in the *Manusmṛti* and other *Dharma śāstras*, as a qualification for disputing questions of law. Thus, Medhātithi (ca. 10th or 11th century A.D.), the very first known commentator of the *Manusmṛti*, was an adept in the *Mimāṁsā* principles.[6]

Unlike the *Mimāṁsā*, the *Vedānta*'s main concern is not with the Vedic injunctions regarding rituals but rather with the philosophical foundations on which ritualism depends. The earliest extant attempt to give a systematic account of *Vedānta* is the *Vedānta-sūtras* (also called *Brahma-sūtras*) which at a very early date became revered as an inspired work. On the basis that this work, attributed to Bādarāyaṇa, contains a refutation of almost all other Indian philosophical systems, scholars have assigned a date as early as the second century B.C. as the time when it was written.[7]

In the eighth century, Gauḍapāda revived the teaching of the *Upaniṣads* by an important commentary on the *Māṇḍūkya Upaniṣad*. Gauḍapāda's disciple, Govinda, was the teacher of Śaṅkara (728-820 A.D.), acknowledged since by orthodox Brahmins as the most authoritative spokesman of the *Vedānta*, and thereby of orthodoxy.

On the basis of the Upaniṣadic mystic intuitions, Śaṅkara proposes knowledge (*jñāna*) as the only direct means of achieving the highest goal of immortality (*mokṣa*) through identifica-

---

3. Chatterjee, S. & Datta, D. *An Introduction to Indian Philosophy*, pp. 338-343.
4. *Ibid.*, pp. 341-343.
5. *Ibid.*, p. 339.
6. Keith, A. B. *The Karma Mīmāṁsā*, pp. 97-98.
7. For instance, Dasgupta, S. *op. cit.*, p. 418.

tion with the impersonal Absolute (*nirguṇa brahman*). His views on social duty and love of God are better expounded in his commentary on the *Bhagavad Gītā*. Throughout his commentary, Śaṅkara presents work (*karma*) as but a means leading to knowledge :

> Devotion to action is a means to the end, not directly, but only as leading to devotion to knowledge; whereas the latter, which is attained by means of devotion to action, leads to the goal directly, without extraneous help.[8]

He goes on to explain that actions are enjoined to the unenlightened whereas the enlightened who has seen the immutable Self has only to renounce all works.[9] For the unenlightened, action is the means of attaining the purity of mind necessary for knowledge.[10] Śaṅkara adds that in spite of the exemption from works, the enlightened may feel obligated to perform his social duty for other reasons such as fidelity to his caste duty or "the purpose of preventing the masses from resorting to a wrong path."[11]

The problem of determining the exact nature of Śaṅkara's views on love of God, referred to as *bhakti* in the *Gītā*, is more complex. When one compares the attention he devotes to the paths of knowledge and work with that of love, it becomes clear that the latter is not treated as an important salvific path.

Compared to other commentators, Śaṅkara treats with coldness many passages dealing with love of God (such as IX. 14, 26, 29, etc..) a coldness which is reflected in his silence or his rather prosaic considerations. Moreover, contrary to other well-known commentators such as Rāmānuja and Madhva, he frequently refers to knowledge and work as the two means—the first direct and the second indirect—of attaining salvation, without including love of God as the third important term of comparison.[12] The explanation for thus minimizing the rôle

8. Śaṅkara's commentary to the *Bhagavad Gītā*, III. 2. My quotations are borrowed from A. M. Sastry's translation.

9. *Ibid.*, II. 21.

10. *Ibid.*, III. 20. IV. 15.

11. *Ibid.*, III. 20.

12. For example: *Ibid.*, II. 10, 54, etc.

of *bhakti* might be sought in Śaṅkara's tendency to identify *bhakti* with *jñāna* in several passages such as VIII.22, XVIII.54, XVIII.55, XIII.11, and XVIII.66.

We may summarize Śaṅkara's views on social duty and love of God by saying that for him social duty, which is a form of *karma*, is necessary for the unenlightened. While it is not imposed on the enlightened, it may nevertheless be advised on at least two grounds: i) his station in life; ii) his desire to serve as an example for the unenlightened. On the other hand, the rôle of love of God is not emphasized on a par with that of social duty. Rather, it is suggested that since *bhakti* is identifiable with *jñāna*, love of God is ultimately not different from love of Self or rather Self-realization. Thus, Śaṅkara shares with the Mīmāṁsakas, although with differing degrees and for different purposes, a common concern for the fulfillment of social duty accompanied with a common tendency to minimize the rôle of love of God.

The influence of both the *Mīmāṁsā* and the *Vedānta* systems in post-vedic Hinduism was considerable. In his study of this period, J. Gonda attributes to Kumārila and Śaṅkara a decisive rôle in the revival of orthodoxy between 700 A.D. and 1600 A.D., which resulted in a definitive absorption of Buddhism within the fold of Hinduism and a greater sense of solidarity among Hindus, particularly of the intellectual class.[13]

The *Dharma Śāstras* may be considered as another instance of Vedic orthodoxy. These documents, the earliest of which are assigned to the period 600 to 200 B.C., deal with righteous conduct, manners and polite behaviour, the administration of the state and justice, and the duties which must be performed in carrying out domestic rituals. The most influential among three in the development and maintenance of Hindu religious practice is the *Manusmṛti*, a metrical Sanskrit work compiled some time before the second century A.D.[14] This law book, intended for the ruling and educated elements of the population,[15] lays heavy stress on the customs and ceremonies which

13. Gonda, J. *Les religions de l'Inde*, Vol. II, pp. 103-121.

14. See Georg Bühler's study of this question in the introduction to his translation of the *Manusmṛti* in *The Laws of Manu.*

15. Lingat, R. *The Classical Law of India*, trans. from the French by J. D. M. Derrett, p. 87.

should surround the life of each individual and accompany him from birth to death. As in the case of the *Mīmāṁsā* and the *Vedānta*, the *Manusmṛti* is based on the authority of the *Vedas*:

> By the Śruti (revelation) is meant the Veda, and by Smṛti (tradition) the Institutes of the sacred law: those two must not be called into question in any matter, since from those two the sacred law shone forth.[16]

Śāstric digests continued to be written down to the British days, and as we shall see in the next chapter exercised a certain influence in medieval North India. In these manuals of moral guidance, as in the *Mīmāṁsā* and the *Vedānta*, the emphasis is laid on the fulfilment of one's prescribed duties and regulations, thereby contrasting with the antinomian emphasis on love of God, which will now be discussed.

2. *Antinomian Theisim*

Antinomian theism tends to regard love of God as an end in itself with the implication that traditional social and domestic regulations, insofar as they are prescribed by tradition, may be dismissed. A relatively early trace of this tendency is found in the Tamil tradition, particularly among the Vaiṣṇavite saints known as the Ālvārs, who rose between the sixth and the ninth century A.D. Thus, Nammālvār is pictured as a contemplative devotee who took up residence under a tamarind tree and remained there in silence and fasting.[17] Likewise, King Kulaśekhara, a Rāma devotee who lived in the ninth century A.D.[18] is especially remembered for having renounced his rich kingdom in order to contemplate and sing the glories of Rāma in the Vaiṣṇavite sanctuaries of Śrīraṅgam and Tirupati, where he spent the rest of his life :

> One night the Lord manifested himself to him and he became a different man on the next morning. His

16. *Manusmṛti*, VI. 10 translated by G. Bühler, *op. cit.*
17. See Varadachari, K. C. *Alvars of South India*, pp. 141, 151.
18. *Ibid*, p. 37.

> heart longed for the spiritual out and out spurning away the material, so much so that he was contemplating on a pilgrimage to Śrīraṅgam... He finally renounced his throne and went to the seat of his Lord, the religious center of Śrīraṅga at first, to be followed by that of Śrī Veṅkateśa over the seven hills, singing the glory of his Lord and expressing his feelings of ecstasy in pure and simple Tamil. (sic)[19]

The implication, in both of the above examples, is that one must renounce worldly concerns in order to become a real devotee.

The *gopī* theme represents a still clearer case of antinomian theism. The exact details of the origins of the *gopī* ideal associated with the Kṛṣṇa cult are not easily determined. The *gopī* story seems to have been already well known at the time of the *Viṣṇu Purāṇa*[20] and the *Harivaṃśa,*[21] as both documents related, around the fourth century A.D.,[22] Kṛṣṇa's sports with the cowherds. However, the most renowned version of the story is found in the *Bhāgavata Purāṇa*, which "is among the latest productions of the Hindu Puranic literature and is undoubtedly the most famous and widely used of the *Purāṇas*".[23] As the *Bhāgavata Purāṇa* attained prominence by the tenth century A.D., it was probably written at least a century before. After a recent and careful study of this question, T. H. Hopkins prudently affirms that it was written "no earlier than A.D. 500 and no later than A.D. 900.[24] On the basis of a possible common historical setting with that of the Āḷvārs, he goes on to suggest A.D. 850 as the probable date.[25]

---

19. Naidu, S. S. R. "Kulashekara Alwar and Rashkhan", *Annals of Oriental Research*, XIV, 1958, p. 2.
20. *Viṣṇu Purāṇa*, V. 13 ff.
21. *Harivaṃśa*, II. 20 ff.
22. "The *Harivaṃśa* clearly cannot be dated later than A. D. 400, and the *Viṣṇu Purāṇa* is so like it in most of its features that it is probable that it belongs to the same general date." (Farquhar, J. N. *An Outline of the Religious Literature of India*, p. 143.
23. Hopkins, T. J. "The Social Teachings of the Bhāgavata Purāṇa", *Krshna: Myths, Rites and Attitudes*, edited by M. Singer, p. 3.
24. *Ibid.*, p. 4.
25. *Ibid.*, p. 6.

It is generally held that the *Bhāgavata Purāṇa* comes from the Tamil land of the Āḷvārs.[26] Mr. D. A. Pai, whom Miss Rukmani quotes approvingly,[27] adds that the *Bhāgavata Purāṇa* is perhaps the work of a body of Tamil ascetics who have lived with the Āḷvārs. However, until more convincing evidence can be obtained, none of the indications given above can be taken as definitive, except for the rather well established fact that the *Bhāgavata Purāṇa* was written between A.D. 500 and A.D. 900.

The story of the *gopīs*, as related in the *Bhāgavata Purāṇa*, could leave no doubt in the hearer's mind that the intensity of the devotee's love of God may justify the forsaking of his social duty to follow the Lord more closely. When moved by an intense devotion to Lord Kṛṣṇa, the *gopīs* are commended for neglecting their duty to follow Him. Thus, upon hearing the notes of Kṛṣṇa's flute, the women of Vraja neglect their duties to get near Him:

> Full of intense longing, some who were milking cows, darted off leaving the milking vessel (uncared for); others left as soon as they had placed the milk on the oven (without waiting for its being boiled) and still others went out without removing the (dressed) porridge (from the hearth); some, who were serving food (to their husbands and other relations) went away neglecting that duty...Though being stopped by their husbands, parents, brothers or other relations, they did not turn back (homeward), infatuated as they were (through love), their mind having been lured away by Śrī Kṛṣṇa.[28]

True, after praising the *gopīs* for having followed Him,[29] Kṛṣṇa gently sends them back to their duties, explaining that "love for Me is fostered not so much by physical proximity as by hear-

26. *Ibid.*, pp. 4-5.

27. Rukmani, T. S. *A Critical Study of the Bhāgavata Purāṇa.*

28. *Bhāgavata Purāṇa*, X. 29. 5-7. Henceforward, this work will be referred to as *B. P.* The quotations from the *B. P.* are taken from the Gītā Press edition.

29. *Ibid.*, X. 29. 23.

ing my praises, looking at Me, meditating on Me or by singing My glories".[30] However, the *gopis* adamantly insist, using a long argument of which the most significant passage is the following:

> As it has been observed by You, the knower of dharma, that the natural duty of women is to render service to their husband and children as well as to the relations of their husband, O beloved One, let such service be done to You, the almightly Lord, the (central) theme of all teachings: for you are the most beloved Friend, (nay) the (very) Self of all embodied souls. Those well versed in the sacred lore surely find delight in You (alone); their own eternally beloved Self; what purpose can be gained through a husband, children and others, who are sources of agony? Therefore, be gracious to us, O supreme Lord: (pray) do not frustrate our hopes centred in You for a long time, O lotus-eyed One.[31]

It is to be noticed that Kṛṣṇa yields to the above argument of the *gopis*, for he "proceeded to delight them out of compassion, though revelling in his own self."[32] In a later passage,[33] a similar episode is related, showing the devotees neglecting their duties to follow Kṛṣṇa, and this time the latter makes no attempt whatever to dissuade them from their course of action.

The example of the *gopis* is illustrative of the view that the intensity of one's devotion, may, in certain cases, be sufficient justification for neglecting one's domestic and social duties. The next chapter will show that this Purāṇic exaltation of antinomian theism exercised an influence in medieval North India, particularly among the *Kṛṣṇa-Sants*.

A more iconoclastic example of antinomian theism is that of the Liṅgāyats, who emerged as a sect between the tenth and the twelfth century A.D.[34] in the Karṇāṭaka and the Mahā-

30. *Ibid.*, X. 29. 27.
31. *Ibid.*, X. 29. 32-33.
32. *Ibid.*, X. 29-42.
33. *Ibid.*, X. 41. 24-31.
34. Dasgupta, S. *op. cit.*, Vol. V, p. 47. See also Bhandarkar, R. G. *Vaiṣṇavism, Śaivism and Minor Religious Sects,* p. 133.

rāṣṭra provinces.[35] The question is still debated whether Basava was the actual founder of the sect. R. C. Bhandarkar believes that he was rather its supporter, thanks especially to his political influences, as he was in charge of the royal treasury[36] under King Bijjala of Kalyāṇa, who acceded to the throne in 1156.[37] Scholars also debate whether, as it is often contended, Basava did away with the Hindu caste stsyem, caste duties and some other traditional customs.[38]

Be that as it may, the Liṅgāyats' expressions of intense devotion (to Śiva), in the poems attributed to Basava and his companions, are accompanied by an attitude highly critical of social structures, accepted conventions, and Hindu religious traditions :

> Classical belief systems, social customs and superstitions (Basavaṇṇa 581, 105), the caste system (Dāsimayya 96), the Vedic ritual of *yajña* (Basavaṇṇa 125) as well as local sacrifices of lambs and goats (Basavaṇṇa 129)—all of them are fiercely questioned and ridiculed.[39]

Of special relevance to us is a *vacana* by Allama Prabhu on the inefficacy of works for spiritual growth, the implication being that love of God does not necessarily call for good works in order to lead the devotee to liberation :

> Feed the poor
> tell the truth
> make water-places
> and build tanks for a town..
> You may then go to heaven
> after death, but you''ll get nowhere
> near the truth of our Lord
> And the man who knows our Lord,
> he gets no result.[40]

---

35. Gonda, J. *op. cit.*, Vol. II, p. 291.
36. Bhandarkar, R. G. *op. cit.*, p. 132.
37. Gonda, J. *op. cit.*, Vol. II, p. 292.
38. Dasgupta, S. *op. cit.*, Vol. V, p. 43.
39. Ramanujan, A. K. *Speaking of Śiva*, p. 30.
40. Allama, 959, quoted by A. K. Ramanujan, *op. cit.*, p. 167.

What seems to be questioned here is the assumption that one must play the rôle expected of him by society and tradition in order to experience genuine love of God. Such conditioned devotion would seem, in the eyes of the Liṅgāyats, to smack of the notion according to which God's love can be commanded by man's actions or virtues:

> All true experience of God is *kṛpa*, grace that cannot be called, recalled, or commended. The *vacanas* distinguish *anubhava* 'experience', and *anubhāva* "the Experience'. The latter is a search for the "unmediated vision", the unconditioned act, the unpredictable experience. Living in history, time and cliché, one lives in a world of the preestablished, through the received (*śruti*) and the remembered (*smṛti*). But the Experience when it comes, comes like a storm to all such husks and labels.[41]

It must not be concluded from the above that having overthrown Brahmanical law, the Liṅgāyats became socially irresponsible. Devara Dāsimayya, the weaver, taught that working in the world was a part of worshipping and reaching Śiva.[42] Nor did they object to religious practices as such. Mr. Ramanujan has shown that the Liṅgāyats' challenging of the existing culture led to the acclamation of a counter-culture.[43]

It has been suggested that Basava and his companions were influenced by the Jains whom they tried to win over to their sect.[44] However whereas the importance attached to the foundation of monasteries by the Liṅgāyats may be seen as traces of Jain influence, their critical attitude towards social inequality is also suggestive of Muslim influence. Yet, despite occasional persecutions[45] the Liṅgāyats, who acknowledge the authority of the *Vedas*, are generally recognized as Hindus, and their socio-political influence attained an apogee in Mysore, where the Liṅgāyat religion was acknowledged as the official

41. Ramanujan, A. K. *op. cit.*, p. 31.
42. *Ibid.*, p. 30.
43. *Ibid.*, pp. 34-37.
44. Gonda, J. *op. cit.*, Vol. II, p. 291.
45. *Ibid.*, p. 294.

state religion from 1350 to 1610.[46]

The antinomian stream may be seen as a dimension of the rise of the post-Vedic devotional trend in India, which has often been interpreted as a reaction against Vedic orthodoxy. J. Gonda, for instance, sees in the Śrī Vaiṣṇava movement an attempt to counter the influence of Vedic orthodoxy.[47] It is significant that the Śrī Vaiṣṇavas cherished the poems of the Āḻvārs[48] and popularized the *Bhāgavata Purāṇa*,[49] both of which, as we have just seen, carried seeds of antinomian theism. This anti-orthodox movement can be seen, then, as an opposition to the one-sided reliance on Vedic injunctions preached by the Mīmāṁsakas, especially Prabhākara and Kumārila, as well as to the advaitic doctrine of Śaṅkara where the insistence on knowledge and to a certain extent on social duty had resulted in an unacceptable minimization of love of God as a path of spiritual liberation. That antinomian theism extended its influence to the immediate context of Tulsī Dās will be seen in the following chapter, as the impact of the *Sant* movement, particularly the influence of Kabīr, is dealt with among the different factors that shaped the religious trends of medieval North India.

3. *Orthodox Theism*

Orthodox theism represents the middle ground between the two conflicting streams just seen, where social duty and love of God stood as two opposite poles. The *Bhagavad Gītā* may be considered as representative of this tendency.

The work of an anonymous author, the *Gītā* forms a small part of the *Mahābhārata*, one of the two greatest Indian epics with the *Rāmāyaṇa*. The exact date of its composition is not yet known. Modern scholars suggest the period between the fifth century B.C. and the second century B.C., the final recension having been made between the fourth and the seventh century A.D.[50]

46. *Ibid.*
47. *Ibid.*, pp. 160-169.
48. *Ibid.*, p. 162.
49. *Ibid.*, p. 184.
50. For instance see Eliot Deutsch's introduction (pp. 3-4) to his translation of the *Bhagavad Gītā*.

The *Gītā* sets forth three spiritual paths whereby one can obtain spiritual fulfillment: knowledge (*jñāna-yoga*), work (*karma-yoga*), and love of God (*bhakti-yoga*). There is no opposition among the three paths. In fact, *karma* normally calls for *bhakti* and *jñāna*. In order for the man of action to achieve spiritual freedom through *karma*, he must detach himself from the fruits of his actions. However, this selflessness (*niṣkāma-karma*) in action is best attained through a new attachment to the Divine :

> Whatever you do, whatever you eat, whatever you offer in sacrifice or give away in alms, whatever penance you may perform, offer it up to me.[51]

Likewise non-attachment to the result of one's actions is more easily achieved through the realization (*jñāna*) that the empirical self, and not the real Self, is the doer of those actions:

> All actions are performed by the *guṇas* of *prakṛti* alone. But he who is deluded by I-consciousness (*ahaṅkāra*) thinks "I am the doer".[52]

This turning away from attachment to all fruits (*phalas*) of the action and from the mistaken identity of the real doer constitutes the preliminary step to what is called "higher *bhakti*", which in turn leads to "higher *jñāna*", wherein the *bhakta* transcends the consciousness of the negative turning away from what is not liberation, in order to attach himself exclusively to the Lord (*Puruṣottama*), and thereby achieving unity with the Divine:

> By devotion (*bhakti*) he knows Me, what my greatness is and what I am really; then having known (*jñāna*) me as I am, he enters forthwith into Me.[53]

From the above, it is clear that *bhakti* leads to *jñāna*, and the latter leads directly to liberation. It is by thus becoming one with Puruṣottama that man will be able to act without attachment in fulfillment of the duty attached to his particular state

51. *Bhagavad Gītā*, IX. 27.
52. *Ibid.*, III. 27.
53 *Ibid.*, XVIII. 55.

of life (*svadharma*). However, rather than following all the steps indicated it would seem that one could achieve the same results by opting either for *bhakti* or for *jñāna*. The two alternatives are compared in the famous answer to Arjuna's query:

> Of those who are thus ever integrated and serve You with loyal devotion, and those who (revere) the Imperishable Unmanifest, which are the most experienced in spiritual exercise?[54]

In his answer, Kṛṣṇa gives priority to those who follow the *bhakti-mārga*, because it is the easier path. He does admit, however, that those who follow *jñāna-mārga* by revering the Imperishable, Unmanifest (or *nirguṇa brahman*) "also obtain me" (v. 4). He even concedes that if one is unable to follow the two preceding paths, then he may receive the prize by just performing actions for His sake:

> For if for such effort you lack the strength, then work and act for Me, make this your goal; for even if you work only for my sake, you will receive the prize.[55]

The *Gītā* also teaches that by thus fulfilling his appointed duty, the devotee conforms to the will of the Lord, who himself created the four-caste system.[56]

Thus, in attempting to promote love of God as the easier way, the *Gītā* does not want to be exclusivistic. Rather, it acknowledges the legitimacy of the three different approaches :

> Arjuna, howsoever men approach Me, Even so do I seek them: for all men follow My path from all sides.[57]

We may conclude from the above that contrary to Śaṅkara's interpretation, the *Gītā* accepts love of God as a possible and distinct means of salvation. In fact, we may even say, on the basis of passages like XII.2, 5, and 6, that the path of love is the most advisable path for it is easier, possible for every one and most pleasing to God. Likewise, the *Gītā* consistently

54. *Ibid.*, XII. 1
55. *Ibid.*, XII. 10.
56. *Ibid.*, IV. 13.
57. *Ibid.*, IV. 11.

teaches that perfection can be reached through work and that the latter is a means to release. In fact, work coupled with knowledge and love of God should be considered as the ideal option. For all, disinterested selfless work is compulsory. It is not only the way to release of the individual: it is also according to III. 20—24, the way of bettering the Universe. In the *Gītā*, therefore, both love of God and social duty are recommended and both are integrated along with knowledge as complementary ways leading to salvation.

The significance of the *Bhagavad Gītā* as a precursor to the *Rāmcaritmānas* should not be overlooked. The *Upaniṣads* insisted on withdrawal from the world (*sannyāsa*)—after the manner of *Yājñavalkya*—as the ideal way of escaping the binding effects of action. Citing King Janaka as an example,[58] the *Gītā* taught renunciation of the fruits rather than of the works themselves. With Buddhism and Jainism the *sannyāsa* ideal was proposed to non-Brahmins as well as to Brahmins. Such spirit of *sannyāsa*, when over-emphasized, could lead members of the society to neglect their appointed duties. The *Gītā* countered such possible consequences by insisting that every one was bound to fulfil his *svadharma*.

The *Gītā* also brought a satisfying meassge to a growing number of Hindus who seemed to incline toward a religion based on the worship of personal God, a tendency which led to a practical deification of Gautama, Mahāvīra and Kṛṣṇa. There again, the *Gītā* , where the Lord Kṛṣṇa plays an important rôle, was better suited than the speculative *Upaniṣads* or the atheistic doctrines of Buddhism and Jainism to answer this need, to the point where it has become "the most revered and celebrated text in Hinduism."[59]

Along with the *Gītā*, the *Vālmiki Rāmāyaṇa* provided another important instance of the epic pattern tending toward the middle road. As can be expected, however, the middle was constantly changing depending on the pressures from the "sides". After having seen how the *Gītā* represents the middle stream, we now see that the *Vālmiki Rāmāyaṇa* played the same rôle but in a different sense.

---

58. *Ibid.*, III. 20.
59. Deutsch, E. *op. cit.*, p. 3.

The composition of the *Rāmāyaṇa* is traditionally attributed to Maharṣi Vālmīki. According to a story found in the *Adhyātma Rāmāyaṇa*,[60] the *Bengali Rāmāyaṇas*[61] and the *Mahābhārata*, where its earliest traces are found,[62] Vālmīki is supposed to have been a robber whose name had been Ratnākara, and who obtained righteousness by repeating during a thousand *yugas* the name "*Rāma*". It is said that at the sight of a male dove killed by a hunter while it was sporting with its mate, Vālmīki uttered the exclamation recorded in *Bāla-kāṇḍa*, 1—4, whereupon a voice from heaven bade him write in the same metric pattern the story of Rāma.

There have been diverging opinions concerning the date of composition of the *Vālmiki Rāmāyaṇa*. In 1893, H. Jacobi suggested the sixth or even the eighth century B.C.;[63] whereas in 1915 A.B. Keith inclined to the fourth,[64] the latter being the most universally accepted view.

It is now generally accepted that Cantos II to VI of the *Vālmiki Rāmāyaṇa* are the work of a single poet, because of the unity of conception and style. It is also generally admitted, since the work of Jacobi,[65] that Cantos I and VII, whose style is characteristic of the later *Purāṇas*, are interpolations, probably added in the first and third century A.D. respectively.[66] In these cantos, Rāma is conceived through out as an *avatāra* of Viṣṇu. However, the *avatāra* theme is also frequent in Canto VI, even more so than in Canto I; this is probably the result of later interpolations.

The task of determining what specific reason Vālmīki had in mind when he set out to write his great Epic is not an easy one. For Dr. Benjamin Khan, Vālmīki's purpose was to show that *dharma* is the supreme object of human life.[67] For Dr. N. K. Devaraja, of the Benares Hindu University, the distinctiveness

60. *Adhyātma Rāmāyaṇa*, II. 6. 64-86.
61. Sen, R. S. D. *The Bengali Rāmāyaṇa*, p. 125.
62. *Mahābhārata*, Anuśāsana Parva.
63. Jacobi, H. *Das Rāmāyaṇa*, pp.18 0-182.
64. Keith, A. B. *Journal of the Royal Asiatic Society*, 1915, p. 7.
65. Jacobi, H. *op. cit.*
66. Bulkey, K. *Rāma-kathā*, pp. 36-37.
67. Khan, B. *The Concept of Dharma in Vālmīki Rāmāyaṇa*, 1965.

of the *Vālmiki Rāmāyaṇa* must be studied against the background of the two sources of Indian culture. One current of thought stems from the pronouncedly secular Vedic Aryans, which advocates a prosperous and orderly life here on this earth. The other current of thought stems from the pronouncedly ascetic non-Aryans, which mainly looks forward to the life beyond, through self-denial. On the basis that the *Vālmiki Rāmāyaṇa* lays great emphasis on *dharma* while making no reference whatsoever to the ideal of *mokṣa*, Dr. Devaraja concludes that the *Rāmāyaṇa* of Vālmīki belongs to the Vedic Aryan tradition.[68]

Dr. R. S. D. Sen sees in the *Vālmiki Rāmāyaṇa* an effort to counter the Buddhist and Jain insistence on monasticism based on celibacy. The numerous cases of young men leaving society to seek *Nirvāṇa* in monasteries or in the wilderness was, according to Dr. Sen, seen as a threat to the ideal of the householder (*gārhastya āśrama*), considered as an essential element of one's spiritual training. The counter-blast was brought about by an increased emphasis on domestic virtues. Thus, a son could attain salvation only by proving his absolute obedience to his father: a brother, by following his elder brother to exile or even to death: a wife, by being supremely devoted to her husband; a servant, by carrying out the orders of his master with implicit submission. Home is the altar, the battle-field, and the paradise of all virtues. True, Rāma, Sītā, and Lakṣmaṇa become forest-wanderers, but they do not do so out of a will to sever all ties with the family and society. On the contrary, if Rāma leaves aside his royal robes and wears bark or rags, he does so in order to keep his father's sacred pledge. Sītā, Lakṣmaṇa, Bharata all accept renunciation, not as a struggle to suppress desire, but out of domestic love. The *Rāmāyaṇa* of Vālmīki is, therefore, according to Dr. Sen, an Epic of domestic life:

> It was the noble voice of the family-bond raised against the clamour of monasteries crying hoarse over renunciation and severance of all earthly ties. The *Rāmāyaṇa* is the greatest teacher of Hindu life, holding the banner of reaction against Buddhist asceticism.[69]

---

68. See Dr. N. K. Devaraja's foreword to Dr. Benjamin Khan's book, *op. cit.*

69. Sen, R. S. D. *op. cit.*, pp. 22-26.

While the views of N. K. Devajara and R. S. D. Sen offer interesting suggestions, one hesitates to follow the former in applying without qualification the word "secular" to the Vedic Aryan tradition, with the possible implication that the Vedic Aryans were not religious and that a religion that seeks to promote or uphold a prosperous and orderly life here on this earth is *ipso facto* secular. Similarly, Dr. Sen's analysis cannot be adopted without reservation, as in the *Rāmāyaṇa* itself there are many sections that praise asceticism and many wanderers and *ṛṣis* who play positive rôles in the story.

No doubt, the safest way of approximating Vālmīki's intention is to consult the *Rāmāyaṇa* itself. The text makes it clear that for Vālmīki traditional duties are of primary importance. Thus, Rāma should be his father's successor as king of Ayodhyā according to a tradition which says that the throne belongs to the eldest son.[70] Sacrifices are performed according to tradition[71] and scriptures,[72] and kings offer the traditional welcome as enjoined by the scriptures.[73]

The rulers and guardians of society are praised for their vigilance in fulfilling their social duties by observing the law. The counsellors of king Daśaratha pass judgment on their sons if they break the law.[74] The kings are praised for their knowledge of *dharma*,[75] and warriors for being fully established in the duties of their caste.[76]

For Vālmīki, caste duties are most important. He notices with satisfaction that no one in Ayodhyā was born of mixed castes, that the warriors were subjected to the learned Brahmins, and the merchants to the warriors.[77] Likewise, he mentions that the citizens were invited to attend the sacrifice, "being

---

70. *The Rāmāyaṇa of Vālmīki*, trans. H. P. Shastri, London: II. 79, 102, 110, Vol. I, pp. 355, 400, 419. Henceforward this translation of the *Vālmīki Rāmāyaṇa* will be referred to as *V. R.* Unless otherwise indicated, my quotations are from this translation.

71. *Ibid.*, I. 13, Vol. I, p. 32.

72. *Ibid.*, I. 8, Vol. I, p. 23.

73. *Ibid.*, I. 11, Vol. I, p. 30.

74. *Ibid.*, I. 7, Vol. I, p. 22.

75. *Ibid.*, I. 32, Vol. I, p. 71.

76. *Ibid.*, I. 44, Vol. I, p. 92.

77. *Ibid.*, I. 6, Vol. I, p. 20.

received in a becoming manner according to their caste". He specifies that invitations were sent to the Brahmins, the warriors, the merchants, the lowest caste."[78]

It is especially in his portrayal of Rāma that Vālmīki highlights the merits of social and domestic duty. Thus, Rāma is shown obeying his father's command, which he considered as his duty, rather than yield to the pressure of his entourage urging him to be inaugurated as heir to the throne of Ayodhyā. In so doing, Rāma is conscious of rejecting another duty, that of succeeding his father according to the traditional rule that the eldest son is the rightful heir, an argument advocated by Bharata to persuade his brother to return to Ayodhyā.[79] This conflict between the unwritten and the written duty is central to the *Vālmiki Rāmāyaṇa*.

The *Vālmiki Rāmāyaṇa* presents many other similar episodes aimed at highlighting Rāma's staunch fidelity to traditional duty. For instance, at the risk of provoking violence he agrees to kill demons in the forest in order to protect the ascetics who live there.[80] He welcomes Vibhīṣaṇa, a demon that came to him from the enemy camp.[81] After Sītā's rescue, Rāma repudiates her against his innermost inclination, in order to assure the people that her conduct with Rāvaṇa had been beyond reproach.[82] In all of these episodes, the same point is made that Rāma chose the difficult decision on account of his duty.

For Vālmīki, Rāma is like his father a "king fixed in his duty",[83] who stands at the very heart of the ideal social order. If the subjects are also fixed in their duty, everything will be as it should, but first the king must set the example of faithfulness to his specific duty as protector and ruler of his people, to the point where "even as he sleeps, he is awake to the ordering of his kingdom."[84]

We must now study to what extent love of God is also present and important in the *Vālmīki Rāmāyaṇa*. On many occa-

---

78. *Ibid.*, I. 13, Vol. I, p. 33.
79. *Ibid.*, II. 98, Vol. I, pp. 390-391.
80. *Ibid.*, III. 8, Vol. II, pp. 17-18
81. *Ibid.*, VI. 11, Vol. III, pp. 25-27.
82. *Ibid.*, VI. 106, Vol. III, pp. 305-308.
83. *Ibid.*, III. 50, Vol. II, p. 105.
84. *Ibid.*, III. 34, Vol. II, p. 71.

sions, particularly in Cantos II to VI, Rāma is likened to Indra, the chief god of the Ṛg Veda and champion of the *kṣatriyas* who, with the help of Maruts, slays demons' chief among whom is Vṛtra. The striking similarities between Rāma and Indra, coupled with the numerous references to Indra in the *Vālmīki Rāmāyaṇa* suggest that Rāma is seen as the successor of the Vedic god. In this respect it is significant that Rāma kills Rāvaṇa with the help of Indra's weapon.

More than a mere successor of Indra, Rāma is also presented as an incarnation (*avatāra*) of Viṣṇu, particularly in Cantos I, IV and VII. We have already seen that modern scholarship considers these as later interpolations. However, they are not necessarily "corrections". They may just as well be the expression of a deeper truth already latent in the original story and gradually discovered by its hearers.

The most overt statement of Rāma's divinity occurs in a long passage in Canto VI, where in answer to Rāma's question: "Who then am I in reality?" Brahmā portrays Rāma as Viṣṇu-*Nārāyaṇa* himself. Indeed Rāma is described in this passage as the supreme Puruṣa, Brahman, the refuge and protector of his devotees who entered a human body in order to kill Rāvaṇa.[85] Even though such an explicit affirmation of Rāma's divine nature is an exception, the many references to the *avatāra* indicate that Rāma devotees loved him as God.

As can be expected however, clear expressions of love addressed to God are less numerous in the *Vālmiki Rāmāyaṇa* than in the later *Rāmāyaṇas*, especially the *Rāmcaritmānas*. The *Vālmīki Rāmāyaṇa* is first and foremost a manual of duty where Rāma is considered as a human hero in the majority of the Cantos. Nevertheless clear instances of love of Rāma as the divine *avatāra* can be found, particularly in the seventh Canto. For example "entertained by the grace of Rāma's affectionate regard," the monkeys and titans spent a month in Ayodhyā which seemed like an hour.[86] Likewise, Lakṣmaṇa and Bharata "in their love for his (Rāma) and their extreme piety, forget that time was passing and thus ten thousand years went by while they devoted themselves to affairs of state."[87] Another

85. *Ibid.*, VI. 119, Vol. III, pp. 339-340.
86. *Ibid.*, VII. 39, Vol. III, p. 515.
87. *Ibid.*, VII. 102, Vol. III, p. 624.

instance occurs later when the inhabitants of Ayodhyā insist upon following Rāma to heaven on the basis that "if thou dost love thy subjects and affection is unsurpassed, let us, with our sons and wives, follow the righteous path with thee'.[88] Finally, after his return to heaven, Rāma, now seen as Viṣṇu himself, gives his subjects a suitable abode, for "they are my devotees and truly deserving, having sacrificed their lives for me."[89]

We may conclude that the *Vālmīki Rāmāyaṇa* is interested primarily in presenting Rāma as the ideal man faithful to his social and domestic duties. The original cantos also present him as the successor to Indra, who kills Rāvaṇa and the demons. The interpolated sections open up another level of meaning whereby Rāma is also considered as the incarnation of Viṣṇu, without necessarily identifying Rāma with Viṣṇu. (The passage quoted above where this identification does occur is an extremely rare exception.) The emphasis given to love of God as devotional Lord is far from equalling in proportion that given to *bhakti* in the *Gītā*. Nevertheless, its rôle seems sufficiently important to classify the *Vālmiki Rāmāyaṇa* with the same stream as the *Gītā*.

By opening up new levels of meaning in the Rāma symbol considered latent in the old levels, the *Vālmīki Rāmāyaṇa* provided the paradigm of the future development which, through the same process of integrating new levels in the old ones, culminated in the *Rāmcaritmānas* where, as we shall later see, love of God emerges as the predominant theme. For this reason, modern Hindus have no difficulty reading back into the *Vālmiki Rāmāyaṇa* love of God as an important theme, thus justifying its inclusion in the same stream as the *Gītā*, namely orthodox theism. That the *Vālmīki Rāmāyaṇa* influenced Tulsī Dās is beyond question, and the degree to which this influence is reflected in the *Rāmcaritmānas* will be studied in the forthcoming chapters of this study.

Along with these passages in the *Bhāgavata Purāṇa* concerning the *gopīs* whose conduct is an example of antinomian theism, other passages of the same *Purāṇa* appearing in different settings reflect the middle stream of orthodox theism, tending to recon-

---

88. *Ibid.*, VII. 107, Vol. III, p. 630.
89. *Ibid.*, VII. 110, Vol. III, p. 636.

cile love of God and social duty. The most important passages illustrating this position are devoted to King Yudhiṣṭhira and to Prince Priyavrata, found in Books I and V respectively. The fact that the latter passages adopt a position different from that underlying the *gopī* stories in Book X presents a difficulty, which is probably due to the inclusion of interpolated passages of different sources and ages.[90]

As he reflects on his rôle in a war which brought about the destruction of so many, Yudhiṣṭhira expresses his dissatisfaction with the traditional views on duty:

> The saving clause found in the scriptures that the destruction of enemies in a righteous war on the part of a monarch seeking the protection of his subjects is no sin, fails to satisfy me. The wrong that I have done in this life to the womenfolk whose husbands and other relations have been slain by me or on my account I shall not be able to expiate through sacrificial performances enjoined on a householder.[91]

In despair, Yudhiṣṭhira calls on Bhīṣma to seek enlightenment on his duties as king. Bhīṣma's answer is illuminating as it provides the king with a new criterion of action: the will of God:

> Indeed no man, O king, can ever discover the intention of Śrī Kṛṣṇa; even seers get bewildered in their seeking to find it out. Therefore, knowing it for certain that all these events depend on the will of Providence, O chief of the Bharatas, follow His will, O ruler of man, and protect the helpless people, as you are their sole monarch.[92]

Prompted by the king's further question, Bhīṣma goes on to explain that this change of perspective does not entail the abolition of the various duties (*dharmas*):

> Thereupon Bhīṣma, who had realized the Truth, dis-

90. Farquhar, J. N. *op. cit.*, p. 231.
91. *B. P.*, I. 8. 50-51.
92. *B. P.*, I. 9, 16-17.

> coursed upon, one by one, the various *dharmas* determined by the innate disposition of men and apportioned with due regard to their *varṇa* and *āśrama* and the twofold *dharmas* severally recommended for those endowed with dispassion and those who are full of worldly attachment, the *dharmas* relating to charitable gifts, the duties obligatory on monarchs, the courses of conduct which are conducive to liberation, the duties of women and the courses of conduct that are intended to propitiate the Lord, both briefly and in detail. He also explained...the four ends of human pursuit, viz., *dharma*, *artha*, *kāma* and *mokṣa* as well as the means to them in their true perspective with the help of many illustrative anecdotes and stories.[93]

The point of this whole passage, therefore, is to show that the will of God provides social duty with a superior ground, Kṛṣṇa being the ultimate source of salvation. Having heard this answer, the king abandons his despair and "with the approval of Śrī Kṛṣṇa ruled his ancestral kingdom with righteousness."[94]

Prince Priyavrata is another example of a ruler whose reluctance to accept his duty could only be overcome by the foregoing argument. As he was about to make a vow of lifelong contemplation, Priyavrata is called upon by his father to "rule over the earth". Now, the prince "did not welcome it, although the command (of his father) was inviolable : for he had through constant absorption of his mind in Lord Vāsudeva completely resigned all the activities of his senses and organs of action to Him and he thought that on his assuming the reins of government (the true nature of) his self would be obscured by (contact with) the nonself, even though the latter had no reality."[95] Having been convinced by Brahmā that his duty was the will of God, the prince accepted the command with the words "Very well !" his head bent low as a token of his smallness."[96]

In the two foregoing examples taken from the *Bhāgavata Purāṇa*, as in the *Gītā*, social duty is not abrogated as a result

93. *B. P.*, I. 9. 25-28.
94. *B. P.*, I. 9. 49.
95. *B. P.*, V. 1. 6.
96. *B. P.*, V. 1. 20.

of the intensity of the devotee's love. Rather, it is given a theological basis : the authority of the divine will, thus making it possible to integrate love of God and social duty.

The three positions described in this chapter, namely vedic orthodoxy, antinomian theism, and orthodox theism, constitute three typical approaches to the problem of relating love of God and social duty. These streams were very much at work in medieval North India and combined to form the immediate background against which the *Rāmcaritmānas* was written. The next chapter will attempt to show under what guise the said currents presented themselves to Tulsī Dās at the time he set out to write his *magnum opus*.

Chapter IV

The Immediate Context

IN trying to account for the religious atmosphere of medieval North India, one cannot overlook the important repercussions of the socio-political situation of the time, which culminated in Akbar's policy of reconciliation between Hindu and Muslims. It is to this situation that we shall first turn our attention, before attempting to describe the religious atmosphere as such.

1. *The Socio-political Context*

It should be pointed out at the outset that the following discussion is not meant to be exhaustive of the socio-political background of Tulsī Dās. The purpose of this section is rather to discuss the elements within the socio-political context of medieval North India that appear to be the most important direct influences on the religious trends of the time in which the *Rāmcaritmānas* was written.

If we accept 1543 as the year in which Tulsī Dās was born, it follows that he was only one year younger than Akbar, whose birth-day is held to be November 23, 1542.[1] Although the latter was officially proclaimed when he was only thirteen as the successor of his deceased father Humāyūn (1507-1556), he did not take the reins of the government until five years later in 1560. Tulsī Dās was therefore seventeen years of age when Akbar began his effective reign, which lasted forty-five years, excluding the five years of regency.

By the time Tulsī Dās was twenty-five years of age, Akbar had already under control Delhi, Lahore, Gwalior, Jaunpur, Mālvā, Allahabad, and Benares, the latter two in 1567. The violence which accompanied these conquests is a well-known historical fact :

1. Majumdar, R. C., Raychaudhuri, H. C. & Datta, K. *An Advanced History of India*, third edition, p. 437.

> Early in May, 1567, he (Akbar) left Āgra in order to crush the rebellion of the Uzbegs, who had been in revolt ever since Hakim's invasion of the Panjab, and had lately marched on Kālpi. He surprised them when the leaders were drunk and their troops in disorder, and in a battle near Allahabad defeated them, Khānzamān being slain and his brother, Bahadur, captured and executed. Several of the leaders taken were trampled to death by elephants, and a reward of a gold coin was paid for every Uzbeg's head. He then marched to Allahabad, and thence to Benares, which closed its gates against him, and in order to punish the citizens the troops were allowed to sack the city.[2]

It is unlikely that Tulsī Dās and his immediate hearers had already forgotten such revolting barbarity within a decade after its occurrence, although, as will be shown later, no explicit reference to such political oppression can be found in the *Rāmcaritmānas*, written only seven years after the conquest of Allahabad and Benares.

From 1567 on, Akbar extended his conquests at a steady pace. In 1574, the year when Tulsī Dās set out to write the *Rāmcaritmānas*, he had already established supreme control over Northern India, including Gujarāt, and was engaged in the process of annexing Bengal to his great Empire.

Akbar's plans for the religious life of India were made public less than a year after Tulsī Dās had started writing his great masterpiece when, in January 1575, he ordered the construction of his "Ibādat-khānā", or "House of Worship", destined to serve as a place for philosophical and religious discussions and debates. In 1580, he loosened his ties with Islam, and in 1582 announced his project concerning a new "Dīn-i-Ilāhi", or "divine Faith", "with the great advantage of not losing what was good in any one religion, while gaining what was better in another".[3]

---

2. Allan, J. & others. *The Cambridge Shorter History of India*, p. 348.

3. Quoted by Allan, J. & others, *op. cit.*, p. 368.

Although Akbar's universal religion did not come out clearly in the open before 1582, it would seem that this event had been prepared, as it were, by a general atmosphere of relative religious tolerance which prevailed during the entire Moghul-Afghan period. In order to appreciate better, by comparison, the political climate of this period, a short description of the preceding era, namely that of the Delhi Sultanate, will be presented.

Although Muslim conquests had been made in India as early as 711 A.D., Muslim suzerainty was not established over the greater part of the sub-continent before the latter part of the thirteenth century under the regin of 'Alā-ud-dīn' who became Sultan of Delhi in 1296 and extended his dominion to the better part of South India. North India, however, had been under the control of the Delhi Sultanate as early as 1229, when Iltutmish, who had acceded to the throne of Delhi in 1210 or 1211 A.D., was nominated Great Sultan by the Caliph of Baghdād. By that time, Iltutmish had already brought under his control Badāūn, Oudh, Benares, Lahore and Swālik, all dependencies of Delhi. As Great Sultan, he extended his dominion further to Bengal, Mālwā and Ujjain. The Delhi Sultanate, whose apogee started with the turn of the thirteenth century A.D., maintained its supremacy in India until the reign of Firuz Tughluq (1351-1388), after which it suffered a steady disintegration to be replaced in the sixteenth century by the Turko-Afghan dynasty, whose rule lasted three centuries.

The Delhi Sultanate is generally regarded as a period during which Hindus and Muslims formed two distinct and hostile communities. On the one hand, the Hindus bore towards the Muslim *mleccha* (impure) an instinctive repugnance. Al-Bīrūnī, one of the few contemporary Muslim historians who had a sincere sympathy for the Hindus, notes that "all their (the Hindus') fanaticism is directed against those who do not belong to them—against all foreigners. They call them *mleccha* i.e. impure, and forbid having any connection with them, be it by intermarriage or any other kind of relationship, or by sitting, eating and drinking with them, because thereby, they think, they would be polluted... They are not allowed to receive anybody who does not belong to them, even if he wished it, or was inclined to their religion. This, too, renders any connection with them quite impossible, and constitutes the widest gulf between us and them."[4] On the other hand, the general attitude of the Muslims towards their Hindu subjects, to whom the former frequently referred as "infidels", was also one of arrogant contempt. Throughout this period, Hindus were not allowed to erect temples unless they paid a discriminatory poll-tax (*jizya*), and Hindu pilgrims had to pay a special fee to visit their own sacred places.[5] The Sultan Fīrūz Tughluq (1351-1388) held more bigoted views by refusing the erection of temples even by Hindus who paid the *jizya* ! Almost all high offices were bestowed upon Muslims, whether Indian or foreign.[6]

The following description of the armies of 'Alā-ud-dīn' (1296-1316) by a fifteenth century historian, Padmanābha, could apply to many of the Muslim campaigns of the time:

> The conquering army burnt villages; devasted the land, plundered people's wealth, took Brāhmaṇas, children and women of all castes captive, and flogged them with thongs and raw hide, carried a moving prison with it, and converted the prisoners into obsequious Turks.[7]

Another vivid description from the pen of a Muslim historian is made of Sultan Sikandar Lodī's (1489-1517) warfare methods:

> He was so zealous a Musulmān that he utterly destroyed the diverse places of worship of the infidels, and left not a vestige remaining of them. He entirely ruined the shrines of Mathurā, the mine of heathenism, and turned their principal Hindu places of worship into caravanserais and colleges. Their stone images were given

---

4. Quoted by V. N. Ghoshal in *The Struggle for Empire*, Vol. 5 of the series *The History and Culture of the Indian People*, Gen. Ed. R. C. Majumdar, Bombay: Bharatiya Vidya Bhavan, 1966 (first published in 1957), p. 501, (Al-Birūnī : first half of the 11th C. A. D.)

5. Majumdar, R. C. "Hindu Muslim Relations", *The Delhi Sultanate*, Vol. 6 of the series *The History and Culture of the Indian Pepole*, p. 620.

6. *Ibid.*, p. 622.

7. Quoted by Dr. K.M. Munshi in the Foreword to *The Struggle for Empire*, p. xv.

> to the butchers to serve them as meat-weights, and all the Hindus in Mathurā were strictly prohibited from shaving their heads and beards, and performing their ablutions. He thus put an end to all idolatrous rites of the infidels there; and no Hindu, if he wished to have his head or beard shaved, could get a barber to do it. Every city thus conformed as he desired to the customs of Islam.[8]

The above must not lead us to think that no degree of sympathetic understanding could exist between the two communities during this period. Historians have shown that there was some degree of mutual harmony and toleration in different spheres of life, particularly in literature, art and architecture.[9] Yet, when all is told, the Delhi Sultanate will be especially remembered for "the ferocity of Muslim bigotry, (which,) renewed at intervals and therefore always of recent memory, fed the ulcer that was eating into the vitals of communal amity."[10]

We now come to the Moghul-Afghan period, which opened with the invasion by Bābur in 1526. With Bābur, who was Akbar's grandfather, began a century and a half of unprecedented political stability and cultural harmony between Hindus and Muslims,[11] a period which attained its apogee under the reign of Akbar.

Contrary to so many of his predecessors, Bābur does not seem to have been a ruthless ruler indulging in needless masscare and indiscriminate destruction. His son Humāyūn lost most of the conquered lands to Sher Shāh (1539—1545) of the Turko-Afghans; the latter proved to be an able administrator, who, though an orthodox Muslim, treated the Hindus with tolerance and justice, thus showing that 'his religious attitude was free from medieval bigotry.'[12] His accidental death having given rise to anarchy and civil wars, Humāyūn

8. Quoted by R. C. Majumdar in "Hindu Muslim Relations", p. 626.
9. For instance, see Majumdar & others, *An Advanced History of India*, pp. 393-415.
10. Majumdar, R. C. "Hindu Muslim Relations", p. 627.
11. Majumdar, R. C. & others, *op. cit.*, p. 368.
12. *Ibid.*, p. 435.

was able to recover a part of the lost territory between 1554 and 1556, though his own accidental death in turn left North India in disorder and famine. The mission of bringing about political unification and economic prosperity was left to his son Akbar, whose rule of forty-five years extended over the whole of Northern and Central India.

It can be said, then, that compared to the atmosphere of intolerance which characterized the Delhi Sultanate, a new spirit of reconciliation emerged under the Moghul Afghans. However, while promoting a certain degree of harmony between Hindus and Muslims, the rules immediately preceding Akbar never questioned the distinctiveness of the two cultures. Akbar would move a step further by proposing a blend of both traditions resulting in a Universal Religion. The latter did not, however, become an official project until 1582 and Akbar's definite break with Islam occurred only in 1580. Thus, by the time Tulsī Dās set out to write the *Rāmcaritmānas*, in 1574, Akbar's intention had not as yet become public policy. However, it seems clear that the ruler's catholicity of temperament and ideals had not been the result of a sudden conversion. A number of factors which seem to have influenced him much earlier, have been analysed and enumerated by Majumdar, Raychaudhuri and Datta:[13]

> Firstly, the influence of his heredity "endowed him with those qualities of head and heart that prepared him to receive the impress of his environments, and reflect it in the best possible way". In spite of their being conquerors, Timur and his descendants were lovers of art and literature and rose above religious orthodoxy, largely owing to their contact with Sufism. Akbar's mother, the daughter of a Persian scholar, sowed in his mind the seeds of toleration.
>
> Secondly, Akbar's early contact with Sufism, during his stay in the court of Kabul, where many Sufi saints had fled away from Persia under the pressure of Safavi persecution, and subsequently the influence of his

13. Majumdar, R. C. & others, *op. cit.*, pp. 450-451.

> tutor, Abdul Latif, impressed upon his mind the worth of liberal and sublime ideals and made him eager to "attain the ineffable bliss of direct contact with the Divine Reality".
>
> Lastly, his Rajput wives and his contact with Hinduism, and the reformation movements of his time, made an impression on his imaginative mind.[14]

That these influences had been at work before 1580 is evidenced by the fact that as early as 1562 Akbar had inaugurated his policy of conciliation by marrying a Hindu princess and admitting Mān Singh, a Hindu, to high office. Again, in 1563 and 1564 he announced the remission of the tax on Hindu pilgrims visiting their sacred places, and the remission of the *jizya*. It seems clear, therefore, that "the main lines of his (Akbar's) policy, directed to obliterating all difference in treatment between Muslims and Hindus, were fixed as political principles while he was still to all outward appearance an orthodox and zealous Muslim and long before his open breach with Islam".[15]

The synthetic trend encouraged by Akbar extended its influence to various fields such as architecture, painting, and music. In architecture, the Moghul period marked a culmination of a process whereby Muslim and Hindu styles were mingled. Sher Shāh's mausoleum, in the district of Bihār, is a blend of Hindu and Muslim architecture. In the mausoleum of Humāyūn, completed in 1569 at Old Delhi, the ground-plan of the tomb as well as the white marble of the exterior are Indian, and the coloured tile decoration typical of Persian builders is absent. The architectural development in India attained its apogee under Akbar, whose "tolerance of the Hindus, sympathy with their culture, and the policy of winning them over to his cause, led him to use Hindu styles of architecture in many of his buildings".[15a] This attitude is illustrated, for example, in many of the buildings of Fatehpur Sīkrī, the imperial capital between 1569 and 1584.

---

14. Allan, J. & others, *op. cit.*, p. 345.
15. Majumdar, R.C. & others *op. cit*, p. 379.

15a. *Ibid.*

The same tendencies can be seen in artistic paintings. In a famous painting dated 1562 showing the arrival of the *Vaiṣṇava* musician Tānsen at the Moghul Court, the fusion of Hindu and Sino-Persian styles is manifest. Likewise, between 1569 and 1584, paintings of artists showing Hindu and Persian influences were used to decorate the wall of Akbar's new capital at Fatehpur Sīkrī, already referred to above.

Like his Moghul predecessors, Akbar also took a great deal of interest in music. Among the thirty-six singers who enjoyed his patronage, the *Vaiṣṇava* Tānsen, referred to above, seems to have been the most renowned.

The spirit of conciliation prevalent in Tulsī Dās' time can help to throw more light on the significance of the *Rāmcaritmānas*. Although this subject will be discussed later, we can already say at this point that Akbar's impartiality towards the Hindus contained both a promise and a threat for the tradition: a promise because a growing atmosphere of tolerance allowed for a reaffirmation of the distinctiveness of the tradition, a threat because group solidarity nurtured by foreign oppression was being undermined as a result of the ruler's growing liberal attitude. Moreover, Akbar's impartiality could just as well be the result of mere disinterestedness towards particular traditions, now considered *dépasseés*. In that sense the *Rāmcaritmānas* was needed not only to reaffirm the Hindu tradition, but also to counter the threat underlying the ambiguous policy of conciliation, which had been in the making for some time in North India.

2. *The Religious Context*

The typology adopted earlier will again provide the guideline for the analysis of the religious context in which the *Rāmcaritmānas* was written. The present chapter will show that the two 'extreme' positions, namely vedic orthodoxy and antinomian theism, were the predominant trends in Tulsī Dās' day. The next chapter will then argue that the *Rāmcaritmānas* contributed to the revival of the middle stream.

Throughout this period, vedic orthodoxy was kept very much alive by numerous publications of commentaries and digests on *mimāṁsā* and *śāstra* regulations. Thus, Pārthasārathi Miśra wrote the *Śāstradipikā* to explain the *Mimāṁsā sūtra*: in 1543 A.D.

Rāmakrṣṇa Bhaṭṭa commented on the *Śāstradipikā* in the *Yuktisnehaprapūraṇi*. Important Śāstraic commenatries were written by Mādhava of Vijayanagar, who composed between 1335-1360 A.D. a work entitled *Kālanirṇaya*; Viśveśvara, who between 1360-1370 A.D. wrote for King Madanapāla a work called *Madanapārijāta*; in the fifteenth century, Kulluka, from Benares, wrote a frequently printed commentary of the *Manusmṛti*; and Raghunandana Bhaṭṭācārya from Bengal wrote around 1500 A.D. an important work on the detailed religious duties of the Hindu, entitled the *Aṣṭāviṁśati Tattva*.

Moving closer to Tulsī Dās' epoch and geographical context, we find that several noteworthy commentaries were produced in Benares in the sixteenth and seventeenth centuries. Thus, the *Bhāṭṭadipikā*, and on a larger scale the *Mimāṁsākaustubha*, both written by Khaṇḍadeva who died at Benares in 1665 A.D. deal fully with the *Mimāṁsā sūtra*.[16] Nanda-paṇḍita, whose activity must be placed between 1595 A.D. and 1630,[17] wrote at Benares a śāstric commentary called *Vaijayanti* in 1622-23.[18] Another Benares writer, Kamalākara-bhaṭṭa, whose literary activity is assigned to the period between 1610 and 1640, composed twelve works concerned with topics of *Dharma śāstra*, the *Śūdrakamalākara*, the *Vivādatāṇḍava* and the *Nirṇayasindhu* being the most famous.[19] Nārāyaṇa-bhaṭṭa, whose works are placed between 1540-1570 A.D., wrote numerous works on *Dharma śāstra*, which are standard works used even now almost throughout the whole of India.[20] A work of a similar type is attributed to Toḍar Mal, the celebrated finance minister of Akbar and an acquaintance of Tulsī Dās, who compiled between 1565-1589 A.D. an extensive encyclopaedia of civil and religious law, astronomy and medicine.[21]

In attempting to explain why such works were flourishing, the importance of the socio-political context of the time must be taken into consideration. In a recent study of the classical law of India, Robert Lingat discusses the effect of the Muslim

16. Keith, A. B. *The Karma-Mīmāṁsā*, p. 12.
17. Kane P. V. *History of Dharmaśāstra*, Vol. I, p. 432.
18. *Ibid.*, p. 70.
19. *Ibid.*, pp. 432-437.
20. *Ibid.*, pp. 419-420.
21. *Ibid.*, pp. 421-423.

take over on the elaboration of śāstric regulations.[22] According to this scholar, Muslim conquests produced a renewal of interest in śāstric digests and treatises, and such renewal is partly attributable to the reactions of the orthodox faithful in regions directly subject to Muslim rule. However, even at the height of Muslim power, an impressive number of similar works also originated in independent Hindu states which enjoyed almost complete internal autonomy. Mr. Lingat concludes that the "flowering of treatises and digests during the Muslim period seems to have been due to the need for a new effort on the part of interpretation to adapt the law to the changes that must have come about in Hindu opinion and manners as a result of the Muslim conquest".[23] He goes on to explain that at a time when the coexistence of two communities effected their respective customs Muslim rulers considered it their mission to maintain the presence of Islam in India. At the same time, Hindu śāstric commentators felt the need to propagate their teaching in order to inform the Hindu population of what were strict duties with which no compromise could be permitted. Thus it is that all over India, authors of repute felt the necessity to appeal to their coreligionists to maintain a faithful observance of the Hindu ethical code.

We have seen that in addition to the *Mimāṁsā* and the *Dharma śāstras*, the *Vedānta* school of philosophy was also central to vedic orthodoxy. It is generally agreed that the influence of Śaṅkara's advaitic views was still prevalent among the North Indian Brahmins of this period. This influence is particularly noticeable in the *Adhyātma Rāmāyaṇa*, which, as we shall see in Part III of the present dissertation, was well known to the disciples of Rāmānanda and no doubt to Tulsī Dās himself.

The most obvious example in medieval North India of the second stream, namely antinomian theism, is the religion preached by Kabīr. Frequently described as the "weaver from Benares", Kabīr lived in the fifteenth century, probably between 1440 and 1518.[24] The tradition that he was a disciple of

22. Lingat, R. *The Classical Law of India*, trans. from the French by J. D. M. Derrett, pp. 259-260.

23. *Ibid.*, p. 260.

24. Farquhar, J. N. *An Outline of the Religious Literature of India*, p. 331.

Rāmānanda does not rest on strong evidence.[25] Whereas at least two of his collections, namely the *Kabīr-granthāvali* and the selection included in the *Ādi-granth,* have adequate claims to be considered as authentic, the *Bijak*, which is later than the former two, is probably a *Kabīr-panthī* recasting.[26]

While the question of classifying Kabīr as a monist *nirguṇi* or as a worshipper of a personal and qualified (*saguṇa*) God is still debated among scholars,[27] what is important for the purpose of this thesis is the fact that love of God played an essential role in his religion. Whereas his writings contain frequent allusions to the mystical absorption of the soul in God, his general attitude is that of the devotee before the Lord "who has bound his heart to His own with gentle bounds".[28] Thus, he entertains relations of the most touching familiarity with God, retains an acute consciousness of his own misery, and counts on the grace of God for his salvation:

> How shall I be saved, O Master, how shall I be saved?
> Here I am full of iniquities !
> Weary, I stand at your threshold
> Who then, if not You, will care for me?
> Let me see your face, open the door !

An important trait of Kabīr's religion, is that God is conceived as a completely spiritual Being, which one should endeavour to discover in the depths of his own interiority. Consequently the illusory manifestations of the divine under the form of *avatāras* should be rejected :

> They say the Lord of the world finding inequalities of the weak and the strong came as Rāma. But Kabīr says, before a one (Rāma) who took birth and died, I cannot bend my head.[30]

25. Bījak, Śabad 77: *One Hundred Poems of Kabīr*, trans. R. Tagore, no. xxix, p. 36. The authenticity of this collection is now considered doubtful.

26. McLeod, W. H. *Guru Nānak and the Sikh Religion*, p. 156.

27. For a recent discussion on the subject, see Vaudeville, C. "Kabir and Interior Religion", *History of Religions*, vol. 3, no. 2, pp. 191-201.

28. Quoted by Vaudeville, C. in "Kabīr and Interior Religion", p. 198.

29. *Ibid.*, p. 198.

30. Quoted by Tara Chand, *Influence of Islam on Indian Culture*, p. 163.

Another relevant trait of Kabīr's religion is the rejection of traditional customs, institutions, and scriptures. It is significant that in a poem attributed to him, he is said to have established a direct causal relation between his conversion to "the Way", i.e. love of God, and his decision to give up all traditional rites and ceremonies:

> O Brother ! when I was forgetful,
> my true *Guru* showed me the Way.
> Then I left off all rites and ceremonies.[31]

This attitude is particularly expected from the *jivanmukti* whose supreme degree of perfection Kabīr claims to have attained :

> Only they who understand the fourth degree, have obtained the supreme position: They never entertain love for pilgrimages, fasting, or for religious ceremonies, purifications, and austerities of the superstitious.[32]

Kabīr extends his condemnation to the caste system and the distinctions between Hindus and Muslims :

> Saith Kabīr, renounce family, caste and lineage; become an ant, and thou canst pick up and eat the sugar.[33]

> Adam who was first, did not know whence came mother Eve. Then there was no Turk (Muslim) nor Hindu.[34]

He is especially critical of the Brahmin caste, who enjoy the privileges attached to that name as a consequence of their birth rather than their degree of virtue:

> How art thou a *Brahmin*? How am I a *Sudar* (sic)?
> How am I of blood and you of milk (i.e. superior)?
> Saith Kabīr, only he who meditateth in God
> Is a *Brahmin* in my estimation.[35]

---

31. *One Hundred Poems of Kabīr*, poem 65.
32. *Ādī Granth*, Kedara 1.
33. *Ādī Granth*, Ramkalī, 12.
34. *Bījak*, Ramaini, 62.
35. *Ādī Granth*, Gaurī 7.

Finally, Kabir rejects the authority of both the *Vedas* and the *Koran*, which he describes as so many "cloaks of falsehood".[36]

Thus, even though he shows by his own example and his declarations[37] that the life of a householder and the exercise of a trade do not have to be forsaken to follow the path of love of God, Kabīr is probably the most iconoclastic of devotees with regards to traditional rituals, social framework and scriptures.

Recent efforts have been made to establish that Kabīr's religion is an original synthesis of medieval yoga and vaiṣṇavite devotionalism, with some elements borrowed from the *Sufi* tradition.[38] Numerous adherents of Tantric yoga in medieval North India belonged to the Nāth sect, known after Gorakh Nāth as *Gorakhnāthis* or *Kānphat Yogis*.[39] *Nāth* influence is particularly noticeable in Kabīr's rejection of Brahmanical authority regarding prescribed ceremonies, *varṇa* distinctions, sacred languages, and scriptures: in his emphasis upon mystical unity with God; and in his search for interiority based on experimental truth.[40]

That the Viṣṇu devotees of the North influenced Kabīr is obvious from the latter's insistence on love as the means *par excellence* of finding God, even though he did not acknowledge the Vaiṣṇavite belief in the *avatāra*. This last trait may be due to the influence of the third strand which composed this tradition, namely Muslim Mysticism, which had been spread by the *Sufis* in North-west India since the thirteenth century. Muslim *Sufis* regarded God as a purely spiritual Being, incompatible with the possibility of a sensible manifestation under the form of an *avatāra*.

The influence of the *Sufis* on Kabīr may also account for the latter's tendency to oppose traditional duties and love of God. The *Sufis* are well known for their antinomian tendencies,[41]

36. *Bījak*, Śabda, 113.

37. "I devote myself to and perform the duties which God assigned me". (*Ādi Granth*, Maru 4.)

38. Vaudeville, C. "Kabīr and Interior Religion". See also McLeod, W. H. *op. cit.*

39. *Ibid.*, p. 152.

40. *Ibid.*, pp. 153, 156. Vaudeville, C. "Kabir and Interior Religion", p. 196.

41. See for instance Trimingham, J. S. *The Sufi Orders in Islam*, pp. 16, 29, 62, etc.. Laoust, H. *Les chismes dans l'Islam*, pp. 119, 156, 282.

and these tendencies were particularly noticeable among medieval Indian *Sufis*.[42] In his study of Sufism in medieval Hindi literature, Charles S. J. White comments on a significant passage found in the *Padmāvat* :

> Someone asks the hero of *Padmāvat*, "Oh, Yogi, tell me what is your caste, station in life and where do you live?" To these and other similar questions the hero replied quite simply that as a yogi he had abandoned all distinctions of caste and the like. Morever, he had ceased to care for the opinion of the world and whether he would be punished or whether he would receive rewards. In fact his personal situation was transcended.[43]

Such disregard for traditional social customs and prescriptions was often severely judged by faithful Muslims who acknowledged the Koranic authority in social and legal matters. The Sufīs defended their antinomian attitude by claiming for themselves a special way reserved for the initiates:

> The Sufī is apparently less free, since he acknowledges the Qur'anic revelation and the principles of Islamic orthodoxy—but he gets around this in his own way by gnosis: without denying the validity of the traditional path, based on the Quar'anic prescriptions he willingly leaves it to the mass of believers, in quest of the joys of "Paradise". He chooses another way for himself the way of love and of intimate experience of God, a way reserved for the initiates only; in this way he will come to a progressive illumination symbolized by the rending of the veils which separate him from the perfect Beauty.[44]

The influence of these views must also be taken into consideration as an element which contributed in spreading the anti-

---

42. Trimingham, J. S. *op. cit.*, p. 98.

43. White, C. S. J. "Sufism in Medieval Hindi Literature", *History of Religions*, vol. 5, no. 11, p. 122.

44. Vaudeville, C. "Kabir and Interior Religion", p. 196.

nomian position in medieval North India, a position which, as will be argued in the conclusion of this chapter, Tulsī Dās could not very well ignore.

The Kabirian insistence on interior religion accompanied by the rejection of traditional religious texts, image worship, formal religious exercises, pilgrimage, and ritual bathing, represented a challenge to the conventional pattern of both Hinduism and Islam, where religion consisted essentially, for a large number of their adherents, of external authority and conventional rituals:

> In the case of the Hindu community this authority was generally accorded to the brahmans and through them to the Vedas and Puranas. The required response consisted in the performance of the customary rites appropriate to a man's station within the caste structure of society. For the Muslim religion also meant loyalty to objective authority. In his case the authority was the Qur'an and its exercise the acknowledged function of the qāzīs. (qāḍī, i.e. judge)[45]

Kabīr and his followers are considered as the most typical representatives of what is known as the *Sant* Movement,[46] whose impact was widely felt throughout North India from the fifteenth century on. The movement included two other important groups, namely the *Kṛṣṇaite Sants* and *Rāmaite Sants* that will now be considered.

The most popular representative of the Kṛṣṇaite saints in the Hindi-speaking region of India is Sūr Dās (ca. 1478-1583),

45. McLeod, W. H., *op. cit.*, p. 151.

46. (Le mot 'Sant') s'applique originellement à l'individu qui a dépassé sa propre individualité et qui a fait l'expérience de l'Etre divin, ou de la Réalité suprême. C'est en général un synonyme de sādhu: 'saint'. Cependant, dés avant Kabīr le terme avait déjá servi á désigner une école, ou pluôt un groupe particulier de bhakta vaiṣṇava, appartenant à la secte Vārakarī (adorateurs de Vitthal) au Mahārāstra. Pour désigner le Vitthal sampradāya c'est-ā-dire la secte Vārakarī, non que les sectateurs des autres sampradāya na soient pas sant—mais ceux-ci sont les Sant par excellence. Deux d'entre eux, Gyandev et Namdev, sont mentionnés par Kabir comme des ancêtres. A leur suite, le terme fut applique à Kabīr et à leurs successeurs, qui leur resemblaient sur plusieurs points. Vaudevillé, C. *Kabīr Grānthāvalī* (Doha), Pondicherry: Institut d'Indologie francais, 1957, p. xiv.

traditionally known as the blind poet of Āgra, and a disciple of Vallabhācārya (ca. 1481-1583). According to a sectarian work, the *Bhāvaprakāsh,* at the age of eighteen, Sūr Dās met Vallabhācāryā who introduced him to the *Bhāgavata Purāṇa.*[47] The blind poet's fame, which supposedly reached Akbar, rests mostly on a collection of poems known as the *Sūrsāgar.* Although he addressed his devotion mostly to Kṛṣṇa, he also acknowledged other *avatāras,* especially Rāma, as is testified to by the fact that he wrote his own abridged version of the *Rāmāyaṇa* where Rāma is acclaimed as the incarnation of the divine.

In the *Sūrsāgar,* Sūr Dās points out that the collection of poems is based on the twelve books of the *Bhāgavata Purāṇa*:

> Vyāsa composed the twelve chapters (sic) of the *Bhāgavata* and recited them to Śukadeva: Sūrdās describes and sings the same ones in the popular language and in *padas.*[48]

In following the *Bhāgavata Purāṇa,* Sūr Dās nevertheless added elements which reflect his own religious inclinations. For example, in the first book of *Sūrsāgar,* which contains some two hundred poems, he insists in a distinctive way on his own unworthiness, on the transitory nature of this world, and on love as the way *par excellence* of attaining God. The emphasis upon the repetition of the Names of Kṛṣṇa and on the pangs of separation are also his own.

Drawing not only from the *Bhāgavata Purāṇa,* but also from other traditions,[49] Sūr Dās likes to dwell at length, in the tenth book of the *Sūrsāgar,* on the details of Kṛṣṇa's birth; the first feeding ceremony and the piercing of the ears; his activities as a child, such as sleeping, playing, stealing butter, grazing cows, and stealing the clothes of the *gopis.* Considerable attention is given in the same book to Rādhā, who was not mentioned in

---

47. Pandey, S. M. and Zide, M. *The Poems of Sūrdās,* an unpublished anthology, South Asia Language and Area Center, University of Chicago, 1962, p. 2.

48. *Sūrsāgar,* Chapter I, pada 225. Al quotations from the *Sūrsāgar* are taken from Pandey & Zide's translation.

49. Pandey, S. M. and Zide, M. *The Poems of Sūrdās,* p. 6.

the *Bhāgavata Purāṇa.* The "bee songs" (*bhramaragitās*), which express in a satirical tone the *gopis*' opposition to Uddhava, a follower of *nirguṇa brahman* and *jñāna-yoga*, are also absent in the *Bhāgavata Purāṇa.* In the eleventh book, Sūr Dās explains at length the three traditional paths of *bhakti*, *jñāna*, and *karma*, with a clear emphasis on the priority of *bhakti*.

For Sūr Dās love of God is the only way to salvation. In his eagerness to promote this way, he repeatedly mocks Uddhava's doctrine favouring knowledge (*jñāna-yoga*).

> The milkmaids say, "Uddhava, you
> force a boat up a dry river..[50]
>
> Uddhava, we are not deserving of Yoga.
> How can a weak woman know the essence of
> knowledge—how can she meditate?
> You tell us to close those eyes where
> the image of Hari lives.
> Oh Bee, such deceitful Words we will not listen to.
> Who wants to suffer, having his ears pierced
> and letting his hair grow long and matted?
> You tell us to give up sandal wood paste
> and smear ashes on our bodies, we who have
> been badly burned by fire of separation from him.
> He for whom a *Yogi* wanders around until he
> forgets himself, is within our hearts.[51]

Sūr Dās' views on the relation between social duty and love of God are revealed in poems dealing with the love of Rādhā and the other *gopis* of Kṛṣṇa:

> When the milkmaids heard the flute in the woods,
> They were disquieted and forgot their household work.
> They did not at all fear family honor or the sanction
> of the Scriptures.[52]

Rādhā is not only fearless of family honour. She forgets her family altogether:

50. *Sūrsāgar*, 87.
51. *Ibid.*, 95
52. *Sūrsāgar*, 56.

Smiling, Giridhar spoke these sweet words.
"Why do you provoke your elders, inviting their anger and being always regretful?
The duty (*dharma*) of a human being is to take care of one's family, home and kinsmen."
Then Rādhā replied, "Let them talk. What can they do by talking? I have forgotten them".[53]

In another passage, the *gopi*, whose eyes are fixed on Hari's face, claims that she has become oblivious of Scriptures, family prestige and tradition:

They (the eyes) follow neither tradition nor scriptures, nor do they care for their family's prestige, they have become contrary.[54]

Not only is the importance of one's social duties diminished as a consequence of one's love of God; life itself seems of no value without Kṛṣṇa's presence:

"Nothing has interested me since my treasure
Kṛṣṇa left me.
I pay no attention to my housework."
A milkmaid says, "Night and day, I repeat his name.
We are not dead, but neither are we living."
So says Sūr Dās.[55]

Here, as in the *Bhāgavata Purāṇa*, the gopīs follow Kṛṣṇa in spite of the latter's protest that a woman's duty is to love her husband and that they should, therefore, return to their home. But the milkmaids do not comply to this entreaty "since they know in their hearts that their real lover is Kṛṣṇa, and he can be attained only through detachment from worldly things, including husbands and children."[56]

Sūr Dās' increased attention given to Rādhā and her attitude towards traditional customs and regulations is another

53. *Ibid.*, 66.
54. *Ibid.*, 70.
55. *Ibid.*, 72.
56. Pandey, S. M. & Zide, M. *The Poems of Sūrdās*, p. 23.

illustration of a significant inclination in the *Sant* tradition toward antinomian theism in medieval North India. Furthermore, his contribution is important to keep in mind as it supports the fact that the *Bhāgavata Purāṇa* had already influenced North Indian piety a generation before Tulsī Dās.

The *Hindi Rāmaite Sants* represent a third stream of the *Sant* Movement. Although there is still very little known about Rāmānanda, scholars generally agree that he was the acknowledged leader of the North Indian Rāmaites of the fifteenth century known as the *Rāmānandis*. The question of the dates of his birth and death has still not received a definite answer. Some[57] suggest ca. 1400-1470, whereas others[58] opt for an earlier date, namely ca. 1300-1411.

One of the earliest available sources of information on Rāmānanda, which unfortunately is not always reliable, is the sixteenth century *Bhakta Mālā*, the Vaiṣṇavite text of Nābhā Dās already referred to. According to this source, Rāmānanda was the disciple of Rāghavānanda, a thirteenth-century Southerner, and a member of the Śrī Vaiṣṇava sect. Born in Allahabad, Rāmānanda is said to have settled in Benares after having taught *Rāma-bhakti* all over India. He is said to have left aside caste barriers, and broken away from his master's sect because of caste restrictions on teaching, eating, and religious life.[59]

It is believed in modern *Rāmānandī* circles that Rāmānanda had been educated at Benares by a Śāṅkara advaitin before being transferred to Rāghavānanda. According to Dr. P. D. Barthwal, Rāmānanda managed to accept both philosophical systems, the advaitic and the viśiṣṭādvaitic:

> The change of masters does not appear to have involved a break with the principles of philosophy that Rāmānanda devotedly learnt during his early years. He seems to have adopted the *Vaiṣṇava Bhakti* only to fit it into the *Advaita* system of Śaṅkarācārya. The rupture

57. Gonda, J. *Les religions de l'inde,* 2 vol., Vol. II, p. 205.

58. Bhandarkar, R.G., *op. cit.*, p. 67; Naidu, S.S.R. *A Comparative Study of Kamba Ramayana and Tulasi Ramayana*, p. 94.

59. Allchin, F. R. *Kavitāvalī*, p. 26.

> that he had with the sect of his new *Guru* must have some connection with his philosophic leanings also. Thus did monistic pantheism and the love of a personal God, the essential characteristic of Vaiṣṇavism, join hands in Rāmānanda.[60]

If this is true, then the Rāmānandī use of both Rāmānuja's *Śribhāṣya* based on viśiṣṭādvaitic principles and the advaitic *Adhyātma Rāmāyaṇa* would be explained by Rāmānanda's double philosophical background.

More lightwill be thrown on Rāmānanda's theology when the question of the authorship of the *Adhyātma Rāmāyaṇa* is definitely solved. J. Gonda sees a similarity between Rāmānanda's doctrine (as reflected by his disciples' teachings) and that of the *Adhyātma Rāmāyaṇa* but is unable to find any historical link between the two.[61] J. N. Farquhar thinks that the *Adhyātma Rāmāyaṇa* may have been the product of some southern Rāmaite sect to which Rāmānanda belonged, a sect based on advaitic theology and *bhakti-mārga*. He suggests that Rāmānanda could have brought the work with him to the North, along with the *Agastya Saṁhitā* and Rāmānuja's *Śribhāṣya*.[62] Many scholars feel that whatever its origin the *Adhyātma Rāmāyaṇa* was an instrument used by Rāmānanda to bring harmony between the Dvaitins and the Advaitins who in his day frequently quarrelled over their differences, sometimes with violence.[63]

In 1943, Mr. R. M. Shastri devoted a long paper to this very question. As his arguments cannot be fully presented here because of their complexity, the author's own summary of his main conclusions will be given here:

> In fine, Rāmānanda, son of Devala, a Kānyakubja Brāhmaṇa, was born at Prāyaga in 1299 A.D. and

---

60. Barthwal, P. D. *Nirguṇa School of Hindī Poetry*, p. 196, quoted by R. M. Shastri in *The Authorship of the Adhyātmarāmāyaṇa*, Ganganath Jha Research Institute, Issue I, 1943.

61. Gonda, J. *op. cit.*, Vol. II, p. 205.

62. Farquhar, J. N. *An Outline of Religious Literature of India*, p. 325.

63. See Mr. Sita Ram's response to Mr. Farquhar's article on the historical position of Rāmānanda, *J. R. A. S.*, LII, pp. 239-241.

> went to Kāśi at the age of 12, and there pursuing higher studies in the *Advaita-Vedānta* and practices in Śaivism and *Rāma-bhakti*, wrote the *Adhyātmarāmayaṇa* as the best synthesis of his achievements in the domain of practical philosophy and religion and a nice specimen of a literary work, before he instituted his own sect which resulted in developing two parallel currents of *Bhakti*, the *Saguṇa* and *Nirguṇa* one, the germs of both having been deposited in this work.[64]

This complex theological heritage would explain, according to this same author, the diversity of theological leanings among Rāmānanda's disciples.[65] The fact that most scholars still hesitate to adopt Mr. Shastri's views invites prudence. Likewise, the attribution to Rāmānanda of a poem found in Guru Nānak's *Granthasāheb* is not firmly established.[66]

Some of the most significant orientations Rāmānanda seems to have imparted to his disciples are the following. He gave *Rāma-bhakti* a decisive impetus in the Northern part of India.[67] With regards to caste distinctions, he took a more liberal attitude than his predecessors in the choice of his disciples,[68] which is testified to by such facts as accepting a Muslim among his followers. Rules of eating such as those enjoined by Rāmānuja seem to have been over-looked.[69] He encouraged his disciples to use modern language for the propagation of the creed,[70] and he gave up the use of Sanskrit altogether. He gave his disciples a distinctive sectmark and a *mantra* ("Om Rāmāya namaḥ") which resembled those of the Śrī-Vaiṣṇavas closely but were yet different.[71]

On the basis of the above, it seems that Mr. A. Barth's

---

64. Shastri, R. M., *op. cit.*, p. 239.
65. *Ibid.*, pp. 236-237.
66. Ranade, R. D. *Pathway to God in Hindī Literature*, pp. 100-103.
67. Dasgupta, S. *A History of Indian Philosophy*, Vol. II, pp. 391-392.
68. Ranade, R. D. *Pathway to God in Hindī Literature*, p. 100.
69. Hopkins, E. W. *The Religions of India*, p. 502.
70. For this question, I have relied mostly on Mr. J. N. Farquhar's article "The Historical Position of Ramananda", *Journal of the Royal Asiatic Society*, LII, 1920.
71. See Farquhar's rejoinder to Mr. Sitā Ram's reply, in *Journal of the of the Royal Asiatic Society*, 1922, pp. 376-378.

contention that Rāmānanda taught "the vanity of merely external observances[72] is not without foundation, although his disciples, except perhaps Kabīr, do not seem to have been conspicuously unorthodox in social matters. We may therefore conclude that to the extent that Rāmānanda was led, on account of the intensity of his devotion, to neglect external observances, we may see another instance of antinomian theism in the movement he promoted.

So far, we have studied the socio-political context of Tulsī Dās' day. We have also studied the extent to which the two "extreme" positions, namely vedic orthodoxy and antinomian theism, influenced the religious climate of his milieu. In order to get a clearer insight of the motives that promoted Tulsī Dās to revive the middle stream, we now ask to what extent the *Rāmcaritmānas* reflects the socio-political and religious situation of the day and to what extent it reveals Tulsī Dās' reactions with regard to this situation.

The task of determining to what degree Tulsī Dās reacted in the *Rāmcaritmānas* to the socio-political trends of his day is not an easy one. Although the expression *kali yuga*, or Dark Ages, appears frequently in the story, the implications are not clear. It is possible that Tulsī Dās may have used the expression as a reference to Muslim domination. However, one could also agree with F. R. Allchin who argues (in the introduction of his translation of the *Vinayapatrikā*) that while the term *kali yuga* was used by the poets who lived in the bitter centuries preceding Bābur as a clear designation of the oppressions of their time, Tulsī Dās continued the ancient usage of referring to his own time with the classical description of Dark Age without necessarily implying a denunciation of Muslim cultural influence or political domination.

Except for these numerous references to the *kali yuga* one looks in vain in the *Rāmcaritmānas* for overt judgements on the socio-political context in which it was written. There are, however, some passages in Tulsī Dās' later works which, according to some probably apocryphal stories, were written in reference to the rulers of his day. For example *Kavitāvali* VII.25

---

72. Barth, A. *The Religions of India*, p. 195.

is seen as an answer to those who praised the generosity of great men and rulers:

> It is your way, O king of kings,
> that whoever seeks your mercy you protect,
> And leave him having mitigated
> his faults, sorrow and poverty.
> Who would abandon him whose very Name is a
> wishing-tree,
> Tulsī, and tend thorn-trees
> or caster-oil plants in its place?
> Who would beg from kings, and who
> endure going from land to land?
> Being pleased one may give great increase,
> but it is more than a mere farthing;
> Before whom else may the hands be held in supplication
> Except the ocean of mercy, King
> of kings and Lord of Sītā—Raghunāth?

Again, *Kavitāvali* VII.27 is considered a reply to those who urged Tulsī Dās to seek the favour and protection of Akbar:

> See the doings of that bearer of the earth
> Who took the five inanimate elements and made this body!
> He who looks after both living and unliving, tell me,
> will he not also care for his servant?
> Tulsī, say then, who else is like to Rāma whose house
> has Lakṣmī for its hand-maiden?
> What care should there be left in the world for the
> man whose salvation is the Lord of the Universe?

What are we to conclude from Tulsī Dās' quasi total silence on the contemporary socio-political situation? It is reasonable to assume that he could hardly be oblivious of the fact that most of his hearers would still remember vividly how in 1567 the gates of Benares had been closed against Akbar and how the latter, after forcing his way in, had allowed his troops to sack the Holy City as a measure of reprisal against its resisting citizens.[73] Yet, one looks in vain for references to these events in the *Rāmcaritmānas* as well as in the other works. Moreover,

73. Allan, J. & others, *op. cit.*, p. 372.

the fact that Tulsī Dās never broke his friendship with, or his appreciation for, his Hindu friend Toḍar Mal, who not only held a high administrative position under Akbar's reign, but seems to have been one of the latter's best friends,[74] suggests that the author of the *Rāmcaritmānas* was not openly critical of Akbar as a politician.

However, one cannot help seeing in the *Rāmcaritmānas* an implicit reaction *vis-à-vis* the universal approach so eloquently preached less than a century previously by such an influential voice as that of Kabīr, a trend which was now reaching its culmination in Akbar. Although we have no direct evidence that Tulsī Dās had Kabir and his followers in mind when he wrote the *Rāmcaritmānas*, yet in the *Dohāvali* (554), one of his later works, he denounces those who expound devotion "with *sakhis*, *śabdas*, and *dohās*", which are forms of verse explicitly associated with Kabīr and Nānak.[75] Furthermore, there is sufficient circumstantial evidence to warrant the view that when he set out to write his *magnum opus*, Tulsī Dās was aware of the religion of Kabīr. The latter had died only half a century before the *Rāmcaritmānas* was composed. He had lived in Benares, where Tulsī Dās had spent some time before 1574. Like Tulsī Dās, Kabīr invoked God under the name of Rāma. Both poets preached love of God as the preeminent path. Finally, the extent of Kabīr's influence was considerable in medieval North India:

> During the middle ages, there was not a single movement for freedom, whether spiritual or intellectual, which did not bear the stamp of Kabīr's influence.[76]

On a number of fundamental religious issues, the author of the *Rāmcaritmānas* is the antithesis of the "weaver from Benares". In fact, one cannot help seeing in the *Rāmcaritmānas* an effort to counter the iconoclastic drive of Kabīr's teachings *vis-à-vis* Hinduism, both as a culture and as a religion. Kabīr's refusal to bend his head before the son of Daśaratha; his designation

74. *Ibid.*, p. 348.
75. Allchin, F. R. *Kavitāvalī*, p. 49.
76. Sen, K. "The Medieval Mystics of North India", in the *Cultural Heritage of India*, Vol. IV, p. 379.

of the *Veda* as a cloak of falsehood; his alleged claim that a conversion to "the Way" or the attainment of *jīvan-mukti* leads to the realization that traditional rites, ceremonies, pilgrimages, fasting, purifications, austerities and "superstitions" are futile; his contempt for the Brahmin caste as an hereditary institution; and above all his contention that in the name of the brotherhood of man, Hindus as well as Muslims should be prepared to give up their differences for the sake of unity—on all of these the *Rāmcaritmānas* takes the opposite stand. When one reads the latter against the background of Kabīr's religion, it becomes all the more apparent that Tulsī Dās' masterpiece represents a vibrant appeal on behalf of the scriptures, rituals and social framework that constitute the precious legacy of the immemorial and venerable Hindu tradition.

Perhaps the most threatening element of Kabīr's religion was its rejection of ceremonial rites and formal worship based on "the *Vedas* and the *Purāṇas*", which, along with the respect for the caste system, play an important rôle in expressing the feeling of identity with Hindu culture and religion. The *Rāmcaritmānas* might be seen as a counter to such a threat, which had become widespread not only in Hindu milieu, but which was also preached by Jain poets such as Munirām Singh, and by the *Bengali Sahajiya Vaiṣṇavas,* especially Caṇḍīdās, who joined the Hindi poets in criticizing Brahmins and their scriptures, authorities, and ways of worship.[77] Time and again Tulsī Dās refers to the *Vedas,* always with a sense of veneration; nowhere does he suggest that devotees should discard traditional "superstitions". On the contrary the *Rāmcaritmānas* is replete with descriptions of the devotees' scrupulously performing the ceremonies and rites enjoined by the scriptures; and his attachment to the traditional order of *varṇas* (castes) with special respect to the Brahmin caste is conspicuously affirmed throughout. For Tulsī Dās, no reason, including social unity, could justify the loss of religious and cultural identity. Such social unity could not be genuine. It is therefore not surprising that in a passage of the *Dohāvali,* quoted by Allchin, in the introduction to his translation of the *Kavitāvali,* Tulsī Dās has spoken disapprovingly of Kabīr and his disciples, who

77. Pandey, S. M. & Zide, M. *Poems from Mīrābāi,* p. 13.

"expound *Bhakti*, while scorning the *Vedas* and *Purānas*",[78] and who "leave the path of Bhakti to Hari and overcome by delusion dream up many new paths".[79]

For Tulsī Dās, there is no inherent incompatibility between genuine love of God and the traditional paths expounded in the *Vedas* and the *Purāṇas*. In other words, respect for the traditional is certification that one's love of God is authentic and not illusory.

This preference for the middle path, where both traditional duties and love of God are upheld, also explains Tulsī Dās' refusal to adopt the approach of the Mīmāṁsakas or the Śāstric scholars then in Benares. While this orthodox approach may have been seen as an effective alternative against the antinomian trend, it failed to give equal insistence to love of God, which was of vital importance to Tulsī Dās. As we shall see later (Ch. VI) the importance attached to love of God also explains Tulsī Dās' reluctance to espouse the *Adhyātma Rāmāyaṇa*'s philosophical approach based on Śaṅkara's advaitic system, no doubt shared by most orthodox Brahmins of his day.

The influence of Sūr Dās is interesting to examine because of his interest in the *Rāmāyaṇa* and especially in the *Bhāgavata Purāṇa* which he popularized in North India a generation before Tulsī Dās through translations in the vernacular. Professor F. R. Allchin has already pointed to striking similarities between Sūr Dās' *Sūrsāgar* and Tulsī Dās' *Vinaya-patrikā*. According to him, such features as the following are found in both: sinfulness of the petitioner; purity and loftiness of the Lord; recital of His divine titles; requests that He should honour them; repeated mentions of notorious sinners that have been saved through His mercy; and the idea of sending a letter of petition to the Lord.[80]

Although Tulsī Dās wrote the *Vinaya-patrikā* in his later years, there is no doubt that by the time he set out to write the *Rāmcaritmānas* he shared many of the views expressed by Sūr Dās. All of the above features listed by Allchin, except the last one, are also found in the *Rāmcaritmānas*. Tulsī Dās does not, however, approve of Rādhā's attitude suggestive of

78. *Dohāvalī*, 554, quoted by Allchin, F. R. *Kavitāvalī*, p. 49.
79. *Ibid.*, 55, quoted by Allchin, F. R. *Kavitāvalī*, p. 49.
80. Allchin F. R. *Tulsī Dās Petition to Rām*, p. 43.

contempt for family duties, scripture and tradition, thus reflecting the antinomian stream.

Finally, in spite of an obvious affinity with the Rāmānandīs, Tulsī Dās seems to have taken his distance *vis-à-vis* some of Rāmānanda's teachings. On the theological level, it has been shown[81] that he followed the syncretistic views attributed to Rāmānanda by accepting both the *saguṇa* and the *nirguṇa* conceptions of the Absolute. However, whereas Rāmānanda had given up the use of Sanskrit altogether, Tulsī Dās wrote several passages of the *Rāmcaritmānas* in the classical language. Moreover, the fact that Rāmānanda accepted a Muslim among his disciples, not to speak of the fact that Kabīr, traditionally considered one of his disciples, promoted a universal brotherhood of men at the cost of one's own religious particularities, suggest a practical syncretistic approach not acceptable to Tulsī Dās.

We have seen that Tulsī Dās lived at a time when antinomian theism was prevalent, a trend which vedic orthodox Brahmins tried to counter by a renewed insistence on śāstric regulations. The next chapter will show that Tulsī Dās took up the challenge by reviving the middle stream through a *rifacimento* of the *Rāmāyaṇa*.

---

81. Macfie, J. M. *The Rāmāyan of Tulsī Dās.*

Chapter V

The Revival of the Middle Stream

AT a time when the Hindu way of life was threatened not only by the socio-political situation of the day but also by the religious and moral trends examined above, it was understandable that Tulsī Dās might think of the Rāmāyaṇic tradition as the one context where the socio-political, religious, and moral dimensions of his heritage are, as we shall see, dealt with in proper balance, thus typifying the central stream. It has already been shown that in an earlier era the Epic tradition, particularly the *Gītā* and the *Rāmāyaṇa*, had affirmed the central position. Tulsī Dās' problem was one of reinterpreting and revitalizing that center in the light of the contemporary situation. This he attempted to do by reviving the *Rāmāyaṇa*.

We have already seen that, compared to the preceding centuries, the Moghul-Afghan period was one of relative stability, and that the socio-political context of Tulsī Dās' time was shaped by the dominating influence of Akbar, whose universalism was at the same time promising and threatening. Because of a growing atmosphere of political tolerance and religious freedom since Bābur invaded India in 1526, the Hindus could affirm publicly their own identity and help their kinsmen to do the same. Yet under such a grandly successful and unchallenged power as that of the Moghuls, the Hindus could not but still feel dispossessed of both their identity as a distinctive culture and of any dreams of political autonomy. By reviving the *Rāmāyaṇa*, Tulsī Dās expressed the political hope needed to counter such feelings of dispossession, and reaffirmed the identity of Hinduism as a distinctive and rich tradition.

Because of its grandeur, the Rāma story could not but reawaken, among the Hindus now under Muslim rule, the nostalgic memory of some past glorious eras, such as that of the Guptas, whose empire comprised all of North India, in the fourth and fifth centuries A.D. In this sense, the Rāma story was more effective as a legend than the Kṛṣṇa story, as it affirmed the socio-political institutions of traditional Hinduism in an unambiguous way. The *Rāmāyaṇa* is of its very nature a story with obvious political overtones. Its central personages are members of the royal family. Rāma, its central hero, is presented not only as the exemplar *par excellence* but also as the prototype of political leadership. Ayodhyā is described as the ideal kingdom and its citizens as the king's praiseworthy subjects.

The social concepts underlying the *Rāmāyaṇa* reveal a constant concern for the Hindu tradition. The caste system is treated as the ideal framework of Indian society. The *guru*, who plays a central rôle throughout the tradition, is treated with veneration. The social customs of the family are respected. Janaka and Daśaratha are frequently shown performing social rites. Women are reminded of the duties proper to their social status. The traditional view that the eldest son should be designated as the father's successor is maintained. The authority of the father as head of the family is treated with consideration. One's oath is, in keeping with social customs, considered as binding.

Thus, the *Rāmāyaṇa* was remarkably suited to revive among its listeners a sense of cultural identity, of pride in the distinctiveness of the tradition, and the possibility of self-reaffirmation —all of which were needed to meet the socio-political challenge of the time.

The social threat accompanying the kind of universalism advocated by Akbar was equally at work in the religious universalism preached by Kabīr, who insisted on the necessity of searching for true religion *beyond* traditional Hinduism and Islam. It was not too difficult to see in such insistence the threatening implication that Hinduism and Islam were both equally rejectable. Kabīr's denial of Rāma as the *avatāra*, of the traditional Hindu divinities, of the divine authority of the *Vedas* and other acknowledged scriptures, of the sacred character of the caste system, of the appropriateness of ceremonial rites and formal worship based on scriptures constituted so many iconoclastic threats to the Hindu way of life.

It is obvious that, seen against such a background, the revival of the *Rāmāyaṇa* would be seen from a Hindu standpoint as a welcome counter-blast and a healthful return to orthodox theism.

As opposed to views such as those of Kabīr, the *Rāmāyaṇa* reminds its listeners that Rāma, the son of Daśaratha, is an incarnation of Viṣṇu; that the other traditional Hindu divinities such as Indra, Śiva, Brahmā, and Umā, have their place in the devotee's spiritual universe; that the Gaṅgā and the Yamunā are to be considered as holy streams; that traditional scriptures are invested with authority; that the *varṇa* system, along with the rôle of preeminence attached to the upper castes, particularly the Brahmins, is to be maintained and respected; that traditional religious rites and practices such as daily bath, austerities (*tapas*), pilgrimages, prescribed sacrifices, birth and investiture ceremonies, morning rites of purification—all these play an important rôle in the life of the Hindu.

It has also been seen that in their zeal to promote love of God as the preeminent path leading to liberation, the other *Sants* of medieval North India, whose influence on the masses seems to have been considerable, also tended to minimize the importance of social duty, a danger which, as we have seen, India had already had to face with the impact of Buddhism. As a devotee, Tulsī Dās was in sympathy with the *Sants*' eagerness to give love of God the predominant role. At the same time, however, he was eager to avoid the excessive position of antinomian theism, where the rôle of social duty was neglected. The affirmation of the one without denying the other led him naturally to the *Rāmāyaṇa*.

Other factors, of course, could explain Tulsī Dās' preference for the *Rāmāyaṇa* rather than (let us say) the *Mahābhārata* or the *Bhāgavata Purāṇa*. The story of Rāma's heroic deeds dominates the *Rāmāyaṇa* throughout, thus giving to the Epic a unity and cohesion not found in the eclectic *Mahābhārata* or the *Bhāgavata Purāṇa*. Furthermore, the very nature of the Rāma story provided Tulsī Dās with the proper mythological, or legendary, material needed to make his *magnum opus* appealing, particularly to the masses. Contrary to such devotees as the Liṅgāyats and Kabīr, the author of the *Rāmcaritmānas* delights in celebrating the mythological setting provided by the story of Rāma (*Rāma-kathā*), whose sequence the reader never loses sight of even though it is interspersed with didactic elements, particularly under the form of hymns and philosophical discourses. Such affirmation about an important facet of the

Hindu tradition, against the possible scorn or indifference of many a Muslim observer, could not but instil in the reader a sense of identity and pride, and solidarity with Hindu socio-political institutions and traditions.

Moreover, apart from his own personal commitment to Rāma, Tulsī Dās' choice of the *Rāmāyaṇa* could have been influenced by the fact that the Rāma cult had already been given a decisive impetus in the Hindi-speaking regions of North India, more than a century before the *Rāmcaritmānas* was written. The fact that Kabīr could use the name Rāma as a synonym for God and not as a designation of Daśaratha's son suggests that his listeners had already learnt to accept that word as part of their religious vocabulary. It is obvious that Tulsī Dās' milieu would be receptive to a new rendering of the *Rāmāyaṇa* to the extent that the Rāma cult had been diffused among the masses.

More research is needed on the growth of Rāma devotion in medieval times. Although it can be safely said, on the basis of Bhandarkar and Bulkey's research,[1] that a Rāma cult arose between the eleventh and the fourteenth century A.D., this in itself is no evidence pointing to the existence of a Rāma community. However, it can be assumed on the basis of several passages in the *Adhyātma Rāmāyaṇa*, that a Rāma community

1. According to Bhandarkar, the first clear evidence of a Rāma-cult is found in a biographical note on Madhva who is represented as having brought, about the year 1264 A.D., the image of Digvijaya Rāma from Badarikāśrama, and having sent Naraharitīrtha to Jagannātha. From the above Bhandarkar concludes that the cult of Rāma must have come into existence about the eleventh century. (Bhandarkar, R. G., *op. cit.*, pp. 46-48.)

Dr. Kamil Bulkey sees in the *Saṁhitās* and the *Purāṇas*, attributed to the Śrī Vaiṣṇava community, the principal witnesses of the process which led to the cult of Rāma. These works, which were composed between the eleventh and the fourteenth centuries, are : the *Agastya Saṁhitā*, the *Kalirāghava Saṁhitā*, the *Vṛhadrāghava Saṁhitā*, and the *Rāghavīya Saṁhitā*; the *Rāmapūrvatāpanīya Upaniṣad*, the *Rāmottaratāpanīya Upaniṣad*, and the *Rāmarahasyopaniṣad*. The *Rāmapūrvatāpanīya Upaniṣad*, whose theological conception is reflected in the *Adhyātma Rāmāyaṇa*, refers to the cult of which Rāma is the object as the incarnation of Brahman :

> The Brahman, spiritual, without a second,
> Without parts and without a body,
> Will nevertheless in its divers manifestations
> Be considered as the object of a cult.

Deussen, P. *Sechzig Upanishad's des Veda*, pp. 805-806.
(The translation from the German is mine.)

existed, probably in the North, at least as early as the fifteenth century A.D. While the *Rāmcaritmānas* gives relatively few references to a specific community whose *raison d'être* is the Rāma cult,[2] the *Adhyātma Rāmāyaṇa* frequently refers to a community of Rāma devotees who fast on special days, who are sacred unto Rāma, who recite the name of Rāma, who worship Rāma,[3] and who "having observed a fast on the Ekādaśī day expound the *Adhyātma Rāmāyaṇa* to an assembly of devout persons."[4]

It is also probable that the Rāma cult had found its most numerous adepts among the uneducated masses. Unfortunately, precise data are still wanting in order to firmly substantiate this claim on the basis of either external or internal evidence. However, it is generally acknowledged that outcastes and women were admitted among Rāmānanda's immediate disciples. Kabīr, traditionally associated with Rāmānanda, was a "weaver from Benares", whose critical attitude towards the educated Brahmins suggests that his followers probably belonged to the lower levels of society. There are indications that Tulsī Dās himself associated with a group of saints composed mostly of low-castes and outcastes, referred to in the first chapter.

In spite of its obvious effort to promote the social position of the upper castes and its rather severe passages on *Śūdras* and women, the *Rāmcaritmānas* itself suggests that Tulsī Dās intended his message of political hope and social conservatism for the devotees of lower classes. The fact that he chose to write his version of the *Rāmāyaṇa* in the vernacular is not without significance. After admitting, in one of his opening paragraphs,[5] to the risk of writing in common speech (*bhāṣā bhaṇiti bhori*) he expresses hope that good men who are not perversely critical—especially those who are devoted to Rāma will listen to the story and praise it with fair words. On the basis of this passage, it may be said that by insisting on writing the *Rāmāyaṇa* in the vernacular despite the probable breath of disapproval from the critical Sanskritized Brahmins, Tulsī Dās gives proof that he wrote for the masses, who were not learned in the sacred language.

2. *H. L. A. R.* I. D. 34, p. 22; II. C. 129, p. 214; II. C. 287, p. 278.
3. *Adhyātma Rāmāyaṇa*, III. 4. 48.
4. *Ibid.*, I. 1. 36-37.
5. *H. L. A. R.*, I. C. 9, pp. 7-8.

Moreover, even though the *Rāmāyaṇa* does not deal *per se* with the situation of the lowly and the poor, as most of Rāma devotees are pictured as well-to-do citizens of the prosperous city of Ayodhyā, Tulsī Dās' concern for the lower-class is nevertheless apparent in more than one respect. Not only is Rāma acclaimed as "friend of the lowly",[6] but this quality is illustrated in one of the most touchnig episodes of the entire *Rāmcaritmānas*,[7] where Rāma is shown clasping to his breast, "as though he were Bharata himself", the chief of the low-caste Niṣādas, explicitly referred to as "this utterly low-born Niṣāda".[8] In the same vein, even though women are described as "inherently impure",[9] they are nevertheless promised the highest bliss if they meditate on the name of Rāma and serve their husbands faithfully.[10]

It is especially in the consideration given to the monkey-devotee Hanumān, presented as the ideal servant (*dās*, lit. "slave") that Tulsī Dās shows his predilection for the lowly. When his portrayal of Hanumān is compared with Vālmīki's, it becomes obvious that the former associates Rāma's monkey-servant with the lowly and the humble. Thus, Hanumān describes himself in the *Rāmcaritmānas* as the "lowest of the low':

> Tell me, do I come of so high a family, a mischievous monkey, the lowest of the low? Why, anyone who mentions our name first thing in the morning has to go hungry the rest of the day! So utterly vile am I. But listen, my friend: even on me has Raghubīr (Rāma) had mercy![11]

This picture contrasts radically with Hanumān's self-description in the *Vālmīki Rāmāyaṇa*:

> I am the son of him who shatters the mountain peaks.. A thousand times am I able without pausing, to encircle Meru.. With my strong arms, churning up the sea,

6. *Ibid.*, III. C. 5, p. 298.
7. This episode will be analysed in detail in the next chapter.
8. *Ibid.*, VI. Ch. 37, p. 430.
9. *Ibid.*, III. C. 4, p. 298.
10. *Ibid.*
11. *Ibid.*, V. C. 7—D. 7, p. 342.

> I can inundate the world with its mountains.. I know of none that surpasses the King of the birds, the Wind-god or myself..[12]

Whereas in the *Vālmīki Rāmāyaṇa,* Sītā addresses Hanumān with terms of respect such as "Hero", "Lion among monkeys", "Destroyer of hostile warriors", "Most skilled of beings",[13] etc., in the *Rāmcaritmānas* she usually calls him "My friend"——a vocative also used by others such as Laṅkiṇī[14]—or "My son".[15] Likewise, Rāvaṇa speaks to Hanumān with contemptive arrogance with clear emphasis on the monkey's lowly stature by birth :

> A wise *guru* have I found in a monkey ! Wretch, your doom is at hand, who dare, base creature as you are, to offer me advice ![16]

Hanumān is not addressed with such contempt in either the *Vālmīki Rāmāyaṇa* or the *Adhyātma Rāmāyaṇa.*

It is significant that Hanumān should be given a predominant rôle as a devotee in the *Rāmcaritmānas,* compared to the *Adhyātma Rāmāyaṇa,* where his importance is diminished and the devotee aspect not emphasized. Tulsī Dās misses no occasion to remind his listeners that Hanumān had constantly "the image of the Lord laid upon his heart";[17] that "his thoughts (were) fixed unceasingly on Raghubīr";[18] that he set out "laying Rāma's lotus feet upon his heart",[19] etc. The scenes describing Hanumān's loving devotion to Rāma and the latter's affection for his servant-devotee are rarely equalled in intensity and emotion. A typical example is the meeting with Rāma upon Hanumān's return from the first trip to Laṅkā : we are told that "again and again the saviour of the gods (i.e. Rāma)

12. *V. R.,* IV. 57, vol. II, pp. 322-323.
13. *Ibid.,* V. 39, vol. II, p. 431.
14. *H. L. A. R.,* V. C. 4, p. 341.
15. For instance, *Ibid.,* V. C. 13—C. 17, pp. 345-347.
16. *Ibid.,* V. C. 24, p. 349.
17. *Ibid.,* IV. C. 23, p. 335.
18. *Ibid.,* V. C. 1, p. 339.
19. *Ibid.,* VI. C. 56, p. 392.

gazed on the monkey with streaming eyes and body trembling with emotion", that Hanumān fell at Rāma's feet crying out in rapturous devotion: "Save me, save me, O Blessed Lord!", that "time after time the Lord would fain have raised him (Hanumān) to his feet, but he would not be raised, so absorbed was he in love", etc.[20] Particularly cherished by Rāma, Hanumān also wins the esteem and affection of Rāma's entourage as well. In addition to Sītā, whose conversation with the monkey-messenger has already been alluded to, Bharat is shown "reverently embrac(ing) him.. his heart overflow(ing) with love, tears pour(ing) from his eyes and trembl(ing)with emotion" and claiming that "at the sight of you all my sorrows have passed away, for today I have met in you my beloved Rāma".[21]

We may conclude from Tulsī Dās' portrayal of Hanumān that the latter typifies the low-born and the humble, and that his prominent rôle as a devotee emphasizes the particular affection of the Lord for the humble servant. We might add that the idealization of Hanumān as the dutiful devotee also provided an alternative to the *gopi* ideal, often considered overly suggestive of antinomianism, if not of immorality, on account of the gopīs' carefree attitude toward traditional moral norms, particularly the dictates of social and domestic duty.

It is clear, from the above, that Tulsī Dās expected his *magnum opus* to be heard from all levels of society, educated and uneducated alike. However, there are also good reasons to believe that he was especially attentive to the needs of the poor and the humble and that this attention reflects particularly in his portrayal of Rāma and some of his devotees such as Guha and the servant Hanumān.

Thus, while the factors that led Tulsī Dās to revive the Rāmāyaṇic tradition might have been many and varied—the list just given in that respect is certainly not exhaustive—the need to reaffirm the middle stream stands among the most fundamental. However, while the *Vālmīki Rāmāyaṇa* represented the central stream insofar as it related love of God to social duty, it consistently maintained that duty played the pre-

20. *Ibid.*, V. C. 32—C. 33, p. 353.
21. *Ibid.*, VII. C. 2, p.432.

dominant rôle as the guiding principle of man's actions. It was inevitable that given the rise of ecstatic devotional religion in medieval North India, with the *gopi* given in many instances as the model devotee, the expectation of the ardent desire of the enthusiast to spend all his time in worship and praise as special calling would also be held by the readers of the *Rāmāyaṇa.* Tulsī Dās himself and no doubt some of his immediate hearers were ardent enthusiasts but could not find within the Rāmāyaṇic tradition the supporting justification for forsaking social duty that Kṛṣṇa devotees found in the *Bhāgavata Purāṇa.*

It was natural, then, that in the new version of the *Rāmāyaṇa* love of God would play the predominant rôle in such a way that the devotee's desire to leave his normal social and domestic duties to spend his whole life in the service of Rāma would be viewed as a justifiable possibility. The challenge consisted therefore in introducing this new vision without weakening the strength of the *Rāmāyaṇa* as a medium capable of reaffirming the Hindu's pride in his heritage both as a socio-political reality and as a religious tradition, and without contradicting the point just made that love of God does not *per se* entail antinomian scorn or disinterestedness *vis-à-vis* traditional social and domestic duty. The following section will show how the *Rāmcaritmānas* played such a rôle.

Part Three

Love of God and Social Duty in the Ramcaritmanas

Chapter VI

The Literary Characteristics of the Ramcaritmanas

IN order to study in proper perspective Tulsī Dās' own views and emphases regarding the two major themes of the present study, namely love of God and social duty, we must first examine the nature of the literary setting in which they are treated. The *Rāmcaritmānas* has distinctive characteristics of its own, mainly because it was meant to be a *rifacimento* of the *Vālmiki Rāmāyaṇa*, written twenty centuries earlier. Furthermore, Tulsī Dās himself declares that the reader is expected to find various elements "culled from other sources too".[1]

We may now affirm, on the basis of careful research done in present years,[2] that the most influential of these sources, besides the *Vālmiki Rāmāyaṇa*, are the *Adhyātma Rāmāyaṇa*, the *Bhusuṇḍi Rāmāyaṇa*, the *Bhāgavata Purāṇa*, and the *Prasanna-rāghava*. Of these, the *Adhyātma Rāmāyaṇa* stands out as by far the most important. The influence of the *Bhusuṇḍi Rāmāyaṇa* is noticeable in the last portion of the seventh canto. The influence of the *Bhāgavata Purāṇa* is less important as a literary source, since it belongs to a different genre, but we shall see that it has been an influential source of inspiration in Tulsī Dās' effort at highlighting the importance of love of God as the central theme of the *Rāmcaritmānas*. The influence of the *Prasanna-rāghava* bears on specific passages and details, of which the most significant will be dealt with in due course.

We have already discussed in the previous section of this study the main features of the *Vālmiki Rāmāyaṇa* and the *Bhāgavata Purāṇa*. Unfortunately, the *Bhusuṇḍi Rāmayaṇa* is not availalbe

1. *H. L. A. R.*, Śloka, p. 2.

2. Vaudeville, C. *Étude sur les sources et la composition du Rāmāyaṇa de Tulsī Dās*, Among the recent studies in the West, this work is the most thorough on the subject.

for consultation. P. C. Bagchi[3] and R. N. Tripāṭhī[4] have commented on it. On the basis of a commentary by M. P. Gupta, C. Vaudeville believes that the manuscript is kept in a temple at Śravaṇakuñja.[5]

The *Prasannarāghava* is a Sanskrit drama attributed to a logician by the name of Jayadeva from Vidarbha who lived around 1200 A.D.[6] The influence of this medieval drama is particularly noticeable in passages belonging to the first and fifth cantos of the *Rāmcaritmānas*.

Because of the special importance of the *Adhyātma Rāmāyaṇa*, we will now give a longer analysis of its nature, even though some of the details of its origin and authorship, about which there is still much uncertainty, have already been discussed in relation to Rāmānanda and the Rāma Sants.[7]

The *Adhyātma Rāmāyaṇa* is traditionally considered as a part of the *Brahmāṇḍa Purāṇa*, dated in the sixteenth century A.D. It was known by Tulsī Dās and by a Marāṭhī poet who died in 1608.[8] The opinion reported previously[9] that it came from the South needs solid corroboration.

The *Adhyātma Rāmāyaṇa* retains the fundamental framework of the *Vālmiki Rāmāyaṇa*, but is only a fraction of its size. Certain portions of the *Vālmiki Rāmāyaṇa* are left out, such as details of the battle, lengthy descriptions of natural scenery or many of the activities of Bharata before he finds Rāma in the forest. The tendency, then, is to leave out the material not immediately related to Rāma as the central figure of the story.

Other portions are added to the original stories. Perhaps the most important among these are the numerous hymns (*stutis*) and philosophical discourses (*gītās*) which in addition to offering speculative comments on the nature of God, man and the universe praise Rāma as the Lord of his devotees.

Finally, the *Adhyātma Rāmāyaṇa* makes a number of changes in the story. While many of these changes are insignificant,

3. Bagchi, P. C. *Introduction to the Adhyātma Rāmāyaṇa*, vol. I.
4. Tripathi, R. M. *Tulsīdās aur unki kavitā*, 2 vol.
5. Vaudeville. C. *Étude*, p. xx.
6. *Ibid.*, p. xix.
7. See above Part II.
8. Bhandarkar, R. G. *op. cit.*, p. 48.
9. Part II.

some are more consequential, for instance the substitution of the real Sītā by a mere shadow, and the frequent reminders that Rāma is merely acting when his behaviour appears too human. It must also be pointed out that the narrator is no longer Vālmīki but Śiva, who related the story to his inquisitive wife Pārvatī. The rôle of Śiva is thereby highlighted, in keeping with Śaṅkara's efforts to make him "orthodox".

For the *Adhyātma Rāmāyaṇa*, Rāma is above all the "One without a second (*advitiya*)",[10] "unmoving (*acala*)",[11] "Truth, Intelligence and Bliss (*saccidānanda*)".[12] In general, the author tends towards the *advaita vedānta* conception of God as the formless Absolute (*nirguṇa brahman*). In keeping with the philosophy of Śaṅkara, he considers knowledge (*jñāna*) as the preeminent path of salvation,[13] love of God and social duties being rungs on the ladder towards knowledge.[14]

This said, it must be pointed out immediately that the *Adhyātma Rāmāyaṇa* does not discourage the reader from following the paths of social duty and love of God. On the contrary, Rāma teaches that union with Him is obtained through the disinterested fulfillment of one's duty (*sva-dharma*):

> Let one, therefore, attain to union with Me by transcending the three attributes of goodness, passion, and darkness, through the performance of duty (*sva-dharma*) without hope of reward.[15]

True, the *Adhyātma Rāmāyaṇa* contains occasional antinomian passages. For instance, in the well-known *Rāmagitā* it is said that "knowledge (*jñāna*) alone is capable of destroying this nescience (*ajñāna*). Action (*karma*) cannot destroy it, as it is born of nescience and is not contrary to it".[16] Again, it says: "Let those who are devoid of devotion to me, roll in the abyss of the *śāstras*. Their's is neither knowledge nor emanci-

---

10. *A. R.* VI. 1. 50.
11. *Ibid.*, III. 8. 19.
12. *Ibid.*, I. 1. 91.
13. *Ibid.*, VII. 5. 9.
14. *Ibid.*, VI. 3. 31. The passage III. 3. 33, where *bhakti* is identified with *jñāna*, is an exception.
15. *Ibid.*, VII. 7. 67.
16. *Ibid.*, VII. 5. 9.

pation even through hundreds of incarnations".[17] However such passages are rare, probably meant to emphasize knowledge (by contrast): furthermore, as we shall see in the next chapter, these antinomian implications are not followed up in practice.

Likewise, for the *Adhyātma Rāmāyaṇa* salvation through knowledge does not eliminate love of God, considered as a means to knowledge so that "he who possesses devotion (*bhakti*) rapidly gains knowledge (*jñāna*) and...thus obtains deliverance (*mokṣa*).[18] Yet, even though love of God and social duty are retained as important themes in the *Adhyātma Rāmāyaṇa*, it remains that the apex is knowledge leading to ultimate absorption with the divine (*nirguṇa brahman*).

We now proceed to a detailed examination of the literary characteristics of the *Rāmcaritmānas*, focussing on the main differences from Tulsī Dās' two main sources, namely the *Vālmīki Rāmāyaṇa* and the *Adhyātma Rāmāyaṇa*. Throughout this section, the abbreviations *V. R.*, *A. D.*, *R. C. M.*, and *B. P.* will be used to designate the *Vālmīki Rāmāyaṇa*, the *Adhyātma Rāmāyaṇa*, the *Rāmcaritmānas*, and the *Bhāgavata Purāṇa* respectively.

The general framework of the *R. C. M.* is that of the *V. R.* The story is divided into seven cantos (*kāṇḍas*) with identical titles except for the sixth *kāṇḍa*, which is entitled *Laṅkā kāṇḍa* instead of the traditional *Yuddha kāṇḍa.*

In terms of its length, the *R. C. M.* is more condensed than the *V. R.*, but not so much as the *A. R.* The first *kāṇḍa* (*Bāla kāṇḍa*) is proportionately the longest, unlike both the *V. R.* and the *A. R.* where the sixth *kāṇḍa* is the longest. In all three versions, the second *kāṇḍa* is second in length, and this is the only canto the length of which is proportionately the same in the three cases. *Kāṇḍas* three, four and five (*Āraṇya kāṇḍa*, *Kiṣkindhā kāṇḍa* and *Sundara kāṇḍa*), are considerably diminished so that together they equate only one third of the length of the *Ayodhyā kāṇḍa*, whereas in both the *V. R.* and the *A. R.* each equates more than half of the length of the *Ayodhyā kāṇḍa*. While the sixth *kāṇḍa* is the longest in both the *V. R.* and the *A. R.*, it is only one third the length of the *Bāla kāṇḍa* in the *R. C. M.* Finally, the seventh *kāṇḍa* (*Uttara kāṇḍa*) is the third

17. *Ibid.*, I. 1. 111.
18. *Ibid.*, III. 4. 51·

longest, which corresponds to the *V. R.* but differs with the *A. R.* where this *kāṇḍa* is the second smallest.

The above indicates that Tulsī Dās felt free to make a number of changes in both of his main sources. The most significant of these changes will be examined in this section.

Before we proceed to examine the structural arrangement of each *kāṇḍa*, it must be pointed out that from a historical point of view it is now acknowledged, mainly on the basis of the research of R. N. Tripathi,[19] M. P. Gupta,[20] and C. Vaudeville,[21] that the *R. C. M.* contains certain sections within its corpus which Tulsī Dās wrote earlier in time. The sections belonging to the earlier stratum are two passages in the first *kāṇḍa*,[22] the entire second *kāṇḍa*, and the first six verses of the third *kāṇḍa*. In addition to the style of these sections, which is simpler, more regular and more personal, the main reason for considering these as separate is that contrary to the rest of the work, where either Śiva or Bhusuṇḍi is presented as the main narrator, here Tulsī Dās himself claims to play that rôle. In fact, he tells us in the opening invocation of the *Bāla kāṇḍa* that he wrote the story of Raghunātha (Rāma) "for his own soul's delight". We mght conclude that these early sections, which are about one fourth of the total, were written as a kind of personal exercise.

Bearing in mind that most Benares brahmins of his day were Śaivites, Tulsī Dās imitates the *A. R.* in setting the rest of the story (excluding the last part of *Laṅkā kāṇḍa*)[23] in the form of a dialogue between Śiva and his wife. This gives the story more solemnity than the preceding parts written to satisfy Tulsī Dās' personal devotion. Here the style is less regular and, as will be shown later, the influence of the *A. R.* is more obvious. We might conclude that the bulk of the text was written after Tulsī Dās had decided to follow the *A. R.* and self-consciously set out to write a new *Rāmāyaṇa*.

The third and latest stratum, written under the influence of the *Bhusuṇḍi Rāmāyaṇa*, is narrated by the crow Bhusuṇḍi to

19. Tripathi, R. N. *op. cit.*, pp. 220ff.
20. Gupta, M. P. *Gosvāmi Tulsīdās*, pp. 264 ff.
21. Vaudeville, *Étude*, pp. 320 ff.
22. *H. L. A. R.* I. S. 1—C. 29: I. C. 184-end.
23. *Ibid.*, I. D. 54—D. 125, pp. 32-62.

Garuḍa, the king of the eagles, desirous of knowing more about Rāma's divine nature. As Miss Vaudeville has shown,[24] the fact that the conclusion to the entire story following the *Bhusuṇḍi* narrative is attributed to Śiva shows a later insertion of the *Bhusunnḍi* section.

With these characteristics of the general framework of the *R. C. M.* in mind, we now proceed to examine the most important features of each *kāṇḍa*.

1. *The Bāla kāṇḍa*

The first *kāṇḍa* contains four main sections, the first three of which owe nothing to the *V. R.* or the *A. R.* The first section[25] presents itself as the prologue of the entire book. After explaining that his work is in accord with traditional scriptures even though it is not written in Sanskrit, Tulsī Dās confesses his unworthiness and inadequateness to deal with such a noble task as writing the story of his Lord.[26] He then goes on to exalt the name of Rāma, which he considers greater than both the impersonal Absolute and the personal *avatāra*, i.e. Rāma.[27] The prologue ends with a description of the *R. C. M.* which is likened to a Holy Lake, hence the title *Rāmcaritmānas* (*Holy Lake of the Acts of Rāma*).[28]

The second section of the *Bāla kāṇḍa*,[29] which shows some influence from the *Śiva Purāṇa*,[30] is narrated by Śiva, who is also the central personage of the entire section. After a short introduction consisting in a dialogue between Yājñavalkya and Bharadvāja, we hear about Śiva and his wife Satī,[31] about the sacrifice of Dakṣa, to which—as in the *B. P.* and against the general tradition—all the gods but Viṣṇu, Brahmā and Śiva were invited,[32] and about the legend of Śiva and Pārvatī.[33]

24. Vaudeville, C. *Étude*, pp. 323-324.
25. *H. L. A. R.*, I. Śloka 1—C. 44, pp. 1-28.
26. *Ibid.*, Śloka 1—D. 18, pp. 1-14.
27. *Ibid.*, I. C. 19—D. 29, pp. 14-19.
28. *Ibid.*, I., C. 30—D. 43, pp. 19-27.
29. *Ibid.*, I. C. 44—C. 104, pp. 28-53.
30. Vaudeville, C. *Étude*, pp. 30-33.
31. *Ibid.*, I. C. 48—D. 59, pp. 29-34.
32. *Ibid.*, I. C. 60—C. 65, pp. 34-35.
33. *Ibid.*, I. C. 65—C. 122, pp. 36-60.

The third section includes six stories dealing with the reasons for the incarnation of Rāma: the story of Jaya and Vijaya, the story of Jalandhara, the story of Nārada's punishment for his pride, the story of Manu and Śatarūpā, the story of Pratāpabhānu and the false hermit, and the story of Rāvaṇa.[34] All but the last of these stories are extensions of Purāṇic tales;[35] the story of Rāvaṇa is related in the last *kāṇḍa* of both the *V. R.* and the *A. R.*[36]

Unlike the preceding section, the fourth section is not new in this sense that it follows the basic outline of the *V. R.* and the *A. R.* in relating the sequence of events. It must be pointed out however that a number of important passages in this section are close to similar passages in the *A. R.* These include the description of Rāma's supernal appearance to his mother Kausalyā,[37] as well as the emphasis upon the childish pranks of Rāma, which the *A. R.* in turn had learned from the *B. P.* at least indirectly.[38] These passages also include five hymns of praise which also appear in the *A. R.*: Brahmā's hymn to Śiva,[39] Kausalya's hymn to her infant child,[40] Ahalyā's hymn to Rāma,[41] Paraśurāma's hymn to Rāma,[42] and Janaka's hymn to Rāma.[43]

Similar instances of Tulsī Dās' preference for the *V. R.* rather than the *A. R.* are not found. There are however, a few details common to both the *R. C. M.* and the *V. R.* and not found in the *A. R.*, but these could have easily been borrowed from other versions of the *Rāmāyaṇa* mentioned in the prologue of the *R. C. M.* For instance, whereas Gandharvas are mentioned in

34. *Ibid.*, I. C. 122—C. 184, pp. 60-85.

35. The story of Jaya and Vijaya is found in *B. P.* III. 15—16; the story of Jalandhara in *Padma Purāṇa,* quoted by C. Vaudeville in *Étude*, p. 64; the story of Nārada, in *Śiva Purāṇa*, II. 2. 2-3; the story of Manu and Śatarūpā, in *B. P.* X. 3. 39—45; the origin of the story of Pratāpabhānu is uncertain: see Vaudeville, C. *Étude*, p. 78.

36. *V. R.* VII. 1—34; *A. R.* VII. 1—2.

37. *H. L. A. R.* I. Ch. 21, p. 88; *A. R.* I. 3. 16—19.

38. *H. L. A. R.* I. C. 201 ff, pp. 93 ff.; *A. R.* I. 3. 52 ff.

39. *H. L. A. R.* I. Ch. 20, p. 86: *A. R.* I. 2, 13—20.

40. *H. L. A. R.* I. Ch. 21, p. 89; *A. R.* I. 3. 20—29.

41. *H. L. A. R.*, I. Ch. 22, p. 97; *A. R.*, I. 5. 43—59.

42. *H. L. A. R.*, I. C. 282, p. 126; *A. R.*, I. 7. 20—45.

43. *H. L. A. R.*, I. C. 338—C. 339, p. 153: *A, R.* I. 6. 59—75.

both the *R. C. M.* and *V. R.* among the deities that presented themselves to Viṣṇu for protection against Rāvaṇa,[44] they are not mentioned in the *A. R.*[45] The celestial celebrations accompanying the birth of Rāma are described in both the *V. R.* and the *R. C. M.*[46] but omitted in the *A. R.* Whereas in both the *R. C. M.* and the *V. R.* Daśaratha is said to have summoned musicians to enhance the celebration,[47] this detail is not mentioned in the *A. R.* Whereas the *R. C. M.* alludes to the descent of the Ganges,[48] which is described in full in the *V. R.*,[49] this event is not spoken of in the *A. R.* It is obvious that none of these traces of possible dependence on the *V. R.* equals in importance the obvious borrowings from the *A. R.* In the latter case, we are dealing with borrowings of elements that are distinctive of this particular version of the story and, especially in the case of hymns and philosophical comments, with passages containing consequential doctrinal additions.

We must also add that while Tulsī Dās follows the basic framework of his two main sources in the latter section of the *Bāla kāṇḍa*, he freely changes details or emphases. The most noticeable additions in the *Bāla kāṇḍa* are the frequent exhortative or laudatory passages commonly expressed in the forms of *dohās* (couplets),[50] and especially the many details added to the account of the marriage of Rāma and Sītā.[51]

Unlike both the *V. R.* and the *A. R.*, where Sītā does not see Rāma before the breaking of the bow, in the *R. C. M.* the two young heroes meet by chance in a garden before the decisive contest. This episode, where the beauty of the scenery and the growing intensity of the love between Rāma and Sītā are described at length, is similar to a parallel passage found in the *Prasannaraghava*.[52] The latter includes other details also retained in the *R. C. M.*: in both accounts the story takes place

44. *H. L. A. R.*, I. Ch. 19, p. 85; *V. R.*, I. 15, p. 39.
45. *A. R.*, I. 2. 7.
46. *H. L. A. R.*, I. C. 190, p. 88; *V. R.*, I. Ch. 18, p. 45.
47. *H. L. A. R.*, I. C. 191, p. 89; *V. R.*, I. 18, p. 46.
48. *H. L. A. R.*, I. C. 209, p. 97.
49. *V. R.*, I. 43, vol. I, pp. 89-92.
50. For instance, *H. L. A. R.*, I. D. 192, p. 198, p. 91; D. 199. p. 92; D. 205, etc.
51. *Ibid.*, I. C. 209—C. 358, pp. 99-161.
52. See Vaudeville, C. *Étude*, p. 104.

in the evening as Rāma and Lakṣmaṇa enter the garden of Mithilā; in both, Sītā is shown going to the temple dedicated to the goddess Girijā; in both, Sītā is obliged to return home because the evening is far advanced.

Many details have also been added in the *R. C. M.* to the description of the kings, of Sītā, of the jealous competitors (including Rāvaṇa; the spectators' reactions are also analyzed at length. These details are not found in the *V. R.* and are only alluded to in the *A. R.* Once again, traces of the *Prasannarāghava* can be seen in these additions.[53] Other changes are made in this same context as Paraśurāma is introduced immediately after the breaking of the bow, whereas in both the *V.R.* and *A.R.* this event occurs only after Daśaratha reaches Mithilā for the wedding ceremony. Likewise, Lakṣmaṇa plays a central rôle in this encounter with Paraśu-Rāma, thereby replacing Rāma, who in the preceding stories was playing the leading rôle. Again, these changes are attributable to the influence of the *Prasannarāghava.*[54] Similar developments are also found in the description of the wedding ceremony, and the return of the newly married couple to Ayodhyā.[55]

Some other additions find their counterpart in the *B. P.* For instance, the miraculous manifestation of Rāma's divinity to Kausalyā[56] is reminiscent of similar scenes in book X of the *B. P.* Again, the description of the city of Mithilā[57] bears a closer resemblance to a passage of the *B. P.*[58] where the city of Mathurā is described. So is the subsequent episode showing Rāma and Lakṣmaṇa visiting the city by night inspired by a parallel episode in the *B. P.*[59] where Kṛṣṇa and Balarāma are seen walking in the streets of Mathurā, thereby provoking the enamoured reactions of the on-looking women. The episode of the breaking of the bow also reveals occasional detailed borrowings from the *B. P.* For instance, it is said that as Rāma was about to accomplish the exploit, each of

53. *Ibid.*, pp. 107-114.
54. *Ibid.*, pp. 115-116.
55. *Ibid.*, pp. 119-126.
56. *H. L. A. R.*, I. C. 199—C. 220.
57. *H. L. A. R.*, I. C. 209—C. 211, pp. 97-98.
58. *B. P.*, X. 41.
59. *Ibid.*

his admirers saw him according to his own attitude of mind.[60] The same observation is made concerning Kṛṣṇa in the *B.P.*[61]

The *kāṇḍa* ends with a short exhortation typical of Tulsī Dās and this practice will be maintained in all of the remaining *kāṇḍas*. Likewise, the practice of beginning each *kāṇḍa* with an opening salutation is followed throughout.

2. *The Ayodhyā kāṇḍa*

As in the last part of the *Bāla-kāṇḍa*, Tulsī Dās follows in the *Ayodhyā kāṇḍa* the main outline sketched in the *V. R.* and the *A. R.* Indeed, it is in this book that the most striking evidences of dependence on the *V. R.* can be found. Examples of these are the descrption of Mantharā at the outset of the coronation as furious,[62] Daśaratha's bending over Kaikeyī touching her with his hand,[63] the king's pleading with Kaikeyī to put an end to her sorrowful state,[64] Kaikeyī's insistence on her husband's loyalty to his promise,[65] and Daśaratha's hope that the sun might never rise again.[66]

Once again, however, Tulsī Dās follows the *A. R.* in adding a lengthy philosophical comment by Lakṣmaṇa to Guha on the nature of God, man and the universe,[67] in a short hymn of praise by Bharadvāja to Rāma,[68] in Vālmīki's extensive hymn of praise of Rāma,[69] in Vasiṣṭha's philosophical comment to Bharata,[70] and in the discussion between Rāma and the boatman.[71]

Among the changes he introduces to this *kāṇḍa*, the most noticeable is the visit of Janaka to Rāma in the forest, which is an occasion for an additional lengthy development to the

60. *H. L. A. R.*, I. C. 241, p. 110.
61. *B. P.*, X. 43. 17.
62. *V. R.*, II. 7, vol. I, p. 174; *H. L. A. R.*, II. C. 13, p. 167.
63. *H. L. A. R.*, II. C. 25, p. 172; *V. R.*, II. 10, vol. I, p. 184.
64. *H. L. A. R.*, II. C. 16, p. 172; *V. R.*, II. 10, vol. I, p. 184.
65. *H. L. A. R*., II. C. 30, p. 174; *V. R.*, II, 12, vol. I, pp. 188-189.
66. *H. L. A. R.*, II. C. 37, p. 177; *V. R.*, II. 13, vol. I, p. 194.
67. *H. L. A. R.*, II. C. 92—C. 94, pp. 198-199; *A. R.*, II. 6.4-15.
68. *H. L. A. R.*, II. C. 107—D. 107, p. 205; *A. R.*, II. 6. 37-39.
69. *H. L. A. R.*, C. 126—D. 131, pp. 212-214; *A. R.*, II. 6. 52-88.
70. *H. L. A. R.*, D. 171—C. 175, pp. 231-232; *A. R.*, II. 8. 3-6.
71. *H. L. A. R.*, II. C. 110—C. 101, pp. 202; *A. R.*, II. 110. 2-3.

story,[72] and is found in neither *V. R.* nor the *A. R.* More important still, is the expansion added to the story of Bharata, whose dilemma occupies the second half of this *kāṇḍa*. This section will be analyzed in the last chapter of the present study, as it is central to the interaction of love of God and social duty as viewed by Tulsī Dās.

3. *The Araṇya kāṇḍa*

Here again, Tulsī Dās follows the pattern sketched by his predecessors. However, apart from the description of Lake Pampā, which is quite similar to the parallel description in the *V. R.*,[73] the influence of the *A. R.* is still apparent here than in the previous *kāṇḍas*, as the general tone of the account becomes more speculative and the characters less real. Although Atri's hymn of praise to Rāma[74] owes nothing to the *A. R.* and Kabandha's hymn to Rāma in the *A. R.*[75] is not found in the *R. C. M.*, the latter nevertheless contains five noticeable passages inspired from the *A. R.* namely Sutīkṣṇa's hymn of praise to Rāma,[76] Agastya's hymn of praise to Rāma,[77] Rāma's philosophical comment to Lakṣmaṇa,[78] Jaṭāyu's hymn of praise to Rāma,[79] and Rāma's didactic exposé to Śabarī.[80]

Moreover, Tulsī Dās adopts an important detail from the *A. R.* in showing Sītā entering the fire before her abduction, to be replaced by an image.[81] This is in accord with the views of the *A.R.* on the world as an illusion (*māyā*).

Apart from Atri's hymn, and the opening salutations and the closing exhortations, which are always distinctive of Tulsī Dās, this *kāṇḍa* contains few additions. The most noticeable is the introduction of an episode showing the sage Nārada paying an

---

72. *H. L. A. R.*, II. C. 270, ff., p. 271 ff.
73. *H. L. A. R.*, III. C. 37—C. 38, pp. 320-321; *V. R.*, IV. 75, vol. II, pp. 159-160.
74. *H. L. A. R.*, II. Ch. 4, pp. 296-297.
75. *A. R.*, III. 9. 30-55.
76. *H. L. A. R.*, III. C. 10—D. 11, pp. 301-302; *A. R.*, III. 2. 27-34.
77. *H. L. A. R.*, III. C. 12, pp. 303-304; *A. R.* III. 3. 18-19.
78. *H. L. A. R.*, III. C. 13—C. 15, pp. 304-305; *A. R.*, III. 4. 19-55.
79. *H. L. A. R.*, III. Ch. 8, p. 315; *A. R.*, III. 8. 44-56.
80. *H. L. A. R.*, III. C. 33—C. 34, pp. 317-318; *A. R.*, III. 10. 22-28.
81. *H. L. A. R.*, III. C. 22, p. 311; *A. R.*, III. 7. 1-4.

unexpected visit to Rāma as the latter was resting by the lake Pampā with Lakṣmaṇa.[82]

4. *The Kiṣkindhā kāṇḍa*

As in the previous book, this *kāṇḍa* generally follows the sequence of events presented in its two main sources, with a clearer dependence on the *A. R.* The latter is apparent in Rāma's philosophical comment to the disconsolate Tārā after her husband's death,[83] which summarizes a parallel comment in the *A. R.*;[84] in Jāmbavān's exhortation to Aṅgad;[85] and in Sugrīva's hymn of adoration to Rāma.[86] However, Tulsī Dās leaves out a long philosophical comment by the sage Sampāti to Candramā.[87]

The most remarkable passage of this *kāṇḍa* for its poetical beauty is Rāma's description of the monsoon season,[88] of which there is a parallel version in the *V. R.* but which is omitted in the *A. R.* Here again the influence of the *B. P.* can be detected. Thus, Tulsī Dās imitates the latter in including details such as the frogs' croaks, which are compared to the recitation of the *Vedas*; the overflowing waters of the streams, compared to the man who has no self-control; the flashes of lightning, compared to libidinous women; and fire-flies, compared to heresies.[89]

There is a popular belief that this *kāṇḍa* was written in Benares. This is a possibility as Tulsī Dās adds to the usual opening invocation in Sanskrit two *soraṭhās* (metres) in Hindi dealing with *Kāśi* (Benares) and Śiva, who is the divine guardian of the Holy City.

5. *The Sundara kāṇḍa*

This last of the short *kāṇḍas*, where Hanumān plays the leading rôle, again follows the outline of both the *V. R.* and the *A. R.* It devotes a beautiful passage to the description of

82. *H. L. A. R.*, III. D. 41—42, p. 321.
83. *H. L. A. R.*, IV. C. 11, p. 329.
84. *A. R.*, IV. 3, 13-35.
85. *H. L. A. R.*, IV. C. 26—D. 26, p. 337; *A. R.*, IV. 7. 9-27.
86. *H. L. A. R.*, IV. C. 7, p. 327; *A. R.*, IV. 1. 76 ff.
87. *A. R.*, IV. 8. 8-52.
88. *H. L. A. R.*, IV. C. 13 ff, pp. 330 ff.
89. *B. P.*, X. 20. 1-17; *V. R.*, IV. 28, 30, vol. II, pp. 237, 244.

Laṅkā[90] which is of the same inspiration as a parallel passage in the *V. R.*[91] but which is only alluded to in the *A. R.*[92] Hanumān's considerations addressed to Rāvaṇa on the theological nature of Rāma find a parallel development in the *A. R.*[93]

Unlike in the preceding *Rāmāyaṇas*, Vibhīṣaṇa is shown meeting Hanumān on the latter's first trip to Laṅkā and indicating to the monkey emissary where Sītā is kept in confinement.[94] However, Vibhīṣaṇa's hymn of praise after transfering his allegiance to Rāma is close to a parallel hymn in the *A. R.*[95]

The first meeting of Hanumān and Vibhīṣaṇa takes place before Hanumān's first encounter with Rāvaṇa. This is new.[96] The description of Rāvaṇa's conversation with Sītā in the grove under the eyes of the hiding Hanumān owes less to the *V. R.* or the *A. R.* than to the *Prasannarāghava*,[97] so does the ensuing conversation between Hanumān and Sītā.[98]

Contrary to his usual practice, Tulsī Dās concludes this *kāṇḍa* with the opening section of the following *kāṇḍa* in both the *V. R.* and the *A. R.* This displaced section deals with Rāvaṇa's repudiation of his brother Vibhīṣaṇa and the latter's admittance among the Rāma fold.

6. *The Laṅkā kāṇḍa*

In general, this *kāṇḍa*, like the *Yuddha kāṇḍa* in the *A. R.*, tends to shorten and simplify the narration as related in the *V. R.* Indeed, more than thirty episodes related in the *V. R.* are left out both in the *A. R.* and the *R. C. M.*[99] However, Tulsī Dās also takes more liberty at departing from the *A. R.*

---

90. *H. L. A. R.*, V. C. 3—Ch. 1, pp. 340-341.
91. *V. R.*, V. 2, vol. II, pp. 338-339.
92. *V. R.*, V. 1. 11.
93. *H. L. A. R.*, V. C. 21—D. 23, pp. 348-349; *A. R.*, V. 4. 8-25.
94. *H. L. A. R.*, V. C. 5—C. 8, pp. 341-342.
95. *H. L. A. R.*, V. C. 46—D. 47, pp. 359-360; *A. R.*, VI. 3. 17-32.
96. *H. L. A. R.*, V. C. 7, pp. 342-343.
97. Vaudeville, C. *Étude*, p. 22.
98. *Ibid.*, p. 223 ff.
99. These include *V. R.*, VI. 25-34,, 40, 45, 47-58, 64,66, 69, 70, 75-79, 81, 84, 97-99, 100. vol. III passim.

in adding expansions and new material, and in frequently deviating from the outline of his predecessor.

There are few indications of dependence on the Vālmīkian account in places where Tulsī Dās departs from the *A. R.* Among the events not related in the *A. R.* are the mandate given to Aṅgada to visit Rāvaṇa before the battle, the intervention of the physician Suṣeṇa to cure Lakṣmaṇa with medicinal herbs, and the description of bad omens accompanying Rāvaṇa's march towards the battle-field, all of which are mentioned in the *V. R.*

However, the instances of dependence on the *A. R.* are more important. In both accounts the bridge across to Laṅkā becomes a pilgrimage site dedicated to Śiva.[100] In both, Kālanemi is sent by Rāvaṇa to throw obstacles in Hanumān's way as he goes to fetch curative herbs on the mountain; in both, Hanumān kills a crocodile who reveals Kālanemi's identity and dies a saving death.[101] In both accounts, the demon Kumbhakarṇa meets Vibhīṣaṇa on his way to the battle-field and congratulates the latter for having become Rāma's devotee.[102] In both, the Sītā that has to undergo the ordeal of fire is illusory.[103] Both narratives present a long hymn to Indra[104] and both report that at the news of Rāma's return to Ayodhyā women ran out to see him thereby neglecting their domestic duties.[105]

A long passage attributed to Rāvaṇa's wife, Mandodarī,[106] is inspired directly from the *B. P.* in a passage where Śiva addresses himself to Kṛṣṇa after the latter's victory over Bāṇa.[107] This passage is not found in either the *V. R.* or the *A. R.*

A number of additions have been made in the *R. C. M.*, many of which are also found in the *Prasannarāghava.*[108] Thus,

100. *H. L. A. R.*, VI. C. 2—C. 6, pp. 367-369; *A. R.*, VI. 4. 1-4.

101. *H. L. A. R.*, C. 57—C. 58, pp. 392-393; *A. R.*, VI. 7. 1-35.

102. *H. L. A. R.*, VI. C. 64—C. 65, p. 395; *A. R.*, VI. 8. 8-16.

103. *H. L. A. R.*, VI. C. 107—D. 109, pp. 421-423; *A. R.*, VI. 13. 19-23.

104. *H. L. A. R.*, VI. Ch. 35—Ch. 36, pp. 425-426;; *A. R.*, VI. 13, 24-32.

105. *H. L. A. R.*, VII. C. 3, p. 433; *A.R.*, VI. 15. 27.

106. *H. L. A. R.*, C. 14—D. 15, pp. 372-373.

107. *B. P.*, X. 63. 34-36.

108. Vaudeville, C. *Étude*, pp. 248-263.

Mandodarī is heard three times supplicating Rāvaṇa to surrender.[109] On his way back from the mountain with the medicinal herbs Hanumān flies over Ayodhyā and Bharata shoots him down by mistake.[110] Rāma fells Rāvaṇa's charioteer but raises him up immediately.[111] Rāma stands in front of Vibhīṣaṇa so as to protect the latter from being hit by Rāvaṇa's spear.[112] The conversation between Rāma and Guha is reported as Rāma first meets him after the end of the battle.[113]

Contrary to his predecessors, Tulsī Dās finishes the sixth *kāṇḍa* by interrupting the end of the story before Rāma reaches Ayodhyā, thus departing once more from the traditional structural arrangement.

We may summarize by saying that while Tulsī Dās takes more liberty from the traditional narrative in both the outline and the content of this *kāṇḍa,* he still depends on the *A. R.* in important matters and shows relatively little evidence of having borrowed directly from the *V. R.*

7. *The Uttara kāṇḍa*

The first part of the *Uttara kāṇḍa* is devoted to Rāma's return to Ayodhyā, his coronation and the ensuing happiness in Rāma's kingdom. Again, many incidents are new, such as Aṅgada and Hanumān's request to stay with Rāma,[114] the meeting with Sanaka in the garden,[115] Rāma's description of the ideal saint and the *kali yuga*,[116] Vasiṣṭha's conversation with Rāma on the merits of loving devotion,[117] and Nārada's hymn of praise to Rāma.[118]

We have already described the last part of this *kāṇḍa* as the Bhusuṇḍi section, which presents the conversation between

109. *H. L. A. R.*, VI, C. 6—C. 7, p. 369; C. 14—D. 15, pp. 372-373; C. 36—D. 37, pp. 383-384.
110. *H. L. A. R.*, VI. D. 58—D. 60, pp. 394-395.
111. *Ibid.*, VI. C. 91, p. 411.
112. *Ibid.*, VI. C. 94, p. 412.
113. *Ibid.*, VI. C. 117—Ch. 37, p. 430.
114. *Ibid.*, VII. C. 16—D. 19, p. 442.
115. *Ibid.*, VII. C. 30—C. 34, pp. 449-450.
116. *Ibid.*, VII. C. 35—C. 40, pp. 450-452.
117. *Ibid.*, VII. C. 46—D. 49, p. 455.
118. *Ibid.*, VII. 49, p. 456.

the crow Bhusuṇḍi and the eagle Garuḍa, bearing on the divinity of Rāma. This whole section is new.

We may summarize the content of this chapter by saying that the *R. C. M.* contains three strata which belong to different periods in time. Most of the story follows the traditional narrative based on the original framework provided in the *V. R.* However, there are sufficient reasons to believe that Tulsī Dās relied mostly on the *A. R.* in rewriting his own version of the *Rāmāyaṇa*, which is longer than the *A. R.* but shorter than the *V. R.* In this sense, the *R. C. M.* presents itself as an expansion of the *A. R.* rather than as a summary of the *V. R.* While depending heavily on the *A. R.* Tulsī Dās nonetheless frequently deviates from the latter in adding new elements of his own or borrowed from other sources. Finally, most of the new material is found in the first and the last *kāṇḍas*.

The above analysis will help us to study in proper perspective the place of love of God and social duty as two important themes in the *R. C. M.* Although the latter must be studied as an organic whole and although one must keep in mind that Tulsī Dās no doubt agreed with the views presented in the sections inherited from his sources, one may nevertheless expect to find the author's most significant emphases in the parts which are his own and in the changes he introduces in dealing with the traditional material.

So far, our analysis has dealt mostly with the structure of the *R. C. M.* In the following three chapters, we will attempt a more thematical analysis, focussing on the interaction of social duty and love of God.

Chapter VII

Social Duty in the Ramcaritmanas

AS we begin the study of the place social duty holds in the *Rāmcaritmānas*, it might not be amiss to recall that as a representative of the "middle stream" Tulsī Dās was confronted with two extreme positions whose attitude towards social duty were at irreconcilable odds. Whereas Vedic orthodoxy stressed the importance of traditional regulations in conformity with the scriptures, namely the *śrutis* (what is heard) and the *smṛtis* (what is remembered), antinomian theism took the opposite stand of promoting love of God as an end in itself with the implication, sometimes made very explicit, that traditional regulations might be disregarded. We shall see that Tulsī Dās' zeal for promoting love of God did not lead him to reject the authority of the scriptures or to despise the value of traditional regulations based on scriptures. After examining to what extent the poet's respect for the scriptures is reflected in the *Rāmcaritmānas*, we shall study the importance attached to social duties dictated by the caste system, the family institution, and the rôle of the *guru*.

A. *The Importance of Scriptures in the Rāmcaritmānas*

The most obvious criterion of a Hindu's respect for his tradition is the place accorded to scriptures. Both the *V. R.* and the *A. R.* gave an important place to traditional scriptures,[1] and this importance reflects in some of the passages Tulsī Dās borrows from them. Thus, as she witnesses her son's supernal manifestation Kausalyā praises him by refering to the *Vedas* and the *Purāṇas* :

> Veda and Purāṇa declare thee beyond illusion (*māyā*), nature's elements and knowledge immeasurable.[2]

Likewise, the corresponding passage in the *A. R.* refers to the *Vedas* :

---

1. These include the *śruti* and the *smṛti*.
2. *H. L. A. R.*, ch. 21, p. 89.

> Knowers of the Vedas declare Thee to be beyond speech, intellect and the rest.[3]

As a young boy we are told in the *Rāmcaritmānas* that Rāma "listened attentively to the recital of the Veda and Purāṇa".[4] Likewise, the *V. R.* notes that Daśaratha's children "took pleasure in the study of the Veda".[5]

However, it is obvious that Tulsī Dās was not rarely conforming to his sources in this respect. On the contrary, he adds references to scriptures even when the sources do not. For instance, in his hymn to Viṣṇu before the birth of Rāma, Brahmā refers to the *Veda*: this detail is not in the preceding versions. Again, the *Rāmcaritmānas* is the only version to describe the infant child as he whom the Veda calls 'Not thus',[6] and to quote Janaka's reference to the *Vedas* when he asks if "the Absolute, which the Vedas called 'Not thus' come to earth in dual form".[7]

Indeed, the emphasis given to traditional scriptures is particularly strong in passages where Tulsī Dās writes independently of his sources. In the very opening *śloka* of the *Rāmcaritmānas* Tulsī Dās makes it clear that the *magnum opus* is to be considered as conform to "all the Purāṇas, the Vedas and the Āgamas." A few stanzas later, he refers to the *Vedās* as a way of authenticating his statement on spiritual benefits accruing from sharing the company of saints.[8] Within the same *caupāi* (a metre or verse consisting of four lines) he refers three times to the *Vedas* as the foundation for distinguishing between the good and the bad:

> It is God who has created all the good and the bad, but the Veda with careful discrimination has distinguished between virtues and faults. The Vedas, the Itihāsas (i.e. the Epics) and the Purāṇas declare that God's creation is a mixture of virtue and vice...the

---

3. *A. R.*, I. 2. 13-20.
4. *H. L. A. R.*, I. C. 203, p. 94.
5. *V. R.*, I. 18, vol. I, p. 46.
6. *H. L. A. R.*, I. C. 201, p. 93.
7. *Ibid.*, I. C. 213, p. 99,
8. *Ibid.*, I. C. 3, p. 4.

> Vedas and the Agamas have made distinction of their merits and demerits.[9]

Tulsī Dās does not hesitate, in the same context, to consider Rāma, whose divine nature he affirms throughout, as the "very essence" of the *Purāṇas* and the *Vedas*,[10] or the "vital breath of the Veda".[11] Consequently, he holds that "the Vedas, the Purāṇas and Āgamas are ever singing his perfection."[12] It is also with the "four Vedas"[13] that he opens the long list of those to whom he extends his reverence as he sets out to write his story. The habit of referring to scripture is maintained throughout.

As a result of his high esteem for traditional scriptures, Tulsī Dās instinctively disapproves of those who say "things as have no warrant in the Veda".[14] As he relates his first narrative of Rāvaṇa's story in the opening section of the *Bāla kāṇḍa*, he describes the wicked demons as those who defied the Vedic law and who never recited the *Vedas* and *Purāṇas*. He adds that the evil Rāvaṇa would inflict various tortures on those who repeated the *Vedas* or *Purāṇas* and banish them from the land.[15] In the same vein, Bharata declares that if he has consented to his mother's perverse manoeuvre which led to Rāma's exile, his guilt would be as serious as "those who recite the Veda for profit" and who "revile the Veda"; he adds that he would deserve a lot similar to those "who abandon the Vedic path and follow the opposite road".[16] Tulsī Dās disapproves of men who walk not on the path of faith "the path approved in scripture...but follow after various heresies and vain imaginings."[17] It is not without significance that among the few whom Tulsī Dās explicitly denounces by identifying them are the "followers of the left-hand path",[18] a clear reference to

9. *Ibid.*, I. C. 6, p. 6.
10. *Ibid.*, I. C. 10, p. 8.
11. *Ibid.*, I. C. 19, p. 14.
12. *Ibid.*, I. C. 12, p. 10.
13. *Ibid.*, I. C. 13—D. 14, p. 11.
14. *Ibid.*, I. C. 115, p. 57.
15. *Ibid.*, I. C. 183, p. 85.
16. *Ibid.*, II. C. 167-168, p. 229.
17. *Ibid.*, VI. D. 100, p. 478.
18. *Ibid.*, VI. C. 31, p. 380.

the left handed Tāntras, who were considered unorthodox as they rejected traditional scriptures.

This said, it must be pointed out that Tulsī Dās also highlighted the value of actions performed according to traditional regulations based on the scriptures. Although he does not refer so frequently as his predecessors on the *Śāstras* as such,[19] he nevertheless praises King Pratāpabhānu for listening to "the holy Śāstras",[20] and Kaikeyī refers to the *Manusmṛti* as a reminder for her hesitating husband that one must keep his promise.[21] Likewise, in describing the funeral rites on the occasion of Daśaratha's death, Tulsī Dās notes that Bharata performed the ceremony "after studying all the Codes (of Manu), the Vedas and the Purāṇas".[22] The *A. R.* also speaks of the *Śāstras* in the parallel passage.[23] In general, however, authoritative scriptures are referred to in the *Rāmcaritmānas* as the *śruti*. Thus, Tulsī Dās speaks about "the Vedas and the Purāṇas and all holy books (*śruti*)".[24] Even though he is not very explicit about *Śāstras* as distinct from ritual in general, he nevertheless imitates both of his predecessors in highlighting the importance of Vedic rites performed on special occasions. Like Vālmīki[25] and the author of the *A. R.*[26] he gives an important place to traditional rituals accompanying important events such as Daśaratha's sacrifice for the obtention of a progeny,[27] the marriage of Sītā and Rāma,[28] and Rāma's installation as king of Ayodhyā.[29] Again, like his two predecessors[30] he is edified by faithful performance of ritual ablutions and devotions. Thus Rāma is shown bathing in the Gaṅgā,[31] he recites evening

19. *V. R.*, I. 66, p. 131; II. 52, vol. I, p. 292, etc.
20. *H. L. A. R.*, C. 155, p. 73.
21. *Ibid.*, I. C. 28, p. 173.
22. *Ibid.*, II. C. 170, p. 230.
23. *A. R.*, II. 7. 108.
24. *H. L. A. R.*, VI. C. 31, p. 449.
25. *V. R.*, I. 12-14, vol. I, pp. 30-34; I. 73, vol. I, pp. 143-145; VI. 130, vol. III, p. 365.
26. *A. R.*, I. 4; I. VII; VI. 15.
27. *H. L. A. R.*, I. C. 188—C. 189, pp. 57-88.
28. *Ibid.*, I. C. 344—c. 348; pp. 155-157.
29. *Ibid.*, VII. C. 11 ff., pp. 437 ff.
30. For instance, *V. R.* II. 51, vol. I, p. 285; *A. R.*, I. 1. 64.
31. *H. L. A. R.*, I. C. 209, p. 97.

prayers with his brother and the guru,[32] and in the morning he bathes after "performing all the rites of purification".[33] Likewise, *guru* Viśvāmitra tells King Janaka to "perform, as is the custom in your family, whatever rites the Vedas prescribe".[34] As the two royal families assemble for the wedding of Rāma and Sītā, the two *gurus* "performed all the rites and ceremonies and usages appropriate to that hour",[35] and so on.

From this point of view, therefore, Tulsī Dās maintains a strictly orthodox position, in conformity with the *V. R.* On this point it is significant to see that the Hindi poet scrupulously avoids certain antinomian statements found in the *A. R.* The latter had denounced Vedic rites in rather strong terms when it declared that those who are devoid of devotion should "roll in the abyss of the *Śāstras*".[36] This opposition between devotion and what is traditionally viewed as good works is made several other times in the *A. R.*[37] Tulsī Dās prefers avoiding such contrasts suggestive of antinomianism; in this he is more orthodox than the Vedāntic *A. R.*

Tulsī Dās attachment to the tradition as codified in the scriptures may also be seen in his attitude towards the Vedic pantheon. This is an important point if one bears in mind the presence of strictly monotheistic Muslims then in authority, and Kabīr's insistence on a unique God.

It is true that Tulsī Dās reserves some of his most severe judgements for the traditionally accepted gods. The latter are pictured as being not only cowardly but jealous.[38] Thus, on the eve of Rāma's coronation "the joyous celebrations at Avadh (Ayodhyā) pleased them no more than a moonlight night delghts a thief".[39] As they feel threatened in their prestige by Rāma's growing popularity they implore Sarasvatī, the goddess of speech, to bring about his exile. Sarasvatī, who reluctantly complies, calls their thoughts base and their deeds

---

32. *Ibid.*, I. C. 223, p. 103.
33. *Ibid.*, see also I. C. 234, p. 107; I. C. 235, p. 108 etc.
34. *Ibid.*, I. C. 283; see also: I. C. 299, p. 133.
35. *Ibid.*, I. C. 320.
36. *A. R.*, I. 1. 111.
37. *Ibid.*, I. 2. 16; III. 2. 35; III. 10. 21; IV. 1. 76 etc.
38. *Ibid.*, I. C. 257, p. 116.
39. *Ibid.*, II. C. 11, p. 166.

low for "they cannot bear to look on another's power".[40] This scene, which is not found in the *V. R.*, is also depicted in the *A. R.* but no motivation is assigned to the gods' intervention.[41] In another scene which is only found in the *Rāmcaritmānas*, the gods are pictured as selfishly dismayed and plunged into despair when they witness that everyone was filled with love for Rāma. Again, they appeal to Sarasvatī begging her to prevent Bharata from bringing Rāma back to Ayodhyā. This time, however, the goddess refuses, leaving the "selfish gods" downcast.[42]

One must, not, on the basis of the above passages, infer that Tulsī Dās was critical of the tradition as such. On the contrary, it was traditional by his time to portray the gods (*devas*) in a similar light, and so Tulsī Dās was simply reflecting an established attitude towards the gods.

In fact, Tulsī Dās freely affirms the existence of the pantheon and in spite of his critical attitude, he generally gives an important place to the gods by frequently referring to them in a favourable light. Thus, he adopts Vālmīki's habit,[43] also followed by the author of the *A. R.*,[44] of showing the gods partaking of the celebrations accompanying joyful events.[45] On several occasions we are told that Rāma incarnated himself for the sake of the gods,[46] a view also found in the *V. R.*[47] and the *A. R.*[48] Devotees, such as King Pratāpabhānu are said to have built "magnificent and marvellous temples" to the gods.[49] In the story of Rāvaṇa narrated in the *Bāla kāṇḍa*, disrespect for the gods is included in the list of vices attributed to the demon king.[50] Time and again, faithful observers of the tradition are exalted for paying service to the gods or worshipping them.[51] Rāma

40. *Ibid.*

41. *A. R.*, II. 2. 44-46.

42. *Ibid.*, II. C. 295—C. 296, p. 281.

43. *V. R.*, I. 18, vol. I, p. 45; I. 73, vol. I, p. 146: VI. 110, vol. III, p. 316; VI. 130, vol. III, p. 369.

44. *A. R.*, I. 3. 14-15; I. 6. 82: VI. II. 79-80.

45. *H. L. A. R.*, I. C. 190, p. 88: I. C. 315, p. 140: I. D. 339, p. 152: I. C. 345, p. 156: I. 350, p. 158, etc.

46. *Ibid.*, I. C. 186, p. 86; D. 192, p. 89, VI. C. 109, p. 423.

47. *V. R.* I. 15, p. 40.

48. *A. R.*, I. 2. 4.

49. *H. L. A. R.*, I. C. 155, p. 73.

50. *Ibid.*, I. C. 183, p. 84.

51. *Ibid.*, I. C. 291, p. 130.

himself is shown worshipping the gods, although Tulsī Dās makes it clear that the gods depend on the Lord's saving power and as such they are sometimes presented as devotees. This can be seen in the following description:

> Rāma...worshipped (*pūje*) them (the gods) and enthroned them in his soul; and the gods were delighted to mark the loving-kindness of the Lord. With exceeding love and gladness the bright eyes of each one reverently drank in the beauty of Rāmacandra's face, as the partridge the light of the moon.[52]

Thus, Tulsī Dās' over-all attitude does not depart from the spirit of the *Vedas* or of the *Manusmṛti,* in which daily offerings to the gods are clearly prescribed.[53]

We conclude that Tulsī Dās' attitude toward the Hindu tradition is one of firm attachment and respect. Throughout his *magnum opus* he frequently refers to traditional scriptures, unambiguously acknowledging their authority. His respect for traditional rituals, including Śāstric regulations, is never denied. He freely draws upon Hindu mythology by affirming the existence of the pantheon which populates the mythology. This respect for orthodoxy will be reflected in the place accorded to domestic duties, to the caste system and to the rôle assigned to the *guru.*

B. *The Importance of Caste Duties in the Rāmcaritmānas*

In the opening section of the first *kāṇḍa*, Tulsī Dās gives a theological foundation for the existence of the *varṇa* system. He explains that creation is essentially a mixture: as God has created good and bad, virtue and vice, pain and pleasure, sin and merit, day and night, saint and sinner, so He has created high caste and low.[54] Indeed, the first characteristics of social deterioration are lawlessness and confusion among the castes.[55]

Tulsī Dās notes with satisfaction that King Janaka's servants "gave men and women seats, the nobles and all of less degree,

52. *Ibid.*, I. C. 318, p. 142.
53. *Manu smṛti,* III. 70.
54. *Ibid.*, I. C. 6, p. 6.
55. *Ibid.*, VII, D. 100, p. 478.

each according to his rank",[56] a detail which his predecessors had failed to note. Likewise, Rāma is seen in the forest receiving the people of Ayodhyā "according to his or her estate".[57]

Even though faith is more important than caste structure,[58] it does not follow that "the rules of caste and the four orders of life" may be neglected.[59] On the contrary, one should be conscious of his own rank, like Rāma who wears his caste-mark on his forehead and declares openly to what *varṇa* he belongs.[60]

Unlike the *V. R.*[61] and the *A. R.*[62] the *Rāmcaritmānas* avoids excluding the lower-caste from the twice-born. The king is hospitable to all, including beggars, who are frequently shown receiving gifts on special occasions of public festivities.[63] However, Tulsī Dās insists that caste identity be maintained and distinctive caste duties observed. Thus, Vasiṣṭha tells Bharata that Brahmins who know not the Veda but abandon religious duty and devote themselves to things of sense should be grieved for. Likewise, Kṣatriyas who understand not statecraft and love not their people as their own lives, Vaiśyas who are rich but niggardly, unpracticed in hospitality or devotion to Śiva, and Śūdras who dishonour Brahmins, are garrulous, ambitious and wise in their own conceits should be grieved for.[64] This new passage is re-echoed in another passage which Tulsī Dās wrote under the influence of the *Bhusuṇḍi Rāmāyaṇa*, where the philosopher described the *kali yuga* as a time of confusion among the castes:

> Brāhmans sold the Vedas...Sūdras gave Brāhmans lessons in wisdom, and putting on the sacred thread accepted iniquitous ashes...The Brāhmans were illiterate, grasping and lascivious, profligate and senseless and the husbands of loose-living outcastes. Śūdras

---

56. *Ibid.*, I. D. 240, p. 109; C. 325, p. 148.
57. *Ibid.*, II. C. 274, p. 272.
58. *Ibid.*, III. C. 33, p. 318.
59. *Ibid.*, VII. C. 96, p. 476.
60. *Ibid.*, II D. 229, p. 254; III. C. 18, p. 307.
61. For emaple, *V. R.* I. 72, vol. I, p. 143.
62. For exmple, *A.. R.*, IV. 4. 12-15.
63. For example, *H. L. A. R.*, I. D. 295, p. 130: C. 303, pp. 134-135: C. 327*i*, p. 148, etc.
64. *Ibid.*, II. C. 172, p. 231.

> indulged in all sorts of prayers and penances and vows and seated themselves on the dais to recite the Purāṇas. Everybody did just exactly what he liked...[65]

Tulsī Dās' uncompromising attitude with regards to caste identity leads him to write such a bold statement as this :

> A Brāhman is to be reverenced even though he curse and beat you and use harsh words—so say the saints. A Brāhman must be revered though he be devoid of goodness and virtue, but a Śūdra never, however virtuous and learned.[66]

On this point, as on so many others, Tulsī Dās is directly opposed to the antinomian attitude of Kabīr which had found its way in Northern India resulting in the rejection of caste distinctions which were intimately linked with the tradition and clearly codified in the prestigious *Manusmṛti*. Even though he does not refer to the twice-born as a separate class excluding Śūdras and Outcastes, yet he teaches in no uncertain terms as we have just seen that caste distinctions are to be rigidly maintained.

We have seen in a previous chapter that Tulsī Dās gave a special attention to the lowly and the humble. We must now examine what place he gave to the Brahmins, who belong to what is usually called the "higher" caste.

It is evident that Tulsī Dās held the Brahmins in high esteem, and that he was particularly mindful of the social duties resulting from their particular situation in society. Rāma declares that Brahmins are his favourite among all men:

> All are dear to me for all are my creation, but the creature I delight in most is man; of men, the Brāhman, and of Brāhmans, the student of the Vedas.[67]

The Brahmins belong to a pure caste,[68] and they are even higher than gods.[69] Even the great Śiva is seen bowing to them.[70]

---

65. *Ibid.*, VII. C. 97-98, pp. 477-478.
66. *Ibid.*, III. C. 31, p. 317.
67. *Ibid.*, VII. C. 84, p. 471.
68. *Ibid.*, VII. C. 105, p. 484.
69. *Ibid.*, I. C. 174, p. 88.
70. *Ibid.*, I. C. 100, p. 51.

It is for their sake, along with that of the gods, the saints and the cows, that Rāma came down to earth as a man.[71] To slay anyone of these would be the worst of crimes.[72]

It is significant that Tulsī Dās addresses the first homage[73] of his work to the Brahmins and gives them the preeminent place among those he mentions in his final benediction.[74] Likewise, he gives devotion to the feet of Brahmins the first place among the nine expressions of faith.[75] He also emphasizes the power of the Brahmin, particularly by relating stories on the consequence of his curse.[76] Most[77] of these are Tulsī Dās' own additions.

It is interesting to see how Tulsi Dās' appreciation for the Brahmin class affected his treatment of the violent encounter between Paraśurāma and Rāma. In the *V. R.*, Paraśurāma wants to provoke a combat against Rāma to satisfy his hatred of the Kṣatriya class, of which Rāma had proven that he was the mightiest by recently breaking the bow:

> In order to avenge the death of his Sire, will he not slay all the warriors anew? Formerly, having destroyed them, his anger was appeased as also his grief; assuredly he has resolved to annihilate the warrior caste once more.[78]

Challenged by his belligerent foe, Rāma answers:

> Thou art a Brahmin and, being a kinsman of Viśvāmitra, I reverence thee: I cannot, therefore, direct a death-dealing shaft upon thee, O Paraśurāma.

He then decides as an alternative to deprive his enemy of his

71. *Ibid.*, I. D. 192, p. 89; C. 121, p. 160.
72. *Ibid.*, II. C. 147, p. 221; II. C. 167, p. 229; III. C. 31, p. 317; IV. C. 17, p. 332; V. C. 44, p. 358; VI. C. 45, p, 387.
73. *Ibid.*, I. C. 2.
74. *Ibid.*, VII. C. 122, p. 497.
75. *Ibid.*, III. C. 15, p. 305.
76. *Ibid.*, I. C. 123, p. 51; D. 174, p. 81; C. 165, pp. 77-78.
77. On the gravity of the slaying of a Brahmin see *A. R.*, II. 7. which corresponds to *H. L. A. R.*, II. C. 167, p. 229.
78. *V. R.*, I. 74, vol. I, p. 147.

power and of his realms, thereby obliging him to withdraw to the Mahendra Mountain.[79]

In the *A. R.* Paraśurāma speaks with even more contempt of the "vile Kṣatriyas" and challenges Rāma to fight with him in a duel after having stringed the bow of Viṣṇu. Rāma "eyeing him angrily snatched away the bow from his hand" and told his impudent adversary that "neither to this world nor the next canst thou go, without my command." Upon hearing such words of bravery Paraśurāma acknowledged Rāma as his saviour.[80]

In the *Rāmcaritmānas* Rāma responds to Paraśurāma's challenge by first trying to placate his anger :

> Lord, it must be one of your servants who has broken (the bow); what is your bidding?

The ensuing verbal confrontation is then led by Lakṣmaṇa and Paraśurāma, where the latter is being ridiculed by Rāma's younger brother. Again Rāma tries to quench the Brahmin's wrath by asking him to excuse the childish impudence of his younger brother. He goes on to call himself Paraśurāma's servant and asking him how he could assuage his wrath. Seeing that his enemy's disposition had still not changed he then repeated his plea by calling him "sage", "master", "noble Brahmin" and by admitting his own inferiority. He added that Lakṣmaṇa was impudent because he mistook the Brahmin challenger for a warrior, given the latter's accoutrement: "Had you come as an anchorite, holy sir, the child would have placed the dust of your feet on his head." Still not satisfied, Paraśurāma repeats his threat, to which Rāma gave a convincing reply by admitting that he will not fight against him on account of his respect for Brahminhood:

> Such is the dignity of Brahman descent that he fears you who fears none other.

Hearing this, Paraśurāma recognized Rāma as his Lord and sang a hymn of praise.[81]

---

79. *Ibid.*, p. 147-150.
80. *A. R.*, I. 7. 1-19.
81. *H. L. A. R.*, I. C. 265—C. 281, p. 119-126.

It is clear that Tulsī Dās tried to avoid attributing to Rāma any sign of impatience, anger or disrespect *vis-à-vis* a Brahmin. Such attitude would not have been in keeping with the over-all treatment given to the Brahmins throughout the *Rāmcaritmānas.*

If Tulsī Dās calls his listener's attention to the importance of the Brahmin and the duties they command, he also reminds the Brahmins their own duties towards society. They are expected to be learned,[82] and to give instructions on religion, morality, detachment and discernment.[83] Although Tulsī Dās goes as far as saying that Brahmins are to be reverenced regardless of their virtue,[84] he nevertheless adds that "The sole mark of a Brahmin (is) not the sacred thread."[85]

In the latter part of the book, which owes nothing to the *V. R.* nor the *A. R.*, Tulsī Dās insists on the importance of doing service to the Brahmins. He praises the citizens of Ayodhyā for doing "humble service to the Brahmins".[86] Śiva declares that "the only vow that pleases Hari (Viṣṇu) is a vow to do service to Brahmins".[87] Service rendered to Brahmins is described as a path leading to Hari.[88]

The Brahmins' relation to the king is also emphasized. The latter is praised for building houses for the Brahmins.[89] As it is frequently mentioned both in the *A. R.* and the *V. R.*, the king gives generous gifts to Brahmins.[90] Viśvāmitra is overheard saying to himself that by leaving his father for the first time to help kill demons in the forest Rāma gave a proof of his devotedness to Brahmins,[91] a detail not found in the *V. R.* nor the *A. R.*

Brahmins are given a prominent place in the public functions of the royal family. They recite the Vedas in the palace;[92]

82. *Ibid.*, I. C. 300, p. 134: II. C. 172, p. 231.
83. *Ibid.*, II. C. 278, p. 274: VII. C. 96—C. 97, pp. 476-477.
84. *Ibid.*, III. C. 31, p. 317.
85. *Ibid.*, VII. D. 100, p. 478.
86. *Ibid.*, VII. C. 20, p. 444.
87. *Ibid.*, VII. C. 104, p. 483.
88. *Ibid.*, VII. C. 121, p. 496.
89. *Ibid.*, I. C. 155, p. 73.
90. *Ibid.*, I. C. 209, pp. 97-98; I. C. 292, p. 130; I. C. 327, p. 149, II. D. 170, p. 230, etc.
91. *Ibid.*, I. C. 207, p. 96.
92. *Ibid.*, I. C. 294, p. 131.

they accompany the king when he welcomes important visitors[93] and they accompany the royal family in important matters such as the search of Rāma in the forest,[94] in public ceremonies,[95] and in the decisive combat between Rāma and Rāvaṇa.[96]

The increased emphasis given to Brahmins in the *Rāmcaritmānas* suggests that Tulsī Dās tended to enhance their prestige. Having lost control of the political power, which was now in the hands of Muslim rulers, it was important for the Hindus to realize that they were not left without spiritual and moral leadership consonant with the tradition, which was the very *raison d'être* of the Brahmin caste. Their rôle had now become vital to the maintenance of the integrity of the tradition, and it was fitting that Tulsī Dās should give them a prominent place in the *Rāmcaritmānas*. We may go further and say that Tulsī Dās' portrayal of Rāma suggests the spiritual and moral leader more than the temporal king. He is even the Brahmin par excellence. This is strongly suggested in the final portion of the story, which owes nothing to the *V. R.* nor the *A. R.* where Rāma is described as "beautiful with the mark of the Brāhman's lotus foot'.'[97] It is also suggested in two episodes where Rāma is shown teaching the Brahmins on the nature and aim of the spiritual quest,[98] and in Nārada's hymn of praise where Rāma is said to bless the Brahmins,[99] two functions which are normally performed by Brahmins. This tendency will be further illustrated in the coming section dealing with the place of the *guru* in society.

C. *The Importance of Traditional Domestic Duties in the Rāmcaritmānas*

The family household is traditionally considered as the basic structure of society and the *Śāstras* devote detailed regulations to its organization.[100] These deal specifically with the duties

93. *Ibid.*, I. C. 205, p. 95; I. D. 214, p. 98; I.C. 312, p. 318.
94. *Ibid.*, II. D. 245, p. 261; D. 253, p. 264; C. 323, p. 293.
95. *Ibid.*, IV. C. 11, p. 330; VII. C. 12, p. 437.
96. *Ibid.*, VI. C. 90, p. 410.
97. *Ibid.*, VII. S. 1, p. 431.
98. *Ibid.*, VII. C. 41, p. 453.
99. *Ibid.*, VII. C. 49, p. 456.
100. *Manu smṛti,* I—IV.

of the son, of the mother, and of the father. It is to their place in the *Rāmcaritmānas* that we shall devote this section of the present chapter.

The ideal son is pictured as respectful, obedient, devoted and affectionate. He performs the religious rituals and he is industrious.

He manifests his attitude of respect by bowing his head before his parents' feet,[101] before the *guru*,[102] and before the Brahmins.[103] One of the characteristics of the demons is precisely the fact that they "honour not mother or father".[104]

The ideal son is obedient. He is subject to his parents' bidding.[105] We are reminded that Rāma went into exile "at his father's command".[106] The son is also obedient to his mother: Bharata "obediently mounted his chariot" at the command of his mother rather than complete on foot the journey in the forest.[107] The son owes obedience to the family *guru*.[108]

Tulsī Dās emphasizes a particular quality of obedience by showing Rāma conforming with ENTHUSIASM to his father's command sending him into exile. In the Vālmīkian version, Rāma accepted the order in perfect serenity :

> On renouncing sovereignty and leaving for exile to the forest, Rāmacandra resembled a great Yogi, and none observed any change of mood in him.[109]

In the *A. R.* Rāma accepted the news with joy:

> To me by living in the forest, there is million times more happiness than in ruling the kingdom.[110]

101. *H. L. A. R.*, I. C. 206, p. 96.
102. *Ibid.*, I., C. 203, p. 94.
103. *Ibid.*, I. C. 305, p. 135.
104. *Ibid.*, I. C. 184, p. 85.
105. *Ibid.*, I. C. 203, p. 94.
106. *Ibid.*, II. C. 165, p. 228.
107. *Ibid.*, II. C. 188, p. 237; this episode is not found in the *V. R.* or the *A. R.*
108. *Ibid.*, I. C. 251, p. 114.
109. *V. R.*, II. 19, p. 212.
110. *A. R.*, II. 3, 74.

In the *Rāmcaritmānas* Rāma is enthusiastic, seeing in the event not only a chance to meet with the sages in the forest but especially an opportunity to act in obedience to his father's command :

> Hear me, my mother: blessed is the son who loves to obey his parents' bidding. Hard to find, mother, in all the world is a son who thus contents his father and mother. It is altogether to my profit that I should go to the forest where I may most easily meet with sages. Herein, moreover, I obey my father's command and follow your advice, my mother.[111]

The ideal son proves his devotedness and affection by speaking to his parents with affectionate words,[112] by being especially diffident towards a parent from whom he has been separated for a length of time,[113] and by comforting a parent in desolation.[114] All of these are exemplified in Rāma's conduct as well as in that of his brothers.

The ideal son strives to acquit himself of his religious duties by submitting at the appointed time to the traditional rituals such as the investment of the sacred thread,[115] by studying, reciting, and teaching the sacred scriptures,[116] and by performing the daily rituals.[117] Finally, he learns young to become industrious: as a prince, Rāma would engage everyday "in the business of the city".[118]

In relation to his brothers, the son is also reminded that he must observe "strict service to his brother...in thought and word and deed".[119] He enjoys being in the company of his brothers,[120] particularly for the daily rites of purification, bath

---

111. *H. L. A. R.*, II. C. 41, p. 178.
112. *Ibid.*, II. C. 53, p. 183.
113. *Ibid.*, I. C. 304, p. 135.
114. *Ibid.*, I. C. 68, p. 189.
115. *Ibid.*, I. C. 202, p. 94.
116. *Ibid.*, I. C. 202—C. 204, p. 94.
117. *Ibid.*, I. C. 235, p. 108.
118. *Ibid.*, I. C. 203, p. 94.
119. *Ibid.*, III. C. 15, p. 305: this detail is not mentioned in the corresponding passage of the *A. R.*, III. 4. 48ff. which deals with the nine means of devotion.
120. *Ibid.*, I. C. 94, p. 94; C. 305, p. 135; II. C. 10, p. 166.

and prayers.[121] He is especially considerate of his senior brother, by serving him obediently and loving him tenderly.[122] In return, the eldest son loves his other brothers dearly, even above his own wife.[123] He contributes to their education, thus imitating Rāma who "told his brother (Lakṣmaṇa) many tales of devotion and continence and the art of kingship and wise judgement."[124]

The domestic duties of the parents are also dealt with in the *Rāmcaritmānas.* As wives, women are given a list of duties, which could be considered as the wife's chapter, in a long passage of the *Rāmcaritmānas* that is not found in the two previous versions of the *Rāmāyaṇa.* Anasūyā, the wife of the saintly sage Atri, advises Sītā above all to pay reverence to her husband, "though he be old, diseased, stupid or poor, blind, deaf, bad-tempered or in great distress".[125] Anasūyā insists on this point. The wife's devotion to her husband's feet is "her one religious duty, her one vow and observance".[126] Sītā could only agree with this since in a previous passage she herself had been heard expressing her admiration for "faithful wives who adore their husbands as gods".[127] Anasūyā then makes a distinction between four grades of faithful wives: i) the best is convinced her husband is the only man in the world: ii) the next considers other husbands as her own brother, father or son: iii) the third in order is chaste for the mere sake of duty and honour; iv) finally, the lowest is the one whom fear alone restrains and want of opportunity. As to the unfaithful wife, she "is cast for a hundred aeons into the depths of the lowest hell".[128]

Tulsī Dās wrote many distinctive passages on women that are particularly harsh.[129] This harshness is repeated in Ana-

121. *Ibid.*, I. C. 223, p. 103.

122. *Ibid.*, C. 196, p. 91; C. 223, p. 103; II. C. 70, p. 190; C. 71, p. 290, etc.

123. *Ibid.*, VI. C. 61, p. 394; see also II. C. 42, p. 178: C. 200, p. 242.

124. *Ibid.*, IV. C. 13, p. 330.

125. *Ibid.*, III. C. 4, p. 298.

126. *Ibid.*

127. *Ibid.*, I. C. 232, p. 107.

128. *Ibid.*, III. C. 4, p. 298.

129. *Ibid.*, II. C. 14, p. 167; C. 27, p. 173; C. 161, p. 227; III. C. 16, p. 306, etc.

sūyā's statement that "women are inherently impure"; she adds, however, that "if she serve her husband faithfully, she wins to highest bliss.[130] She concludes her long exposition by saying that those who meditate on Sītā's own name will be faithful wives, thereby explicitly proposing to the female listener an ideal and a model wife to be imitated.

With regard to her children, the good mother is shown accompanying her husband and the *guru* for the investment of the sacred thread to their sons thus showing her interest in the children's religious education. She gives good advice to her children in kindness and simplicity,[131] and even speaks to them with authority when necessary.[132] Above all, the good mother is the one whose love for the children is boundless. Among the many passages in the *Rāmcaritmānas* where such love is portrayed,[133] we could select for demonstration the scene which shows Kausalyā giving her blessing to Rāma as he prepares to leave for his sylvan exile. The same scene is described in both the *V. R.* and the *A. R.* The *V. R.* devotes a long passage to Kausalyā's numerous wishes for her sons. This is followed by a brief description of the queen's emotional feelings, which is one of the most moving in the whole story:

> Although a prey to grief, she spoke in cheerful tones with deep emotion, in a quivering voice, and the illustrious princess bent over her son, placed her arms round him and embraced him.[134]

After invoking the protection of the gods, her emotions are once more described in these terms:

> Thereafter, her eyes full of tears, having completed the benedictory rites, she circumambulated Rāghava reverentially, and, her gaze fixed on him, she embraced him tenderly again and again.[135]

---

130. *Ibid.*, III. S. 5, p. 298.
131. *Ibid.*, II. C. 176, p. 232.
132. *Ibid.*, II. C. 53, p. 183; C. 188, p. 237.
133. *Ibid.*, I. D. 200, p. 92; II. C. 52, p. 183 C. 68, p. 189; C. 245, p. 260, etc.
134. *V. R.* II. 25, vol. I, 227.
135. *Ibid.*, II. 25, vol. I, pp. 227-230.

The *A. R.* is particularly brief in its description of Kausalyā's physical expression of motherly love:

> On hearing this, Kausalyā became greatly confused and fell into a swoon; then she got up and (was) in great pain and sunk in the ocean of sorrow.[136]

Tulsī Dās describes the scene in the following way:

> She blessed him and clasped him to her bosom and lavished on him ornaments and raiment. Again and again his mother kissed his face, with tears of love in her eyes and trembling with emotion. Again she took him on her lap and pressed him to her heart, and the milk of love poured from her fair breasts. Her gladness and affection were indescribable, as when a beggar becomes rich as Kuvera. Reverently gazing on his beauteous face his mother spoke in tender tones.[137]

What distinguishes Tulsī Dās' description is the warmth and the spontaneous simplicity of the mother's love. Like Vālmīki, Tulsī Dās notes Kausalyā's reverence, but in the new description Kausalyā is no longer shown circumambulating her son nor is she trying to dissimulate her feelings by attempting to speak in cheerful tones.

Tulsī Dās pays less attention to man's obligations as a husband. Nevertheless he reminds him of his duty to be true to his wife,[138] by not looking with a lustful eye at "a younger brother's wife, a sister, the wife of a son and a virgin maid."[139] He should strive to love his own wife as dearly as Rāma loved Sītā.[140] As head of a household and as father, he is shown tolerating "no display of valour against gods or Brāhmans or votaries or cows."[141] He performs the appointed religious rites and ceremonies[142] and gives proper hospitality.[143] He

136. *A. R.*, II. 4. 7.
137. *H. L. A. R.*, II. C. 52, p. 183.
138. *Ibid.*, VII. C. 20, p 444.
139. *Ibid.*, IV. C. 9, p. 329.
140. *Ibid.*
141. *Ibid.*, I. C. 270, p. 122.
142. *Ibid.*, I. C. 188, p. 87.
143. *Ibid.*, I. C. 195, p. 91; C. 308, p. 136, etc.

gives gifts to Brahmins[144] and guests[145] and shows a high respect for the *guru.*[146] He rejoices at the birth of his children[147] and educates them in the strict observance of their duties,[148] in collaboration with his wife and the family *guru.*[149] Above all, he gives love, kindness, and solicitude to his children,[150] by considering them as dear to him as his own life.[151]

Again, Tulsī Dās reaffirms the orthodox position. Unlike Rādhā in the *Sūrsāgar*, it is clear from the above that Tulsī Dās avoids statements which might suggest that "family, home and kinsmen" may be forgotten.

D. *The Rôle of the Guru in the Rāmcaritmānas*

We now study the importance of the *guru* in the *Rāmcaritmānas* both insofar as he plays a rôle within the family circle and insofar as he is the king's personal adviser and preceptor.

Tulsī Dās describes the *guru* as the ocean of wisdom who considers the universe as a plum in the hollow of his hand.[152] He is the physician,[153] whose words are the rays of the sun to disperse the deep darkness of powerful ignorance.[154] The dust of his feet are "sweet to the taste and fragrant and full of the flavour of love, delightful powder of the ambrosial root that heals all life's attendant ills.[155] The brightness of the nails of his feet is compared to the brightness of jewels which scatters the darkness of ignorance.[156]

In the opening verses he pays homage to the *guru*, whom he likens to Śiva.[157] Again and again different members of the

144. *Ibid.*, I. C. 209, pp. 97-98.
145. *Ibid.*, I. C. 194, p. 90.
146. This will be discussed in the next section dealing with the *guru.*
147. *Ibid.*, I. C. 191, p. 89.
148. *Ibid.*, I. C. 291, p. 130.
149. *Ibid.*, I. C. 209, p. 94.
150. *Ibid.*, I. C. 151, p. 72; C. 288, p. 129; C. 305, p. 135, etc.
151. *Ibid.*, I. C. 206, p. 95.
152. *Ibid.*, II. C. 182, p. 234.
153. *Ibid.*, VII. C. 117, p. 494.
154. *Ibid.*, I. S. 1, p. 2.
155. *Ibid.*, I. C. 1, p. 2.
156. *Ibid.*
157. *Ibid.*, I. Śloka 1, p. 1.

family are shown bowing their head before his feet.[158] Respect to the *guru* is frequently reminded as an important duty.[159] He is considered as sacred, and to kill him would be as serious an offence as to kill a Brahmin or a cow.[160] He is given a place of honour in royal circles.[161]

His rôle as a family preceptor is important not only as a religious figure,[162] but also as a confidant[163] and as a consultant.[164] He is pictured as a comforter of the family[165] and he is affectionately attached to each of its members.[166] He relates sacred stories and tales[167] and takes part in their festivities.[168] In return, the family misses no occasion to show him affection[169] and devotedness.[170] His rôle as educator is not overlooked[171] and he is also seen admonishing the members of the household.[172]

The *guru* is often seen giving commands to different members of the family. This point deserves special consideration as we are dealing with an aspect of the *guru* particularly emphasized in the *Rāmcaritmānas*. Upon learning that Daśaratha wished to have a progeny, *Guru* Vasiṣṭha summoned Śṛṅgi and commanded him to perform a sacrifice.[173] This was not so in either the *V. R.*, where the king himself invited Śṛṅgi to assist him in the sacrifice,[174] not in the *A. R.*, where the *guru* let the king

158. *Ibid.*, I. C. 328, p. 149; D. 353, p. 158; C. 355, p. 160; II. C. 9, p. 165.

159. *Ibid.*, I. C. 183, p. 84; VII. 38, p. 451; C. 104, p. 481.

160. *Ibid.*, I. C. 147, p. 221; VII, D. 99, p. 477.

161. *Ibid.*, I. p. 214, p. 98.

162. *Ibid.*, I. C. 202, p. 94.

163. *Ibid.*, I. D. 45, p. 28; C. 188, p. 87; C. 234, p. 107; D. 293, p. 130; II. C. 3, p. 163; VII. C. 3, p. 433.

164. *Ibid.*, I. C. 188, p. 87; C. 206, p. 95; D. 286, p. 127; II. D. 70, p. 190.

165. *Ibid.*, II. S. 151, p. 223.

166. *Ibid.*, I. C. 356; II. C. 184; p. 235; C. 259, p. 266; C. 268, p. 270; C. 291, p. 279, etc.

167. *Ibid.*, I. C. 356, p. 160.

168. *Ibid.*, I. C. 191, p. 89.

169. *Ibid.*, I. C. 357, p. 160; II. C. 200, p. 242; C. 243, p. 254; I. C. 223; p. 103.

170. *Ibid.*, I. C. 291, p. 130; II. C. 9, p. 165; C. 259, p. 266 etc.

171. *Ibid.*, I. C. 202.

172. *Ibid.*, II. C. 278, p. 274.

173. *Ibid.*, I. C. 188, p. 87.

174. *V. R.*, I. 12, vol. I. p. 30.

himself bring Śṛṅgi to the palace in order to perform the sacrifice with them both.[175]

Again, at the contest organized by Sītā's father to determine who was to be her husband, Rāma awaits the *guru*'s command before bending the bow.[176] The episode is related differently in the *V. R.* where the *guru* asks Rāma to look at the bow. Rāma looks at the bow and declares that he will take it into his hand, raise it and bend it. The king and the *guru* agree and "on the assent of the *guru*", Rāma raises the bow.[177] Likewise, in the *A. R.* the *guru* orders the bow to be shown to Rāma, without commanding the latter to bend it.[178] Thus, the *Rāmcaritmānas* is the only version where Rāma is clearly given a command by the *guru* to bend the bow.

The same obedient attitude towards the *guru* is seen in the following episode. Upon receiving the visit of Vasiṣṭha, who comes to announce the king's decision to install him as king, Rāma addresses the *guru* as his master and expresses his readiness to obey his command :

> Though the coming of a master to a servant's home is a source of joy and a foe to sorrow, yet were it more fitting, Lord, and customary that you should graciously send for your servant at need. But in that my Lord has laid aside his right as Lord (*prabhu*) and done me this loving favour, this house today is sanctified. Now command me, holy saint, and I will do your bidding, for it is a servant's joy to do his master (*svāmi*) service.[179]

This is new: in the preceding versions, Rāma does not speak a word to the *guru*.

Tulsī Dās insists on this point. Thus, Bharata presides at his father's funeral rites "upon the guru's bidding".[180] This is not new in itself since both of his sources mention the same

175. *A. R.*, I. 3. 5.
176. *H. L. A. R.*, I. C. 251, p. 114.
177. *V. R.*, I. ch. 67, vol. I. pp. 133-134.
178. *A. R.*, I. 6. 23.
179. *H. L. A. R.*, II. C. 9, p. 165.
180. *Ibid.*, II. D. 169, p. 230.

point.[181] However, Tulsī Dās adds an insistence of his own by saying that Bharata "carried out a thousand times over" all the orders the *guru* gave him. In the same context, Vasiṣṭha summons Bharata and tells him to act in obedience to the king's command. This is understood by the entourage as the *guru*'s own command since the ministers say, "Be sure to obey the *guru*'s command", which is echoed by Kausalyā's remark that "your *guru*'s commands are for the best."[182] No such comments on the *guru*'s authority are found in the preceding versions of the episode.

The same stress on the *guru*'s prestige is again found in a further episode of the *Rāmcaritmānas*. Worried by the people's fasting in the forest as they await Rāma's acceptance to return with them to Ayodhyā, Rāma asks the *guru* to set out with them all for the city. He then remembers the *guru*'s authority and corrects a possible impression of lack of respect: "I have said enough and presumed too greatly; so act, holy master, as seems good to you". The *guru*'s reply is significant:

> O Rāma, perfectly righteous, home of compassion, it is like you to suggest it. But the people are wearied, let them take rest for two days and enjoy the sight of you.[183]

Once again, this conversation which highlights the *guru*'s ascendency is not reported in the *V. R.* or in the *A. R.* In the whole conversation which ensues, prompted by Bharata's effort at persuading his brother to return as king, the *guru* again plays a major rôle. Thus, it is Vasiṣṭha (rather than Bharata as in the other versions), who takes the initiative of opening the conversation by asking Rāma to devise "a plan which will benefit the citizens and your mothers and Bharata".[184] Rāma's reply is significant:

> Lord, it is you who must decide. The good of all lies in regarding your wishes, in cheerfully obeying your

---

181. *V. R.*, II. 76, p. 349; *A. R.*, II. 7. 109-110.
182. *H. L. A. R.*, II. C. 175, p. 232.
183. *Ibid.*, II. C. 248, p. 262.
184. *Ibid.*, II. C. 257, p. 266.

> commands and acknowledging them as truly wise. First, then, whatever you bid me do, I will dutifully obey your instructions, and next, holy father, I will engage without reserve in whatsoever service you impose.[185]

This addition is completely new. The rest of the conversation is mostly carried by Rāma and Bharata although Vasiṣṭha's dominating presence is still very much in the picture. He bids Rāma and Bharata to speak, he is frequently referred to by the two brothers and he himself is again occasionally heard. It is important to note, however, that while approving Rāma's above-quoted words the *guru* nevertheless refused to comply by taking a decision. Giving as a reason that Bharata's affection disturbed his judgment, he conceded all his authority to Rāma. This marks the emergence of an important theme, namely the will of God, that will be dealt more at length in the last chapter of the present study. It is also a first indication that in Tulsī Dās' eyes Rāma is the ideal *guru*; again this aspect will be treated later when the social rôle of the *guru* is dealt with.

There are several other instances of this same emphasis on the *guru*'s authority. The two brothers are shown, in another new passage, asking their *guru* permission to pluck flowers,[186] and to return to rest.[187] Likewise, in preparation for Rāma's coronation, the citizens are shown zealously carrying out the *guru*'s orders :

> Obedient to the great sage's word, each one set about his own special business. Each carried out the orders the high sage had given him, as it seemed, before he was bidden.[188]

This last description concurs with a parallel passage in the Vālmīkian account,[189] but the *A. R.* offers a slight variation in that Vasiṣṭha confides the minister with the responsibility of carrying out the king's orders.[190]

185. *Ibid.*
186. *Ibid.*, I. C. 224, p. 103.
187. *Ibid.*, I. C. 235, p. 108.
188. *Ibid.*, II. D. 6, p. 164.
189. *V. R.*, II. 3, vol. I, pp. 164-165.
190. *A. R.*, II. 2. 1-16.

In the same vein, Tulsī Dās adds another anecdote showing Rāma immediately after meeting with his mothers again since his exile, and asking permission to the *guru* "to go with them, and the citizens, with the permission of the high sage".[191] In describing the return of the citizens of Ayodhyā in the capital city, Tulsī Dās adds another note of his own when he writes that "all the men and women of the city, in obdeience to the *guru*'s instructions, settled down peacefully in Rāma's capital".[192] Finally, upon arriving at Ayodhyā Bharata is shown going to the *guru*'s house and asking his permission to live in observance of the ascetic rule. The *guru* agrees but gives him his instructions before he leaves. This episode is not found in the *A. R.* It is recorded in the Vālmīkian version, with a few variations; Rāma is shown asking permission "to his holy guru and the elders", and not to Vasiṣṭha alone in his own residence; secondly, Vālmīki does not say that Rāma received "instructions" from his *guru*, as Tulsī Dās significantly adds.

Thus, as Tulsī Dās rewrote a story where the family *guru* was assigned an important rôle, he added an insistence of his own which highlights still more the importance of that rôle. The same tendency characterizes the portrayal of the *guru*'s social rôle as the king's adviser, thus suggesting that Rāma is less the ideal king than the *guru* par excellence.

Admittedly, the king is given an important place in the *Rāmcaritmānas* and his virtues are highlighted especially as they are personified in the person of Rāma. Rāma is[193] repeatedly referred to as King of Kosala.[194] He identifies himself as a Kṣatriya[195] and as the son of a king, who observes the rules of royal conduct.[196] He is seen with an army of four divisions,[197] with rich possessions.[198] He crowns new kings,[199]

191. *H. L. A. R.*, II. C. 245, p. 260.
192. *Ibid.*, II. C. 322, p. 292.
193. *Ibid.*, VI. C. 71, p. 399; C. 92, p. 412; D. 100, p. 417; C. 106, p. 421, etc.
194. *Ibid.*, II. D. 229, p. 254; III. C. 18, p. 307.
195. *Ibid.*, III. C. 2, p. 325.
196. *Ibid.*, IV. C. 23, p. 235.
197. *Ibid.*, II. C. 222, p. 251.
198. *Ibid.*, II. C. 185, p. 236.
199. *Ibid.*, VI. C. 105, p. 420.

gives orders to his subjects,[200] and rules over a prosperous city.[201] The good king is pictured as true to his word,[202] as a man of high integrity,[203] and as the upholder of righteousness.[204] He is the treasure-house of sound judgment, virtue and wisdom.[205]

The bad king is also given an important place. We are often reminded that Rāvaṇa is a demon king.[206] His vices are also shown, thus contrasting with the good kings' qualities. He is described as lacking in piety,[207] his four typical vices are conciliation, bribery, punishment, and the causing of dissension.[208]

By contrast, the duties of the king are brought to mind either by word or by example. The good king consults his *guru* and the Brahmins,[209] and the ministers.[210] He learns the science of statecraft[211] and listens every day to "the holy Śāstras, the Vedas and the Purāṇas".[212] He generously distributes gifts to the Brahmins,[213] the ministers and beggars.[214]

In spite of its importance, the rôle of the king is less emphasized in the *Rāmcaritmānas* than that of the *guru*. Rarely do we see a king commanding a *guru*. One such rare instance shows Daśaratha ordering Vasiṣṭha to make Rāma regent and prepare for the celebration and then sending him to Rāma's abode to announce the news of his coronation.[215] In another instance, Rāma is seen instructing the *guru* as to the care of the citizens during his exile,[216] and summoning them with others after his return from the forest to instruct them in their duties.[217]

200. *Ibid.*, VI. C. 107, pp. 421-422.
201. *Ibid.*, VII. C. 26, p. 446.
202. *Ibid.*, I. C. 246, p. 112; II. C. 40, p. 178.
203. *Ibid.*, I. C. 291, p. 130.
204. *Ibid.*, II. D. 30, p. 174; II. C. 53, p. 183.
205. *Ibid.*, II. C. 257, p. 266.
206. *Ibid.*, VI. C. 8, p. 370; V. C. 50, p. 361; VI. C. 44, p. 387.
207. *Ibid.*, VI. D. 38, p. 384.
208. *Ibid.*, VI. C. 38, p. 384.
209. *Ibid.*, I. D. 286, p. 127.
210. *Ibid.*, II. C. 5, p. 164; D. 253, p. 264; II. D. 273, p. 272.
211. *Ibid.*, III. C. 19, p. 309; IV. C. 12, p. 331.
212. *Ibid.*, I. C. 155, p. 73.
213. *Ibid.*, I. D. 193, p. 89.
214. *Ibid.*, I. D. 308, p. 136.
215. *Ibid.*, I. C. 9, p. 165.
216. *Ibid.*, II. C. 80, p. 194.
217. *Ibid.*, VII. C. 41, p. 453.

On the other hand, we see the king obeying the *guru*. Thus, Daśaratha takes permission from the *guru* before setting forth for a procession.[218] Likewise, he is shown twice asking permission of the *guru* before performing the family rites,[219] and he awaits the *guru*'s word before making his entry in the wedding hall with his retinue.[220] Again Sītā's father, king Janaka, takes permission of the *guru* to see his own daughter.[221] These details are new.

The importance of the *guru* in the life of the king is acknowledged by Rāma when he says :

> In the absence of my father only the favour of the *guru* has helped me: else would any people, my household and my family have all been ruined together with myself.[222]

He emphasizes the place of the *guru* in public social life as well as in the domestic circle:

> All the affairs of the state, our honour and good name, religion, our land and wealth and homes—all these the *guru*'s power will protect, and all will be well at the end. Both you and I and all our companies, at home or in the forest, are guarded by the *guru*'s grace.[223]

Upon returning to Ayodhyā as king, Rāma immediately summons all his comrades together and directs everyone to touch his *guru*'s feet, adding the following explanation:

> The *guru* Vasiṣṭha is to be reverenced by the whole of my house; it is of his grace that the demons were slaughtered on the field.[224]

Rāma thus continues in his father's traces, who was seen "humbly worshipping his *guru*'s lotus feet with exceeding devotion in his

218. *Ibid.*, I. C. 299, p. 133.
219. *Ibid.*, C. 310, p. 138; C. 349, p. 157.
220. *Ibid.*, C. 344, p. 156.
221. *Ibid.*, C. 286, p. 277.
222. *Ibid.*, II. C. 305, p. 285.
223. *Ibid.*, D. 305, p. 286.
224. *Ibid.*, VII, C. 8, p. 435.

heart.[225] This new insistence in the *Rāmcaritmānas* on the importance of the *guru* produces a subtle shift of emphasis from the king to the *guru*. Not only is there more emphasis on the importance of the *guru* as such, but the overall picture that is presented of Rāma himself is more suggestive of the ideal *guru* than the ideal *rājā* (king). This general impression is created in a number of ways.

First, Tulsī Dās significantly leaves out passages of the *V. R.* that were meant to highlight the duties of the kingly office. Thus, in the Vālmīkian version, Bāli, who was hit from behind by Rāma's arrow, addressed reproaches by reminding Rāma of his royal duties:

> Self-mastery, forbearance, loyalty, fixity of purpose, good-will and heroism are the virtues of kings, O Prince... Equanimity of soul, liberality, forbearance, justice, loyalty, constancy and courage are the characteristics of a king, O Prince...In temporal and spiritual matters, as well as in the dispensing of reward and punishment, a king should be wholly given up to the task of government...etc.[226]

In the *A. R.*, Bāli is also heard reminding Rāma about the duties of a king and a protector of *dharma*, although the insistence is not so strong as in the *V. R.*[227] In the *Rāmcaritmānas* there is but one allusion to the king's duty when Bāli tells Rāma that the latter has come down from heaven "to further righteousness".[228]

Likewise, in the *V. R.* the *guru* Viśvāmitra who was welcomed by Daśaratha inquired about the latter's kingdom,[229] and similarly *guru* Vasiṣṭha was heard asking King Viśvāmitra several questions on the state of the kingdom.[230] These are omitted in the *Rāmcaritmānas*.

Likewise, upon proposing to the elders and counsellors that Rāma be installed as his successor, King Daśaratha gives a long

225. *Ibid.*, I. C. 349, p. 158.
226. *V. R.*, IV, 17-18, pp. 206-214, passim.
227. *A. R.*, IV. 2. p. 51-63.
228. *H. L. A. R.*, IV. C. 9, pp. 328-329.
229. *V. R.*, I. 19, p. 47.
230. *V. R.* I. 52, vol. I, p. 107.

list of qualities that are necessary to fulfil the royal office all of which Rāma possesses.[231] Again, this is omitted in the *Rāmcaritmānas*.

In two distinct passages of the *V. R.* Rāma's father and *mother* remind their son of his royal duties.[232] No such reminders are found in the *Rāmcaritmānas*.

Quite significantly, a somewhat lengthy passage in Vālmīki's version[233] where Rāma is seen questioning Bharata concerning the discharge of his royal duties is completely omitted in the *Rāmcaritmānas*. In the same vein, Tulsī Dās leaves out the opening section of the third *kāṇḍa* in the *V. R.* which also deals entirely with the duties of the king.[234]

It is not obvious that Tulsī Dās was actually making a conscious choice when excluding such passages. We have seen that his main source was the *A. R.* and this version also excludes the same passages. The fact remains, however, that Tulsī Dās chose not to stress the royal figure in the same way as he emphasized the rôle of the *guru*. In this sense his tendency to de-emphasize the importance of the king can be said to be conscious.

The same tendency may be observed in the distinctive CHANGES Tulsī Dās brings in his portrayal of Rāma. Thus, for Rāma Bharata is to replace him on the throne of Ayodhyā mainly on the ground that without a king "Avadh would be left quite desolate, and *guru*, father, mother, subjects and kinsfolk would all have to bear the burden of intolerable pain." He adds that "that king in whose realm the subjects he loves are sad assuredly merits hell".[235] In the corresponding passage of the *V. R.*, which is left out by the *A. R.*, the argument hinged on the necessity to protect and defend the people and to regard their needs. This suggests the powerful ruler, and it is not retained in Tulsī Dās' portrayal.

The same contrast appears in the description of the people's motive for following Rāma into the forest rather than staying in Ayodhyā without him. In the *V. R.*, the people's main argu-

231. *Ibid.*, II. 2, vol. I, pp. 160-164.
232. *Ibid.*, II. 3, 4, vol. I, pp. 166, 169.
233. *Ibid.*, II. 100, vol. I, pp. 393-398.
234. *Ibid.*, III. 1, vol. II, p. 4.
235. *H. L. A. R.*, II. C. 71, p. 190.

ment had to do with lack of security, whereas in the *A. R.* it was sorrow that impelled them to follow Rāma.[236] Tulsī Dās also notes that the people were distressed and frightened at the thought of living without Rāma as their king. However, he adds another motive which becomes the most important one: "How can luxury's delights constrain those who love the lotus feet of Rāma?"[237] Again, it is not first and foremost on account of his royal power that Rāma is needed. On the human level, his leadership is more spiritual and moral than temporal.

A further illustration of this tendency can be made by a comparison of the three accounts of Rāma's visit to Śṛṅgavera, the capital city of Guha, king of the low-caste Niṣādas. In the *V. R.* Guha welcomes Rāma in these words:

> O Great-armed Warrier, be thou welcome, this country is wholly thine! We are thy servants, thou art the master, this kingdom is thine, issue thy commands. Here are dishes of various kinds and confections and wines at thy disposition as also excellent beds and provender for the horses.[238]

The *A. R.* reports Guha's welcome address in the following terms:

> Having touched thy person I have become very happy. This kingdom of the Niṣādas is at thy service, O thou best of Rāghus, I am thy servant dependent upon Thee, I shall live. Do thou, O best of Raghus, protect us. Come we will go to our city, do thou sanctify my house. Take thou the fruits and roots which I have collected there for thy sake. Do thou be gracious unto me. I am, O best of gods, thy slave.[239]

Tulsī Dās first quotes Guha and then adds a distinctive comment of his own :

---

236. These passages will be discussed at length in the last chapter of this study.
237. *Ibid.*, II. C. 84, p. 195.
238. *V. R.*, II, 50, vol. I, p. 284.
239. *A. R.*, II. 5, 64-67.

> "Now, O Lord, that we have seen your feet, we have all found a lord. Blessed are we that you have come among us, O king of Kosala! Happy that earth, that forest, road and hill, wherever, Lord, you have set your feet! Happy those birds and beasts that haunt the woods, that have beheld you and crowned their lives with joy! Happy, too, are all we and our families, who have feasted our eyes on your presence! It is a fair spot you have chosen to dwell in, and one where you may stay at ease in every season. We shall do you all possible service, protecting you from elephants, lions, snakes and tigers. We, O Lord, are familiar with every step of the wild woodlands, the hills and caves and chasms. We shall take you out hunting in this place and that and show you lakes and springs and other spots where there is water. We and all our kinsfolk are your servants, Lord; hesitate not to give us your commands."
>
> That Lord whom the Veda cannot define nor the mind of the sage comprehend, the home of compassion, listened to the words of the Kirāts as a father to the prattling of his child. Nothing but love is dear to Rāma; let him who will understand this understand.[240]

Again, the royal figure in Rāma is de-emphasized in Tulsī Dās' version. He is still called "King of Kosala" but Guha's words do not suggest that he sees Rāma as a Great-armed Warrior, a Master or a Protector. Rāma's presence brings above all spiritual joy, fatherly love and brotherly compassion.

The same subtle changes are repeated over and over again. Besides the above, the most significant instances are the descriptions of Rāma's actions as leader of his army in the battle against Rāvaṇa. Typical is the description of Rāma's plans for the attack on Laṅkā. The Vālmīkian narrative of the scene opens with a description of Rāma as "King of men, the Sovereign of the Monkeys, the Son of the Wind, Jāṁbavān the King of the Bears, the Titan Vibhīṣaṇa with Bāli's son Aṅgada and Saumitra..." Thereafter Vālmīki shows Rāma's

240. *H. L. A. R.*, II. D. 135—C. 137, pp. 216-217.

counsellors drawing up the plans, under the leadership of Vibhīṣaṇa, who reports the result of the discussion to Rāma. It is he, Rāma, who then assumes the rôle of commander in chief by giving precise orders. Vālmīki ends his description by noting that "at the head of his great army which spread over the earth, the magnanimous Rāma set out for Laṅkā with a joyous and exultant air, resolved to destroy his enemy".[241]

Tulsī Dās' corresponding description does not retain the list of prestigious titles. Vibhīṣaṇa does not report the counsellors' plan, nor does Rāma assume direct command after the discussion. Instead, we are told that the leaders impressed on the commanders the power of the Lord, and that the soldiers "bowed their heads before Rāma's feet". Rather than ending by describing the splendour of Rāma, the king, Tulsī Dās describes the army who went "dauntless in the power of the Lord".[242]

These and other similar episodes emphasize Rāma's spiritual power rather than his temporal power. The result is that Rāma emerges as the ideal *guru* without ceasing to be the *rājā* of the *Rāmāyaṇa*.

It is not without significance that Rāma is frequently and explicitly described in the *Rāmcaritmānas* as the *guru*. Thus Bharata addresses him as "my father, my mother, my friend, my *guru*, and my master".[243] Śiva tells his wife that "there is no *guru* in the world, no father, mother, brother or lord so kind as Rāma".[244] Aṅgada addresses him as "my Lord, my *guru*, my father and my mother".[245] Upon hearing Rāma's speech shortly after his coronation, the *gurus*, Brahmins, and sages clasped the feet of the Lord and said, "You, O gracious Lord, are our mother and our father, our *guru* and our brother, dearer to us than life itself; you, O Rāma, are our selves, our property, our homes, our never-failing friend, the suppliant's comforter !"[246] The sage Atri calls him "the eternal *guru* of the world."[247] It is significant that Vasiṣṭha, the *guru* par

241. *V. R.*, VI, 27, vol. III, pp. 89-91.
242. *H. L. A. R.*, VI. C. 39, pp. 384-385.
243. *Ibid.*, II. C. 298, p. 282.
244. *Ibid.*, IV. C. 12, p. 330.
245. *Ibid.*, VII. C. 16, p. 442.
246. *Ibid.*, VII. C. 45, p. 454.
247. *Ibid.*, III. C. 4, p. 297.

excellence in the *Rāmāyaṇa,* is among those who, in the final portion of the story acclaim Rāma as *guru.*

By thus emphasizing Rāma's spiritual power, Tulsī Dās allayed a possible malaise among the listeners who might have had some difficulty in accepting emphasis on kingly prestige when the Muslims were actually in power. As Rāma had been in former times the paradigm of the ideal king, so could he become the model of the ideal *guru* at a time when Hinduism could not rely on civil authority to maintain the integrity of the tradition.

We conclude this chapter by saying that on the question of social duty Tulsī Dās unambiguously reaffirms the orthodox position. Unlike Kabīr, who denounced the *Vedas* as so many cloaks of falsehood, he acknowledges the authority of the scriptures and considered their injunctions as normative. Unlike Kabīr again, he reaffirms the binding character of caste duties. Unlike Sūr Dās, he emphasizes the importance of domestic duties. Finally, the *Rāmcaritmānas* enhances in a distinctive way the rôle of the *guru* by portraying Rāma as the *guru par excellence.* The subtle shift of emphasis from Rāma the *rājā* to Rāma the *guru* enabled Tulsī Dās to remind his fellow Hindus that the loss of political power to foreign rulers did not entail the deprivation of spiritual and moral leadership capable of maintaining the integrity of the religious heritage.

Chapter VIII

Love of God in the Ramcaritmanas

BEFORE we proceed to study in detail the theme of love of God in the *Rāmcaritmānas*, it is important to recall briefly the living alternatives with which Tulsī Dās was confronted when he set out to write his *magnum opus*. The first set of living alternatives was provided by his own religious education, which he received in early infancy. We know from his writings that as a child he was initiated into the devotion to Rāma by a group of Rāma *sants* who had rescued him after seeing his misery. We know also that his early piety was nourished by the *Rāmāyaṇa*, which because of his age he had to hear over and over again before he could grasp its meaning.[1] Moreover, the fact that he used the *A. R.* as his main literary source in writing the *Rāmcaritmānas* is evidence that he also knew this medieval version of the story. Although he had some acquaintance with other medieval versions of the *Rāmāyaṇa*, we shall limit ourselves once more to the *V. R.* and the *A. R.* as the two main sources of living alternatives regarding the question of love of God.

Another source was the Purāṇic tradition, particularly through the *Bhāgavata Purāṇa*. Traces of the latter can be found in the *Rāmcaritmānas*, and we have seen that its impact in North Indian piety was already noticeable by the time the *Rāmcaritmānas* was written.

A third main source of living alternatives was the religion preached by Kabīr. We have seen that Tulsī Dās could hardly have been unaware of this tradition although he makes no explicit references to it in the *Rāmcaritmānas*.

While Vedic orthodoxy was still alive at the time of Tulsī Dās, we may consider for our purpose the Vedāntic *Adhyātma Rāmāyaṇa* as sufficiently representative of that tendency although it does not adopt the extreme Mīmāṁsic position which denies a place to love of God. Likewise, while the *Sufis* provided a

1. *H. L. A. R.*, I. C. 31, p. 20.

distinctive alternative of their own, the most significant traits of their influence were also found in the religion of Kabīr, to which we shall limit ourselves in order to avoid unnecessary dispersion.

We shall see that Tulsī Dās' approach to love of God coincided with none of the alternatives just enumerated. The following analysis will attempt to delineate the main features that combined to give to his piety a distinctiveness of its own.

It must be pointed out that this section will not attempt to give a complete account of Tulsī Dās' theology as such. This would require a thesis in itself and it has been attempted elsewhere.[2] Rather, in this chapter we try to determine, on the basis of the *Rāmcaritmānas*, the importance Tulsī Dās attached to love of God as a salvific path.

A. *The Emergence of Love of God as the Central Theme of the Rāmcaritmānas*

The first important question to be asked is to what extent Tulsī Dās considered Rāma, the son of Daśaratha,, as divine? In other words, when he speaks about love of Rāma, are we to understand that he implies love of the Absolute?

The answer to this question is given in a countless number of adjectives describing Rāma's nature. In one of the opening passages of the *Bāla kāṇḍa*, Tulsī Dās describes Rāma as "one, desireless, without form or name, unborn, True Being, Consciousness and Bliss (*saccidānandamaya*), Spirit Supreme (*paraṁdhāmā*), all-pervading, universal... single-minded, almighty, Lord of all".[3] In another passage, Śiva explains to his wife that Rāma is "the impersonal (*aguṇa*), formless, invisible, unborn". He goes on to say that "Rāma is the sun, True Being, Consciousness and Bliss (*saccidānanda*), untouched by the shadow of the night of delusion. He is the Blessed Lord, whose being is Light itself, and in him is no place for a dawn of wisdom. Sorrow and joy, knowledge and ignorance, self-conceit and pride—these are the lot of mortal man; but Rāma as all

2. For instance, Vaudeville, C. *Étude sur les sources et la composition du Rāmāyaṇa de Tulsī Dās,* Macfie, J. M. *The Rāmāyaṇa of Tulsī Dās.* Whaling, F. "The Growth and the Religious Significance of Rāma in North India", a Ph. D. Thesis, Harvard University, Mass., 1973.

3. *H. L. A. R.*, I. C. 13, p. 10.

the world knows is the all-pervading Absolute (*brahman*) Supreme Bliss, God on high from everlasting".[4]

It is clear from the above and from numerous other similar affirmations[5] that Tulsī Dās has moved far beyond Vālmīki in his conception of Rāma as the Absolute. We have seen that in the later portions of the *V. R.* Rāma was presented as the successor of Indra and the incarnation of Viṣṇu. In the *Rāmcaritmānas*, Rāma clearly transcends both Viṣṇu and Indra, as he is now identified as the Supreme Absolute.[6]

On the other hand, while he shares with the author of the *A. R.*, the view that Rāma is the Absolute, he disagrees with him by proclaiming his preference for *saguṇa* Rāma rather than *nirguṇa* Rāma. He says so in more than one place. For instance, Bhusuṇḍi says that "all the sages whom I questioned told me that God is present in all creation; but this doctrine of the impersonal (*nirguṇa*) did not satisfy me; I became ever more attached to the Absolute made personal (*saguṇa brahman*)".[7] In another passage, the personified *Vedas* again proclaim their preference for *saguṇa brahman* without condemning those who mediate on *nirguṇa brahman*:

> Let those who contemplate the Absolute, from everlasting and without a second, attainable only by intuition, beyond intellectual reach, speak of It and know It; we, O Lord, hymn unceasingly thy glory as personal.[8]

In the same vein, Indra sings, "Some there are who contemplate the impersonal Absolute which scripture hymns as the unmanifest; but I delight in the king of Kosala, the Lord Rāma himself in personal form".[9]

---

4. *Ibid.*, I. C. 116, pp. 57-58.
5. Examples: *Ibid.*, I. C. 144, p. 69; D. 198, p. 91; C. 196, p. 91; C. 338, p. 133; II. C. 93, p. 199, etc.
6. There are a number of passages where Tulsi Dās explicitly says that Rāma transcends Viṣṇu: e.g. I. C. 146, pp. 69-70; I. C. 217 p. 101; II. 241, p. 259, etc.
7. *Ibid.*, VII. C. 105, p. 484.
8. *Ibid.*, VII. C. 12, p. 439.
9. *Ibid.*, VI. C. 35, p. 425.

From this last quotation, it is also clear that Tulsī Dās acknowledges Rāma both as the Absolute and as the divine *avatāra*. Insofar as he accepts Rāma as the incarnation of the Absolute he differs from Kabīr who, as already seen, refused to bow his head before the son of Daśaratha.

Summing up, we may say that Rāma is unambiguously presented in the *Rāmcaritmānas* as the divine Absolute, and that while Tulsī Dās does not reject the *nirguṇa* conception of the Absolute he differs from the author of the *A. R.* by prefering the *saguṇa* form and he disagrees with Kabīr in accepting the son of Daśaratha as the human incarnation (*avatāra*) of the Absolute.

This said, we now proceed to show that love of God is the central theme of the *Rāmcaritmānas* thus differing from both the *V. R.* and the *A. R.* which present duty and knowledge respectively as the supreme salvific paths. This change of emphasis was effected in a number of ways in the *Rāmcaritmānas*. The most noticeable are the exclusion of certain passages, the addition of others, and the changes within the portions of the original story that have been maintained.

We have seen in the foregoing chapter that Tulsī Dās, like the author of the *A. R.*, excluded a remarkable number of important passages of the original story which dealt with the duties related to the royal office. In addition to these, Tulsī Dās decided to leave out many portions of the story that are not immediately concerned with Rāma, and consequently not conducive to emphasize love of God. Some examples of these are the narrative of how Vālmīki created the metrical form for the *Rāmāyaṇa*,[10] Sumantra's tales to Daśaratha containing predictions related to the birth of Rāma,[11] the description of how Ṛṣyaśṛṅga was brought to king Romapāda's court,[12] Viśvāmitra's account of his ancestry and the dynasty of king Kuśa,[13] the marriage of the sage Brahmadatta with the hundred princesses,[14] and so on. We have seen that the most conspicuous exclusions are those of passages dealing with many incidents

10. *V. R.*, II.
11. *Ibid.*, IX.
12. *Ibid.*, X.
13. *Ibid.*, XXXII.
14. *Ibid.*, XXXIII.

of the combat in the forest where Rāma is not in the picture, and the entire *Uttara kāṇḍa*, of which the *A. R.*, presents a summarized version but which Tulsī Dās excludes completely, probably due again to the mass of tales not related to Rāma, at least in an immediate way.

While he followed the *A. R.* in eliminating many sections not immediately related to Rāma, Tulsī Dās added some new sections, many of which are his own.[15] We have already seen that these added sections are new. We must now see to what extent they are meant to highlight the importance of love of God.

An important category of additions consist in the introductory and concluding sections of each *kāṇḍa*. All fourteen poems are centred on Rāma. All seven introductory hymns are devoted to expressing the poet's love of Rāma, to whom are also added Śiva (in all seven *kāṇḍas*), the *guru*, Vāṇī and Vināyaka (in *kāṇḍa* I), Sītā (in *kāṇḍa* I and IV), Lakṣmaṇa (in *kāṇḍa* III), Bhavānī (in *kāṇḍas* I and IV), and Bhagavān (in *kāṇḍa* V). Likewise, all concluding sections are exhortations either to worship Rāma (*kāṇḍas* III, IV, VII), to hear or recite the story of his deeds (all *kāṇḍas*) or to praise his devotees such as Bharata (*kāṇḍas* II) and Guha (*kāṇḍa* IV).

The other category of additions are the short pauses written in the form of *dohās* or *soraṭhās* (Hindi couplets) which are inserted in the corpus of the story to allow the author to make a personal comment. While a small proportion of these are devoted to other subjects than Rāma, such as the *guru*, Hanumān, Sītā, Śiva and his wife, and a number of purely moral exhortations,[16] the majority either extol the merit of hearing or reciting the story of Rāma,[17] praise the glory fo Rāma,[18] or address a prayer of worship directly to Him.[19]

Other major additions, the substance of which was borrowed from other sources than the *V. R.* or the *A. R.*, are found, as we have previously seen,[20] in the first half of the *Bāla kāṇḍa* and

15. Part 3, Ch. VI.

16. Out of 76 such passages in the *Bāla kāṇḍa*, 23 are devoted to all these combined. The proportion is about the same in the other *kāṇḍas*.

17. There are 21 such passages out of 76 in the *Bāla kāṇḍa*.

18. There are 26 such passages out of 76 in the *Bāla kāṇḍa*.

19. There are 6 such passages out of 76 in the *Bāla kāṇḍa*.

20. Part II. 1.

the concluding section of the book which forms the major portion of the *Uttara kāṇḍa*. The first half of the *Bāla kāṇḍa* begins with a prologue[21] where love of God is immediately presented as the central theme of the story. After paying his homage to Rāma and to all creatures, good or bad, Tulsī Dās implores the saints to bestow on him devotion (*rati*) to the feet of Rāma.[22] He insists that the aim of his enterprise is above all to tell a story of Rāma's virtue which Rāma devotees will welcome.[23] After admitting a feeling of awe when confronted with the Lord's infinite power, he recalls that Rāma "has taken bodily form and wrought all manner of works, simply to do his faithful servants good, a Lord of perfect grace who loves his suppliant people. He bestows his affection and gracious favour on his own, and in his loving-kindness has refrained from wrath. Raghurāja restores what is lost and befriends the poor".[24]

A long development within the prologue deals with the NAME of Rāma. In this passage, Tulsī Dās declares that the Name is greater than the two forms of the Absolute—impersonal and personal. He goes on to explain that both forms are made known by the Name. The Absolute "within the heart" (*nirguṇa*) which leaves every creature miserable and sad is made manifest by uttering the Name of Rāma. So also while Rāma in his incarnate form (*saguṇa*) is physically limited in his action, he can easily reach out to all devotees who invoke his Name. It seems that in this passage the word "Name" is synonymous with "Love", Tulsī Dās was not interested in philosophical subtleties; rather he wanted to propose the most beneficial, or salvific, way of considering God, namely as Supreme Love.

The prologue ends with a comparison between the story of Rāma and a beautiful lake. Again love of God is the central theme, as we are told that "for those who have no faith...and love for Raghunāth, the Lake is inaccessible".[25]

After the prologue comes a long dialogue between Śiva and Pārvatī, introduced by a short preliminary dialogue between sages Yājñavalkya and Bharadvāja. It may seem strange that

21. *H. L. A. R.*, Ś. 1—D. 43, pp. 1-27.
22. *Ibid.*, I. D. 3, p. 4.
23. *Ibid.*, I. C. 8.—C. 9, pp. 7-8.
24. *Ibid.*, L. C. 13, p. 10.
25. *Ibid.*, I. C. 38, p. 26.

Tulsī Dās should add of his own initiative such a long development where Śiva, and not Rāma, is the prominent figure. Indeed, Tulsī Dās writes that Bhavānī and Śiva are the Mother and Father of the whole world ![26] Such an emphasis can be explained in two ways. First, we must not forget that Tulsī Dās was writing in the Benares area, where devotion to Śiva was strong. Second, the point of this section is given at the end where we are told that "those who are not devoted to Śiva's lotus feet can never dream of pleasing Rāma".[27] Insofar as devotion to Śiva leads to love of Rāma, it is important in Tulsī Dās' eyes.

The last part of this new section[28] relates a series of Purāṇic tales dealing with the incarnation of Rāma. The first story tells us about Jaya and Vijaya, reincarnated as Rāvaṇa and Kumbhakarṇa as a result of a Brahminical curse, thus, causing one of Rāma's incarnations. It is said that Rāma came down to save them.

The second story deals with another Rāma devotee, namely Jalandhara, who was reborn as Rāvaṇa, again as a result of a curse. Out of mercy, Rāma "slew him in battle and granted him final release (*paramapada*)".[29]

The next story relates Nārada's self-pride and his subsequent punishment by Viṣṇu, followed by his deliverance which allowed him to depart to *Brahma loka* singing the praise of Rāma's virtues. The point of the story is made in the final verse:

> The Lord is sportive and acts for his suppliants' weal; he is to be found of those that worship him, one who eases every pain. There is no god or man or sage whom his powerful illusion (*māyā*) does not lead astray. This remember and worship in your heart the Lord of mighty illusion.[30]

The story of Manu and his wife Śatarūpā relates the example of king Manu who renounced his kingdom and went with his wife to practice *tapas* in order to obtain a vision of Hari-Rāma.

26. *Ibid.*, I. C. 81, p. 42.
27. *Ibid.*, I. C. 104, p. 53.
28. *Ibid.*, I. C. 122—C. 184, pp. 60-85.
29. *Ibid.*, I. C. 124, p. 61.
30. *Ibid.*, I. C. 140, pp. 67-68.

Hari rewarded him by showing him His supernal manifestation and, at the request of Manu himself, by promising to become the king's son.

The fifth story deals with Pratāpabhānu, king of the Kekayas, who even though he was guiltless and a fervent devotee of Viṣṇu reincarnated as Rāvaṇa, the result of another Brahminical curse, thus causing Rāma's reincarnation in order to deliver him. Only Rāma can deliver one from a Brahmin's curse.

Unlike the first five stories, the last one summarizes a long section of the *Uttara kāṇḍa* in the *V. R.*[31] The aim of this story is to explain the origin of Rāvaṇa who became of evil form by the power of a Brahmin's curse, though he was "pure, stainless and incomparable".[32] This situation led to the actual incarnation of Rāma and the eventual saving death of Rāvaṇa.

It is clear that the dominant aim of this section is to enhance the love of God for his devotees which causes him to take a human form in order to save them. This marks a departure from the *A. R.*, which gives equal importance to three reasons for the incarnation of Rāma; accomplish the work of the gods, bring rescue to the devotees and kill the demons.[33] While Tulsī Dās explicitly admits the other reasons offered in the *A. R.*,[34] he definitely emphasizes love for his devotees as the first reason.

The other major addition is the final portion of the whole book, found in the *Uttara kāṇḍa*.[35] Here again, the central theme is love of God. Complying with Bharata's request, Rāma explains the characteristics of the saints.[36] Having finished enumerating the virtues of the saints—among which he includes the virtue of those who think of nothing but His name—and by contrast the list of sinners' vices, Tulsī Dās notes that Rāma's listeners could not contain their love.[37]

---

31. *V. R.*, VII. 1—34, vol. III, pp. 375-487.
32. *H. L. A. R.*, I. C. 176, p. 82.
33. *A. R.*, I. 6. 57; II. 2. 23; II. 5. 27; IV. 1. 15; IV. 6. 56; VI. 15. 7, 49, etc.
34. *H. L. A. R.*, I. D. 121, p. 60.
35. *Ibid.*, VII. C. 30—end.
36. *Ibid.*, VII. C. 34-41.
37. *Ibid.*

The next episode shows the sage Nārada who constantly came and sang of Rāma's holy deeds to the gods,[38] thus prompting the latter to "awake from their contemplative trance and listen attentively". This is followed by a long passage reporting Rāma's speech to all the citizens, including the *guru*, the sages and the Brahmins. This passage is crucial. After explaining that it is a blessing to be a human being, Rāma explains emphatically that "the way of devotion (*bhagati*) to me.. is an easy path and leads to bliss". He then contrasts love of God with knowledge (*jñāna*), which is "hard to pursue". Even though he does not condemn *jñāna* as such he adds that "he is not dear to me if he (the pursuer of *jñāna*) lack faith (*bhakti*")).[39]

This episode is followed by Vasiṣṭha's visit to Rāma where we learn that the *guru* accepted his office as family preceptor for the sake of unceasing devotion to Rāma's lotus feet. Here, Rāma becomes the Supreme *guru*. Vasiṣṭha closes by asking a boon: "Let my love for my Lord's lotus feet never grow less as life succeeds life".[40]

This section of the narrative ends with a hymn in which Nārada sings the virtues of Rāma, after which the old sage "departed to Brahmā's realm, laying the ocean of beauty on his heart".[41] After a transitional section on the merits of the *Rāmāyaṇa*, we pass to the last section devoted to the dialogue between Bhusuṇḍi and Garuḍa.[42]

In the first part of the Bhusuṇḍi-Garuḍa section, Bhusuṇḍi relates, in a summarized form, the story of Rāma to Garuḍa. This is followed by a number of considerations and autobiographical accounts where again the main emphasis is on love of God. We are told once more that Rāma assumed the form of a king "for the sake of his worshippers".[43] We are warned that if a man "aims at final release (*nirvāṇa*) without worshipping Rāma, he is but a beast without tail or horns".[44] It is

---

38. *Ibid.*, VII. C. 40—D. 42.
39. *Ibid.*, VII. C. 41—C. 45, pp. 453-454.
40. *Ibid.*, VII. C. 46—C. 47, p. 455.
41. *Ibid.*, VII. C. 49, p. 456.
42. *Ibid.*, VII. C. 53—end.
43. *Ibid.*, VII. D. 72, p. 465.
44. *Ibid.*, VII. D. 78, p. 468.

interesting to notice how Tulsī Dās reverses the Vedāntic order of priority in the following statement:

> Ignorance affects not the servants (*dās*) of Hari, for knowledge (*jñāna*), sent by the Lord, possesses them. Hence, Garuḍa, the servant is not destroyed, but his devotion (*bhagati*) to his master grows ever stronger.[45]

Bhusuṇḍi relates how he was awe-stricken by Rāma's supernal manifestation and how the Lord checked the influence of his *māyā* "when (he) saw that I was distraught with love".[46] He also relates how he obtained the gift of devotion to Rāma.[47] He reports the Lord's declaration, that he prefered to all men, including Brahmins and the student of the *Veda*, his own servant who looks to Him for refuge and whose trust is in no other.[48] In a long development, we are told that the way of *bhakti* is the only sure way of salvation.[49]

Bhusuṇḍi then relates a confrontation with his *guru* as a result of the latter's statement that Śiva and Brahmā worship Rāma. As a result of his obstinate opposition to this doctrine, Bhusuṇḍi was punished by Śiva himself. Bhusuṇḍi repented and was granted the boon of devotion to Rāma.[50] Reincarnated as a Brahmin, Bhusuṇḍi tried to find an ascetic who would teach him how to contemplate the Lord, but they all taught him the doctrine of the impersonal which did not satisfy him: "I became ever more attached to the Absolute made personal".[51] Neither would the Ṛṣi Lomaśa, whom he met on Mount Meru, teach him how to worship *saguṇa brahman*. A confrontation ensued and Bhusuṇḍi was transformed into a crow by the Brahmin's power. Rāma then enlightened Lomaśa who was thereby enabled to impart to his disciple "unwavering faith in Rāma".[52]

---

45. *Ibid.*, VII. C. 77, p. 468.
46. *Ibid.*, VII. C. 81, p. 469.
47. *Ibid.*, VII. C. 82, p. 470.
48. *Ibid.*, VII. C. 84, p. 471.
49. *Ibid.*, VII. D. 96—D. 104, pp. 476-480.
50. *Ibid.*, VII. C. 101, p. 480.
51. *Ibid.*, VII. C. 105, p. 484.
52. *Ibid.*, VII. C. 108, p. 487.

The final strophes are devoted to an explanation of the relation between *bhakti* and *jñāna*, which culminates in the proclamation that "Śiva, Brahmā, Śukadeva (son of Vyāsa), Sanaka and his brethren and Nārada, sages preeminent in apprehension of the divine, all agree...in this doctrine—one must love the lotus feet of Rāma. Veda, Purāṇa and all the holy books proclaim that without faith in Raghupati there is no peace".[53]

We now study the main corpus of the story, where Tulsī Dās follows the general outline sketched in the *V. R.* and the *A. R.* We will stop at the most significant passages only, first dealing with the new inserted material not yet examined.

The most noticeable insertion within the *Bāla kāṇḍa* is the episode relating Rāma's visit to the garden of Mithilā with his brother Lakṣmaṇa.[54] There, Rāma and Sītā see each other for the first time. The whole scene is meant to show the intense love between Rāma and Sītā. The latter's love is especially highlighted:

> Then with firm resolve she drew Rāma into her heart and turned to go...Pretending to look back at a deer or a bird or a tree, she turned again and again and as each time she beheld the beauty of Raghubīr, her love grew ever greater.[55]

Of course, the author does not say whether Sītā recognized the Lord in Rāma at this point, but this is implicit because the listener has been led to consider Rāma as the *avatāra* throughout. Sītā's love of Rāma, here as elsewhere in the story, is therefore the devotee's love of God.

The *Ayodhyā kāṇḍa* contains two major additions, the first of which, namely the special development on the story of Bharata's dilemma, will be dealt with in the last chapter of this study. The other addition introduces a new episode, namely Janaka's visit to Rāma at Citrakūṭa, in the forest.[56] Although we are not explicitly told why the king of Mithilā left his capital

53. *Ibid.*, VII. C. 117, p. 494.
54. *Ibid.*, I. C. 224—C. 236, pp. 103-108.
55. *Ibid.*, I. C. 231, p. 106.
56. *Ibid.*, I. C. 270, ff. pp. 271 ff.

city, the description of his feelngs as he arrived at Citrakūṭa makes it sufficiently clear that it is out of love for Rāma that he went to find him in the forest:

> So eager and delighted were they (Janaka and his retinue) to see Rāma that no one felt the least fatigue or weariness from their journey; for their souls were with Raghubar and the princess of Videha, and who without a soul can feel bodily pain or pleasure? Thus Janaka and his retinue came forward, intoxicated with love.[57]

It would seem that Tulsī Dās also meant to give more emphasis to Bharata's love for Rāma by showing Janaka as an admirer of Rāma's brother-devotee. Tulsī Dās draws our attention to "so self-restrained a one as Janaka", who was, like the others, overwhelmed by Bharata's love for Rāma.[58]

The *Araṇya kāṇḍa* presents a new hymn of praise not found in the *A. R.* In this hymn, Atri addresses the Lord as love of his devotees, gracious and tender-hearted, the eternal *guru* of the world, lover of love. He concludes by asking Rāma to grant him devotion (*bhakti*) to his lotus feet.[59] The *Araṇya kāṇḍa* ends with Nārada's visit to Rāma, which again is a new insertion. After asking Rāma a boon, namely that the name "Rāma" be the greatest of all names, the sage wants to know why Rāma would not allow him to marry. The core of Rāma's answer is contained in the following passage:

> Those who worship me, relying on none other, I ever guard as a mother guards her child...The wise are like my grown-up sons, but my servants who rely not on themselves are like my infant children. My servant depends upon my strength, the wise man on his own, but both have lust and anger for their foes. With this in mind the learned worship me and even when they attained to wisdom forsake not their devotion (*bhagati*).[60]

57. *Ibid.*, I. C. 275, p. 273.
58. *Ibid.*, I. C. 317, p. 290.
59. *Ibid.*, III. C. 4, pp. 296-297.
60. *Ibid.*, III. C. 41, p. 322.

The answer rejoices Nārada who then asks Rāma to enumerate the qualities of the saints. Rāma enumerates a number of them, which culminate in loving devotion to Him: "They love me most sincerely... (and) are ever singing or listening to my sportive acts."[61]

The *Sundara kāṇḍa* presents a new episode which shows Hanumān and Vibhīṣaṇa meeting before Hanumān's first encounter with Rāvaṇa. The intent, once again is clearly to emphasize love of God. As he awakes, Vibhīṣaṇa utters the name of Rāma. Upon seeing Hanumān; he feels an instinctive affection for him, wondering if the monkey now disguised as a Brahmin is not Rāma himself. Complaining that he lives in Laṅkā "like a wretched tongue between the teeth", and that "there is in my heart (no) devotion to his lotus feet", he asks Hanumān if Rāma will have mercy on him. Hanumān answers that "even on me has Raghubīr had mercy". The author adds that Vibhīṣaṇa also gave Hanumān the needed information concerning Sītā's whereabouts. The main emphasis of the episode, however, is on Rāma's love and not on the information given to Hanumān.

We have seen that several episodes were added to the *Laṅkā kāṇḍa*. An important one is the three long interventions of Mandodarī in an attempt to dissuade her husband Rāvaṇa from resisting Rāma's power. The *A. R.* reports only one such intervention,[62] where the demon's wife reminds her adamant husband that Rāma has taken a human form for his sake and therefore he should submit to him. In all three interventions recorded in the *Rāmcaritmānas*, Mandodarī adds an important element by insisting that Rāvaṇa should give up his resistance in order to worship Rāma.[63]

The episode relating Bharata's shooting of Hanumān by mistake is also meant to show the mutual love between Rāma and his devotee. In his effort to arouse the injured monkey Bharata makes this significant pledge:

> If in thought and word and deed I have unfeigned love for Rāma's lotus-feet, and if Raghupati is

61. *Ibid.*, III. C. 44, p. 323.
62. *A. R.*, VI. 10. 44-54.
63. See Ch. VI. note 109, p. 99.

> graciously inclined towards me, may the monkey recover from his weariness and pain.

We are told that Hanumān immediately sat up, saying, "Glory, glory to the Lord of Kosala !"[64]

The new episodes showing Rāma on the battle-field raising up Rāvaṇa's charioteer,[65] and standing in front of Vibhīṣaṇa as a way of protecting him from Rāvaṇa's spear[66] are also obviously meant to show Rāma's love for his devotees.

The final episode in the *Laṅkā kāṇḍa* relating Rāma's visit to Guha at the latter's home is also new. The scene culminates in Guha's confession of love:

> Now, all is well with me, for I behold those lotus feet which Brahmā and Śaṅkara adore, O Rāma, home of bliss, whose every wish has been fulfilled, I worship thee ! Rāma, I worship thee ![67]

The greater part of the *Uttara kāṇḍa* contains additions, and these have already been dealt with. The above analysis shows once again that Tulsī Dās' additions were meant to highlight the centrality of love of God as the *leitmotiv* of his story.

We now turn to the modification that Tulsī Dās brought to the material inherited from the *V. R.* and the *A. R.* This material can be divided into two main categories. The first comprises the sequence of events, most of which are related both in the *V.R.* and the *A. R.* The second category comprises the hymns and philosophical comments inspired from the *A. R.* It is obvious that we will have to make a selection, as Tulsī Dās' modifications are numberless. We shall therefore examine only the most typical among the important ones.

The *Bāla kāṇḍa* of the *V. R.* relates Viśvāmitra's request to obtain the help of Daśaratha's sons, Rāma and Lakṣmaṇa, in order to destroy the demons who create impediments to the performance of the sage's sacrifice.[68] The *A. R.* relates the

64. *H. L. A. R.*, VI. C. 59, p. 393.
65. See Ch. VI, note 111, p. 99.
66. See Ch. VI, note 112, p. 99.
67. *H. L. A. R.*, VI. C. 117, p. 430.
68. *V. R.*, I. 18-20, pp. 47-53.

same event but adds a detail to Viśvāmitra's motivation: he had come to "know of the supreme self's incarnation as such through *māyā*".[69] The *Rāmcaritmānas* adds another motivation—besides the one suggested in the *A. R.*—which emphasizes the sage's love of Rāma:

> Then the great sage bethought him that the Lord had become incarnate to relieve earth of its burdens. He thought, "I will make this excuse to go and see his feet..; thus shall I feast my eyes on the Lord, in whom all knowledge and detachment and virtue dwell.[70]

As Viśvāmitra and the two princes arrive at Janaka's court, the king's whole attention, according to Vālmīki, was first focussed on the sage. After a while Janaka asked Viśvāmitra about the two youths. The sage's answer is followed by a long comment from Janaka's *guru* Śatānanda, the eldest son of Gautama, whose mother Rāma had just restored to life. Most of Śatānanda's comment, however, is a praise to *guru* Vasiṣṭha. In the *A. R.*, Janaka first worshipped Viśvāmitra, and then he enquired of Viśvāmitra who were "those lions amongst men resembling gods attracting his heart forthwith like Nara and Nārāyaṇa".[71] Having heard the sage's answer, the king worshipped the two princes according to rites. In the *Rāmcaritmānas*, the princes arrived only some time after Viśvāmitra. As they entered and sat by the sides of their *guru*, the spectators' eyes "were filled with tears and they trembled with emotion".[72] The king himself exclaimed his wonder, asking the sage if these were the Absolute come to earth in dual form. He "gazed time and again at the Lord with a thrill of emotion and passionate devotion in his heart".[73] In this episode, as in the previous one, it is clear that Tulsī Dās goes far beyond the *A. R.* in emphasizing love of God as the central theme.

Again in the episode showing Lakṣmaṇa's farewell to his mother, Tulsī Dās modifies the details to emphasize love of God.

---

69. *A. R.*, I. 4. 1.
70. *H. L. A. R.*, I. C. 204, p. 95.
71. *A. R.*, I. 6. 7.
72. *H. L. A. R.*, I. C. 212, p. 99.
73. *Ibid.*

In the *V. R.*, Sumitrā tells her son to consider Rāma as his own father, Sītā as his mother and the forest as Ayodhyā.[74] The same advice, which is not found in the *A. R.*, is repeated in the *Rāmcaritmānas*. However, Tulsī Dās attributes a significant addition to Sumitrā thus presenting her as a Rāma devotee:

> May your devotion to the feet of Sītā and Raghubīr constant, selfless and never-wearying.[75]

The devotee's love of God is sometimes said in the *Rāmcaritmānas* to cause one's fatigue to vanish. This is shown in the comment added to a scene showing Rāma, Lakṣmaṇa, Sītā and Sumantra bathing in the Gaṅgā: "To say that he was weary, by thinking on whom the burden of all weariness is removed, is but to use a conventional phrase".[76]

Tulsī Dās thus multiplies the occasions to remind the reader/listener that love of God is the central "message" of the *Rāmcaritmānas*. This tendency is again seen in the episode showing Rāma asking a boat-man to help him cross the Gaṅgā. In relating this episode, which is not found in the *V. R.*, the author of the *A. R.* clearly stressed the *power* of the Lord. The boatman refuses to allow Rāma to ride in his boat because he knows that the dust of the Lord's feet has the power to transform a stone into a woman. Rāma allows him to wash his feet and is then allowed to ride in the boat.[77] In the *Rāmcaritmānas*, the boatman is clearly presented as a devotee and the scene is clearly intended to show the Lord's *mercy*. We are told that the boatman washed Rāma's lotus feet "in an ecstasy of bliss" and that the gods rained down flowers and enviously praised him, crying, "None is so meritorious as thee". The text also adds that by allowing the boatman to wash his feet, Rāma was being merciful: "He, the merciful (*kṛpāl*)...made request of a boatman."[78]

Whereas in the *V. R.* the scenery surrounding Citrakūṭa filled Rāma with delight and made him forget his banishment

74. *V. R.*, I. 40, vol. I, p. 263.
75. *H. L. A. R.*, II. C. 75, p. 152.
76. *Ibid.*, II. C. 87, p. 197; see also II. C. 275, p. 273.
77. *A. R.*, I. 6. 18.
78. *H. L. A. R.*, II. C. 100—C. 102, p. 202.

from Ayodhyā,[79] in the *Rāmcaritmānas* it is the very presence of Rāma which gladdens his surroundings at Citrakūṭa. In a long passage this idea is suggested by such statements as these : "The very beasts were glad when they beheld the beauty of Rāma... All creatures that had eyes, gazing on Raghubar, forgot their sorrows..."[80]

In the *Aryaṇya kāṇḍa* all three versions of the *Rāmāyaṇa* relate the story of Śarabhaṅga who had waited for the Lord's coming before mounting the funeral pyre. In both the *V. R.* and the *A. R.*,[81] the ascetic enters the fire and then goes to *Brahmaloka* in Indra's chariot. In addition to his ascetic practices, the *A. R.* mentions that he meditated (*jñāna*) on Rāma, and that he was his devotee (bhakti). The sage dies by asking Rāma and Sītā to ever abide in his heart. In the *Rāmcaritmānas*, Śarabhaṅga also practised asceticism and asks Rāma to dwell in his heart. Tulsī Dās adds that the sage went to Vaikuṇṭha (Viṣṇu's, i.e. Rāma's heaven) and that "he was not absorbed into Hari because he had received the gift of separate devotion (*bhedābheda*) before he died."[82]

Tulsī Dās imitates the *A. R.* in explaining the act of dying at the hands of Rāma as an act of divine mercy. He goes further in this direction however by saying, unlike the *A. R.*, that fourteen thousand enemies of Rāma died crying "Rāma ! Rāma !"[83] In the *A. R.* Rāvaṇa himself chooses to be killed by Rāma in order to "enjoy the kingdom of heaven".[84] Tulsī Dās attributes the same motivation to the King of demons but is more explicit in saying that Rāvaṇa thereby hoped to worship the Lord.[85] Elsewhere, Tulsī Dās had been still more explicit about Rāvaṇa's interior devotion as he described him as being enraged against Sītā and yet finding delight "in mental adoration of her feet".[86]

---

79. *V. R.*, II. 56, vol. I, p. 303.
80. *H.L.A.R.*, II. C. 137 ff., pp. 217 ff.
81. *V. R.*, III. 5, vol. 2, p. 11; *A. R.*, III. 2. 11-12.
82. *H. L. A. R.*, III. C. 7, p. 300.
83. *Ibid.*, D. 20, p. 309.
84. *A. R.*, III. 5. 60.
85. *H. L. A. R.*, III. C. 21, p. 310.
86. *Ibid.*, III. C. 26, p. 313.

The same insistence is made in the story of Mārīca who was asked to take part in Rāvaṇa's scheme to kidnap Sītā. In the *V. R.*, Rāvaṇa forces him to comply;[87] in the *A. R.*, Mārīca complies after realizing that if Rāma killed him he would "be released from this ocean of worldly life".[88] In the *Rāmcaritmānas* the dominant motivation is loving devotion to Rāma's feet.[89]

An episode unique for its moral implications is the slaying of Bāli. All three versions report the incident but with different modifications. In the *V. R.*,[90] Bāli reproaches Rāma for having hit him from behind; Rāma counters with a number of excuses and Bāli apologizes. In the *A. R.*,[91] Bāli both apologizes and prostrates himself before Rāma, whom he recognizes as God, and implores his permission to attain to His supreme abode. In the *Rāmcaritmānas*,[92] Bāli's body is restored to health but he asks the boon to be reborn in any womb whatsoever provided he be devoted to Rāma's feet.

The crossing of the bridge to Laṅkā is another typical episode meant to highlight the importance of love of God. In the Vālmīkian version, the monkeys who build the bridge are the centre of attraction. Even the gods look down to see them at work![93] The *A. R.* is very concise except for an addition concerning a Śaivite pilgrimage site which, as we have seen, is also mentioned in the *Rāmcaritmānas*.[94] In the *Rāmcaritmānas*, all eyes are on Rāma. Even the creatures of the deep come forth to gaze at him, the "source of mercy". The crossing of the bridge has become in the *Rāmcaritmānas* a long description of a pilgrimage to Rāma.

Also typical of Tulsī Dās is his habit of inserting in his description of the final battle recurrent reminders that Rāma's servants had their hearts on the Lord. Thus, Sugrīva, Jāṁbavān and Vibhīṣaṇa took counsel together "with their thoughts

87. *V. R.*, III. 38, vol. III, p. 81.
88. *A. R.*, III. 6. 36.
89. *H. L. A. R.*, III. C. 24, p. 312.
90. *V. R.*, IV. 18, vol. II, pp. 210-214.
91. *A. R.*, IV. 2. 64 ff.
92. *H. L. A. R.*, IV. C. 10, p. 329.
93. *V. R.*, VI. 22, vol. III, pp. 51-55.
94. *A. R.*, VI. 4. 1-4.

fixed on the jewel of the Solar race".[95] The army pounces every where on Rāvaṇa's palace "singing the praises of Rāma".[96] The monkeys trample down the throng of demons "by the power of Rāma".[97] Hanumān sets out "laying Rāma's lotus feet upon his heart".[98]

Many other instances can be adduced to show that even when dealing with his sources Tulsī Dās never lost sight of his central theme and that he made the necessary modifications in order to make it emerge forcefully. The most important among these other passages are the numerous hymns and philosophical comments inspired by the *A. R.* These have all been listed in a previous chapter.[99] In order to avoid repetition, we shall deal with a limited number of them considered as representative. These will include Ahalyā's hymn to Rāma, Paraśurāma's hymn to Rāma, Vālmīki's hymn of praise to Rāma, Lakṣmaṇa's philosophical comment to Guha, and Rāma's philosophical comment to Lakṣmaṇa. Then, we shall conclude with a comparative study of the treatment given to Rāma's visit to Guha in both versions of the story.

Ahalyā's Hymn to Rāma

In the *A. R.* Ahalyā's hymn to Rāma dwells at length on the theological nature of Rāma, on Rāma's relation with creation, on the misconceptions that people who are deluded by *māyā* have of Rāma, on Ahaylā's incapacity to comprehend the true nature of Rāma, and on her prayer for constant devotion to the feet of Rāma.[100] In the corresponding hymn, Tulsī Dās summarizes in the opening statement the first four of the original themes: "Glory to Raghurāī, whom only wisdom may reveal". All the rest is a development of the fifth theme, namely loving devotion to Rāma. Ahalyā admits her sinfulness, she asks the Lord to purify her and to save her from rebirth, she sings her joy of being able to feast her eyes on the saviour, and

95. *H. L. A. R.*, VI. C. 39, p. 385.
96. *Ibid.*, VI. C. 40, p. 386.
97. *Ibid.*, VI. C. 42, p. 386.
98. *Ibid.*, C. 56. p. 392.
99. Ch. VI. pp. 85ff.
100. *A. R.*, I, 5. 43-58.

she asks the boon of loving devotion to Rāma.[101] It is clear that Tulsī Dās has shifted the emphasis in favour of loving devotion to God.

Paraśurāma's Hymn to Rāma

In the *A. R.*, Paraśurāma's hymn to Rāma contains two different sections. Verses 22-30 are inserted within its corpus to explain how Paraśurāma became a foe of the Kṣatriya caste and how his encounter with Rāma happened according to predictons. The hymn proper deals with the following themes: Rāma's essential nature, Rāma's relation with *māyā*, the worldly ignorance caused by *māyā*, the relation between the *ātman* and the *buddhi*, the means of escaping the world of *māyā* (i.e. company of saintly devotees, worship of the Lord and search of knowledge under a *guru*), and a prayer to obtain loving devotion to the saintly devotees.[102] In the corresponding hymn, Tulsī Dās abandons his predecessor's efforts to grasp the nature of the Lord *in se*. Rather, the whole hymn sings the glory of the Lord's attributes by which the Supreme communicates with his devotees: God is hymned as the fire that burns the harmful demons, as the friend of gods, Brahmins and cows, as the dispeller of sin, as the bringer of virtues, joys and beauties, and as the friend of Śiva.[103] Here again, the shift of emphasis is clear. In the first instance interest is focussed on the ultimate nature of God, man and the universe. In the second, God is approached as the loving saviour of his devotees.

Vālmīki's Hymn to Rāma

In the *A. R.* Vālmīki's hymn to Rāma describes those whose heart is the temple of Rāma. Most of the characteristics enumerated are usually associated with knowledge (*jñāna*): enjoying a peaceful disposition, looking upon all with equal eye, cherishing no enmity to any creature, etc. Nevertheless, love of God is also clearly mentioned, but as a secondary theme: "Those whose minds have become firm by incessant devotion to thee, those who are always devoted to the service of thy feet,

101. *H. L. A. R.*, I. D. 210, p. 97.
102. *A. R.*, I. 7. 20-45.
103. *H. L. A. R.*, I. C. 282, p. 126.

those whose sins have been washed off by the recitation of thy name (are thy Temple)".[104] The first portion of Vālmīki's hymn in the *Rāmcaritmānas* has nothing in common with the corresponding hymn in the *A. R.* Strangely enough, this portion is philosophical in tone dealing with themes usually found in the hymns of the *A. R.* such as God's ultimate nature, the world as *māyā*, the salvific value of knowledge.

The second portion deals with the same subject as the hymn of the *A. R.*, namely Rāma's mystical abodes. This passage as deals exclusively with themes associated with love of God: fitting abodes of God are those who yearn for God's presence, who sing the glory of God, who worship the feet of Rāma and none other, who fulfill their duties, who practice the saintly virtues of which charity and loyalty are the most important, and those who live in spiritual detachment from all that is not the Lord.[105]

Lakṣmaṇa's philosophical Comment to Guha

In this passage of the *A. R.* Lakṣmaṇa tries to console Guha, who grieves over Rāma's situation, by pondering on the nature and consequences of *karma* which no one can avoid unless he acquires wisdom: "The wise do not... show joy on occasions of joy nor sorrow on occasions of sorrow, but patiently bear the advent of the pleasurable and the painful and are not deluded, knowing all to be *māyā*".[106] Here, Tulsī Dās follows the *A. R.* very closely except for the very last sentence where he adds loving devotion as the culminating point: "Remember this, my friend, and rid yourself of delusion; be devoted to the feet of Sītā and Raghubīr".[107]

Rāma's Philosophical Comment to Lakṣmaṇa

As in the previous case, Tulsī Dās stays very close to the *A. R.* in reporting Rāma's philosophical comments to Lakṣmaṇa. Both texts follow the same outline: Rāma explains how one obtains release through knowledge (*jñāna*); he enumerates the

104. *A. R.*, II. 6. 52-60.
105. *H. L. A. R.*, II. C. 127—C. 131, pp. 213-214
106. *A. R.*, II. 6. 5-15.
107. *H. L. A. R.*, II. C. 92—C. 94, p. 199.

means of acquiring knowledge; he proposes devotion (*bhakti*) as the easier and safer way: he enumerates the means of obtaining devotion.[108]

There is however a crucial difference between the two approaches. For the author of the *A. R.* *bhakti* is a MEANS to *jñāna* :

> He who possesses devotion (*bhakti*) rapidly gains knowledge (*jñāna*) and realization thus obtains deliverance (*mokṣa*).[109]

For Tulsī Dās, love of God is independent from knowledge (*jñāna*). Indeed, knowledge depends on faith:

> From the performance of duty (*dharma*) springs detachment; from austerity, knowledge (*jñāna*); knowledge brings release—so says the Veda. But, brother, it is faith (*bhagati*) in me that quickly melts my heart and brings bliss to the faithful. Faith is its own support; it needs no other stay. On it depends all knowledge, material and divine (*gyāna bigyāna*).[110]

Thus, while Tulsī Dās borrows from the *A. R.* the idea of inserting hymns and philosophical comments, and while he sometimes deals with the same themes, he does not depart from his fundamental position which considers love of God as the preeminent salvific path. Without being exclusive, it is nevertheless a self-sufficient path; it is the easier one and the preferable one for Tulsī Dās. I have not been able to find in the *Rāmcaritmānas* one single hymn or philosophical comment borrowed from the *A. R.* where the balance is not tilted in favour of loving devotion. This process has been sufficiently illustrated in the above examples, and it is not necessary to pursue it further.

We conclude this first portion of the present chapter by showing how Tulsī Dās' tendency is once more apparent in dealing with the story of Guha. Once again, the treatment

---

108. *A. R.*, III. 4. 19-54; *H. L. A. R.*, III. C. 13—C. 15, pp. 304-305.
109. *A. R.*, III. 4. 51.
110. *H. L. A. R.*, III. C. 15, p. 305.

given in the *Rāmcaritmānas* is compared to the parallel treatment in the *A. R.*

Rāma's Visit to Guha

In the *Adhyātma Rāmāyaṇa*, Rāma's visit to Guha is described in these terms :

> Then approaching Guha who was standing with folded hands, Rāma said, "My friend, do thou go to thy city, the beautiful Śṛṅgavera. Thinking of me, do thou enjoy things obtained by thee through thy own exertion. At the end of life thou shalt attain to my own form, there is no doubt in this." So saying he gave him celestial ornaments and having bestowed upon him a wide kingdom communicated to him the highest wisdom. Embraced by Rāma, Guha returned home happy.[111]

Nothing is more instructive than the comparison of this description with that given by Tulsī Dās, who sees in Guha an "utterly low-born Niṣāda" purified by loving devotion to Rāma:

> At the news (of Rāma's arrival) Guha came forward in an ecstasy of love and blissfully drew near to the Lord: and when he saw the Lord and the princess of Videha, he fell unconscious to the ground. Beholding his marvellous devotion, Raghurāī joyfully raised him and clasped him to his bosom. He clasped him to his breast, even Lakṣmī's lord, the treasure-house of grace, the chiefest of the wise. He seated him close beside himself and asked him how very he fared. Guha humbly replied, "Now all is well with me, for I behold these lotus feet which Brahmā and Śiva adore. O Rāma, home of bliss, whose every wish has been fulfilled, I worship thee ! Rāma, I worship thee !"[112]

In the *Adhyātma Rāmāyaṇa*, Guha welcomes Rāma standing still with his hands folded, which reveals above all an attitude

111. *A.R.*, VI. 16. 18-19.
112. *H. L. A. R.*, VI. C. 37, p. 430.

of reverence; in the *Rāmcaritmānas*, Guha's behaviour reveals the intensity of his love, causing him to run towards Rāma upon hearing of his arrival, and then losing consciousness upon seeing him. In the first instance, the devotee is struck by Rāma's grandeur; in the second, he is enraptured by Rāma's saving and loving presence.

In the *Adhyātma Rāmāyaṇa*, Rāma sends Guha to the city, enjoining his devotee to think of Him and to enjoy the fruit of his own efforts. In the *Rāmcaritmānas*, Rāma affectionately clasps Guha to his bosom, and rather than sending him away to "think" about Him and enjoy the fruit "of his own exertion", he enters into an intimate conversation with his devotee. It is more important for Tulsī Dās to be in the very presence of Rāma than merely to think about him. It is easier to obtain salvation through God's grace, than to achieve it through one's own efforts. Finally, in the *Adhyātma Rāmāyaṇa*, Guha is granted material wealth and wisdom (*jñāna*), whereupon he happily leaves Rāma. In the *Rāmcaritmānas*, Guha is seen finding his happiness in worshipping the object of his devotion. Love, not wisdom, still less material wealth, is the devotee's only reward in the *Rāmcaritmānas*.

From the above, it can be said that whereas the author of the *Adhyātma Rāmāyaṇa* reveals speculative interests in the nature of God and creation, Tulsī Dās prefers a practical language more conducive in bringing the reader to submit to the salvific power and love of Rāma. Whereas the *Adhyātma Rāmāyaṇa* is especially concerned with the possibility of reconciling the path of *bhakti* with the supreme path of *jñāna* leading to *nirguṇa brahman*, Tulsī Dās' aim is to extol love of God as the privileged path leading to liberation in union with the Lord (*saguṇa brahman*).

The above comparisons show that Tulsī Dās transferred the pivotal axis of his two sources. The *Vālmiki Rāmāyaṇa* emphasized social duty without denying love of God; Tulsī Dās emphasizes love of God without denying social duty. The *Adhyātma Rāmāyaṇa* emphasized knowledge as the path *par excellence* leading to the formless Absolute, without denying the rôle of social duty and love of God; the *Rāmcaritmānas* insists on the preeminence of love of God, without denying the value of knowledge and social duty.

B. *The Ecstatic Quality of Love of God in the Rāmcaritmānas*

Having established that love of God emerges clearly as the central theme of the *Rāmcaritmānas* we must now study the special ecstatic quality which characterizes devotion as it is portrayed in the Hindi *Rāmāyaṇa*. We will see that this characteristic is noticeable in both joyful and tragic contexts.

Upon learning, through the sacrifice ceremony, that he will have a progeny, Daśaratha's heart is gladdened. According to the *V. R.*, Daśaratha was "in the height of joy".[113] The *A. R.* says nothing on the king's emotions in this context. In the *Rāmcaritmānas* it is said that "the king was in an ecstasy of bliss; his heart could not contain his joy".[114]

While the *V. R.* is silent on the king's feelings at the birth of his sons, the *A. R.* says that "he became immersed in a sea of joy" and that "he shed tears of joy".[115] Tulsī Dās describes Daśaratha's joy in these terms:

> When Daśaratha heard of the birth of His son, his joy was like the joy of the blessed; in his soul was love supreme and he trembled with delight. He would have risen, but composed himself... (His) heart was filled with perfect bliss.[116]

Tulsī Dās also adds that the king summoned minstrels, the *guru*, the Brahmins to look at the peerless child and sing the charms of his beauty. All the queens, the handmaids and the citizens also came to admire "in ecstasies" Rāma and his three brothers.[117]

Again in the *Rāmcaritmānas* Janaka displays the same ecstatic emotion as he sees Rāma for the first time. He is described as losing all consciousness of self, inarticulate with emotion, overwhelmed by love, with a thrill of emotion and passionate devotion in his heart.[118] The *V. R.* does not describe Janaka's emotional feelings at this point, while the *A.R.* merely notes that

113. *V. R.*, I. 14, vol. I, p. 38.
114. *H. L. A. R.*, I. D. 189, p. 87.
115. *A. R.*, I. 3. 36-37.
116. *H. L. A. R.*, I. C. 191, p. 89.
117. *Ibid.*
118. *Ibid.*, I. C. 212—C. 214, p. 99.

Janaka "knowing the two youths to be deserving of worship worshipped them according to rites".[119]

In the scene showing Rāma going to Janaka's garden where he met Sītā for the first time, Tulsī Dās describes the citizens of Mithilā "running like beggars that run to spoil a treasury" and young women gathering at the lattice-windows of their houses, gazing "with passion on Rāma's graceful form".[120] This, as we have seen, is a new passage, in which the atmosphere is obviously close to that of the *Bhāgavata Purāṇa*.

It is also interesting to compare how the three versions describe Daśaratha's emotions upon learning the news of Rāma's wedding. In the *V. R.*, Daśaratha is said to have been "in the height of joy".[121] The *A. R.* is just as laconic : "He became immersed in joy".[122] In the *Rāmcaritmānas* Daśaratha is pictured reading the letter carrying the news with his eyes full of tears, trembling with emotion, his heart full of joy. Rāma's brothers also "felt a thrill of joy and could scarce contain their feelings of affection". "Overpowered by affection", the king hastily read the letter of invitation to the *guru* and to the ladies of the court, who were "filled with joy...and overwhelmed with affection and delight". The news eventually spread to the whole city and the people "were wild with joy" and adorned the city "for the love (they) bore him". The poet ends this description, not found in the preceding versions, by saying that "great was the rejoicing, and it seemed to overflow in all directions".[123]

Upon meeting his two sons again after their first sojourn in the forest, Daśaratha is said in the *V. R.* to have enjoyed "supreme satisfaction".[124] In the *A. R.* it is said that "he smelt Rāma on the forehead and repeatedly embraced him, filled with joy as if he had attained to the bliss of Brahman".[125] In the *Rāmcaritmānas* Daśaratha, upon seeing Janaka and the two boys, "rose in joy and advanced, as one who feels bottom in a sea of

119. *A. R.*, I. 6. 17.
120. *H. L. A. R.*, I. C. 217, p. 101.
121. *V. R.*, I. 68, vol. I. p. 135.
122. *A. R.*, I. 6. 35.
123. *H. L. A. R.*, I. C. 287—C. 294, pp. 128-130.
124. *V. R.*, I. 69, vol. I, p. 137.
125. *A. R.*, I. 6. 43.

bliss..." Not able to contain his joy, "he clasped his sons to his heart and eased the intolerable anguish he had borne, like a dead man quickened to new life."[126]

The wedding ceremony gave Tulsī Dās another occasion to emphasize the devotees' ecstatic admiration. In the *V. R.* little effort is made at describing the emotions of the on-lookers. We are told that Janaka had his eyes suffused with tears of joy as he wedded Lakṣmaṇa to his daughter Ūrmilā, and there is a short description of the celebrations that accompanied the ceremony:

> In the midst of immense splendour, a rain of flowers fell from the sky. To the sound of celestial gongs, hymns and music, troops of Apsarās danced with Gandharvas broke into paeons of praise, while the nuptial ceremony...was taking place, a marvel indeed :[127]

Here again, the *A. R.* is more laconic. The place of marriage "resounded with the sounds of drums and was filled with people dancing and swinging." Besides, the mothers are shown embracing Sītā (who was weeping) and giving her good advice "with tears in their eyes".[128] The *Rāmcaritmānas* describes at length the feelings of Rāma's admirers. Upon seeing the two princes as they went to the royal palace, the ladies of the court rose in delight, the queens "in rapturous joy scattered gifts and waved the lustral lamps about their heads. In an ecstasy of devotion they looked on Rāma's beauty; constrained by love, again and again they touched his feet. They felt no shame, for their hearts were filled with affection; no words can tell the love they could not but feel". As she entrusted Sītā to Rāma, her mother "clasped his feet, as though her speech were sunk in the quicksand of love". Indeed, all the queens "laid up in their hearts his sweet and charming image and grew faint with love." Janaka's emotions are again described: his heart overflowed with love his composure fled, the strong restraints of his wisdom

---

126. *H. L. A. R.*, I. C. 305, p. 135.
127. *V. R.*, I. 74, vol. I, p. 146.
128. *A. R.*, I. 6. 48-81.

were broken down, and his eyes brimming over with tears of love. The courtiers were all "overpowered with emotion" and the queens are again described as "so overcome with joy and rapture that they waxed faint and could not move". The citizens gazed at Rāma "with brimming eyes and trembling limbs". Even Sarasvatī, the goddess of speech, "ransacked her store of similes, but none could she find as they all seemed too trivial, and she could only fix her gaze upon them (the newly wed) entranced by their beauty."[129]

A similar stress on intensive love for Rāma is again noticeable in the long passages Tulsī Dās devotes to describe the reactions of forest-dwellers upon seeing Rāma. Such developments find no parallels in the two preceding versions of the story. The forest-dwellers are described as constrained by love, trembling with emotion and with tears in their eyes, enchanted, in a blissful state no tongue can describe". Other spectators would "draw his beauty into their hearts by the pathway of their vision, unable to move or think or even speak good words".[130] Gods and sages come to admire him.[131] The lowly tribes gaze upon Rāma with devotion:

> They stood there all about him like painted figures trembling with emotion, and their eyes overflowed with tears. When Rāma perceived that they were all beside themselves with love, he received them with honour and spoke to them kindly.[132]

Thus, everywhere Rāma passes, he provokes intense loving reactions. Tulsī Dās does not miss an occasion to underline this fact, and his insistence finds no parallel in the *V. R.* or the *A. R.*

The most obvious case of emotional mysticism is reported in a scene of the *Rāmcaritmānas* which owes nothing to the *V. R.* or the *A. R.* or to any other source. The scene describes a sage by the name of Sutīkṣṇa as he welcomes Rāma to his hermitage. The sage's rapturous delight is described in these vivid terms:

---

129. *H. L. A. R.*, I. C. 333—C. 346, pp. 151-156.
130. *Ibid.*, II. C. 110—C. 116, pp. 207-209.
131. *Ibid.*, II. C. 132—C. 134, p. 215.
132. *Ibid.*, II. C. 135, p. 216.

> The wise sage was so utterly absorbed in love that his state was beyond description. He lost all sense of direction on the road; he knew not who he was or where he was going; at one time he would turn and go back and then again advance; at another he would dance, singing of Rama's virtues. Even more profound grew the sage's love and devotion, while the Lord watched him, hiding behind a tree. Seeing his exceeding love, Raghubīr...manifested himself in his heart. The sage stood motionless in the middle of the road, and every hair on his body stood erect as on a jackfruit. Then Raghunāth drew near to him, rejoicing to see his servant's emotion. Rāma tried every means to awaken the sage, but he awoke not, for he was absorbed in the bliss of contemplation. Then Rāma withdrew his form as a king and revealed himself as the four-armed in his heart, and the sage started up in agitation like a serpent distressed by the loss of its jewel. Seeing before him dark-hued Rāma, the home of bliss, with Sītā and his brother, the great sage fell prostrate at his feet, lost in love and greatly blessed.[133]

Emotional intensity is also portrayed to illustrate the devotee's pain caused by separation from Rāma. We shall demonstrate this by analyzing the description of Daśaratha's death which occurred shortly after Rāma's departure for his sylvan exile.

The *V. R.* gives a much more lengthy and pathetic account of the old king's death,[134] which is considerably shortened in the *A. R.*[135] This may be seen as a result of the philosophy in the *A. R.* which views worldly events, including human tragedies, as illusory. After relating how the turn of events was the result of a *muni's* curse, Daśaratha, in the *V. R.*, dies in sorrow exclaiming:

> Alas, O valiant Rāghava ! Alas, Thou who hast robbed me of strength by thy departure ! Alas, Thou who

133. *Ibid.*, II.. C. 9. p. 301.
134. *V. R.*, II 58—64, vol. I, pp. 306-322.
135. *A. R.*, II. I7. 16-51.

> art full of filial devotion, thou, my support ! Alas, Thy virtuous Sumitrā ! Woe unto thee, my cruel enemy, Kaikeyī, O obliquy of thy Race.[136]

The narrator sadly adds that the king "who was distraught on account of the exile of his beloved son, passed away at midnight and under the weight of suffering yielded up his life."[137]

The *A. R.* also says that Daśaratha died "greatly agitated with sorrow", and that his last words were:

> O Rāma ! O son ! O Sītā ! O Laksmaṇa ! mines of all good qualities, through separation from thee I am meeting my death caused by Kaikeyī.[138]

In the *Rāmcaritmānas* Daśaratha's sorrow is also mentioned but the king overcomes that sorrow before dying as he realizes that his body is impeding him from going in the presence of Rāma. He dies therefore with a cry not of despair but of love for Rāma, which reaches a climax of ecstasy in these words:

> Crying, "Rāma, Rāma !" and again "Rāma !" and yet again, "Rāma, Rāma !" and "Rāma !" the king, parted from Raghubar, abandoned his body and entered the abodes of the gods.[139]

Tulsī Dās hastens to make it explicit that Daśaratha's death was glorious because he died "for the loss of Rāma" as he had lived "in the face of Rāma".[140]

Several other instances could be adduced to illustrate the same tendency; the most important among these will be dealt with in the last chapter of this study. The above makes it sufficiently clear that Tulsī Dās consistently added a special insistence on the ecstatic quality of loving devotion which gives to the *Rāmcaritmānas* a distinctive place in the *Rāmāyaṇic* tradition.

It must be added, however, that the mystical ecstasy portrayed in the *Rāmcaritmānas* has characteristics of its own. While

136. *V. R.*, II 64, vol. I, p. 322.
137. *Ibid.*
138. *A. R.*, II· *R.* 46-47.
139. *H. L. A. R.*, II. C. 155, p. 224.
140. *Ibid.*

it is more emotional than the type of devotion advocated in the *Bhagavad Gītā,* it is also more restrained than the devotion advocated in the *Bhāgavata Purāṇa.*

In the *Gītā,* which the Vedāntins recognize as authoritative, the ideal devotee is portrayed as self-controlled, free from joy and impatience, fear and excitement. He neither rejoices nor hates, neither grieves nor desires. He is alike to enemy and friend, to pleasure and pain.[141] He renounces all actions to God, is "intent on Him", and worships with complete discipline and meditation. Having restrained his senses he is equal minded and rejoices in the welfare of all beings.[142]

This type of devotion characterized by self-control, dispassion and indifference is obviously not the same as the devotion advocated in the *Rāmcaritmānas.* As we have seen, the latter emphasizes ecstatic emotions accompanied with abundant tears, horripilations, thrills of joy, overflowing rejoicings, dancing and singing. Devotees are often pictured as unable to contain their emotion, as overpowered by affection, as overwhelmed with delight, as wild with joy, as growing faint with love, as having lost all sense of direction. In this sense, therefore, Tulsī Dās clearly departs from Vedic orthodoxy.

On the other hand, Tulsī Dās avoids the display of unrestrained behaviour sometimes suggestive of eroticism, typified in the *lilās* of Kṛṣṇa as a child and as a lady charmer. For instance, while Tulsī Dās adopts from the *A. R.* the description of the child Rāma, obviously inspired from the description of the child Kṛṣṇa in the *Bhāgavata Purāṇa,* he avoids showing Rāma crying and being so mischievous that when he could not obtain immediately from his busy mother something to eat, he grew angry, "broke the vessels containing milk, curds and butter with stick and threw down the whole of it".[143] Such behaviour would be too undisciplined for Tulsī Dās.

As Rāma grows, he keeps in the *Rāmcaritmānas* the same distinctive blend of charming affection and dutiful restraint. Unlike Kṛṣṇa who provokes wherever he goes the most unbridled display of mystico-erotic passions, Rāma's passage arouses

141. *Bhagavad Gītā,* XII. 13-19.
142. *Ibid.,* XII. 1-8.
143. *A. R.,* I. 3. 53-55.

unambiguous love and pure joy.[144] The description of his first love follows the same tendency. The poet tells us that after seeing Sītā, Rāma "drank in the beauty of her face as the bee sips honey from the lotus". As he confides to his brother how much he thinks of Sītā to the point of being disturbed by his love, he immediately recalls his moal duties:

> Men of the house of Raghu never even in thought set feet upon the road of evil; that is their nature. So I fell in perfect confidence, for I have never even dreamed of looking on another's wife. Few in the world are those honourable men who turn not their back on the foe in battle nor even in thought let their eyes rest on another's wife nor send a beggar empty away.[145]

For Tulsī Dās love and duty go hand in hand. In the same vein, the descriptions of the beauty of Sītā avoid giving details suggestive of eroticism. Such details are uttered by Rāvaṇa in the Vālmīkian version of the story :

> How even, sharp and white are thy teeth, how large thy slightly reddened eyes with their dark pupils, how well proportioned and rounded are thy thighs and how charming thy legs, resembling the tapering trunk of an elephant ! How round and plump are thy cheeks, like unto the polished fruit of the Tala trees; how enchanting is thy bosom, decorated with pearls.[146]

In the parallel passage of the *A. R.*, Rāvaṇa tells Sītā that he burns with love for her and he invites her to abandon her life with a *muni* to enjoy the pleasures of life with him.[147] In this respect, Tulsī Dās simply says that Rāvaṇa "spoke of love".[148] The same tendency can be observed regarding Rāvaṇa's impu-

---

144. Except perhaps for one passage inspired from the *Bhāgavata Purāṇa*, where the on-looking damsels of Mithilā are shown gathered at the lattice-windows to gaze "with passion" on Rāma's graceful form. (*H. L. A. R.*, I. C. 217, p. 101.)

145. *H. L. A. R.*, I. C. 228, p. 105.

146. *V. R.*, III. 46. vol. II. p. 96.

147. *A. R.*, III. 7. 45-46.

148. *H. L. A. R.*, III. C. 26, p. 313.

dent words to Sītā in the groves of Laṅkā as they are reported in the *V. R.*[149] It can also be observed in Tulsī Dās' description of Sītā's beauty as she enters the garden of Mithilā, which shows more restraint in the *Rāmcaritmānas* than in the parallel passage of the *Prasannarāghava* from which it is inspired.

We may say, therefore, that while Tulsī Dās draws closer to antinomian theism insofar as he adopts the North Indian *sants*' tendency of stressing ecstatic mysticism, he nevertheless refuses in this respect to portray Rāma and his devotees on the Purāṇic model of Kṛṣṇa and the *gopis*. Here again, he stands between two "extremes".

We conclude this chapter by saying that Tulsī Dās' approach to love of God is distinctive from all the alternative with which he was confronted as he set out to write his *magnum opus*. Unlike Vālmīki, he considered Rāma as God, the Supreme Absolute. Unlike the author of the *Adhyātma Rāmāyaṇa* he considered loving devotion not as a mere means to knowledge but as the preeminent salvific path. Unlike the promoters of the unbridled mystico-erotic devotion, Tulsī Dās did not dissociate mystical ecstasy from moral duty. Unlike Kabīr, he acknowledged without hesitation Rāma, the son of Daśaratha, as the *avatāra* par excellence. In this sense, therefore, the distinctiveness of Tulsī Dās' spirituality allowed him to offer a new alternative to the religious aspirations of his time.

This chapter has attempted to show that love of God has emerged, with Tulsī Dās, as the *leitmotiv* of the *Rāmāyaṇa*. The previous chapter had studied to what extent social duty was an important theme in the *Rāmcaritmānas*. There remains to be seen, in the final chapter, how social duty and love of God are interrelated in Tulsī Dās' *magnum opus*.

---

149. *V. R.*, V. 20-22, vol. I. pp. 383-390; *H. L. A. R.*, V. C. 9, p. 343.

Chapter IX

The Ideal Devotee

THE historical part of this dissertation dealing with the immediate context of the *Rāmcaritmānas* has shown that the devotees of medieval North India often experienced a tension between their loving attachment to God and the traditional dictates of social and domestic duties. While this tension is absent in the *Vālmiki Rāmāyaṇa* and is rarely reflected in the *Adhyātma Rāmāyaṇa*,[1] it is given a place of importance in the *Rāmcaritmānas*.

In certain cases the tension between love of God and social duty as illustrated in the *Rāmcaritmānas*, does not entail serious repercussions. For instance, upon seeing Rāma as he happens to pass by, admirers are frequently shown temporarily abandoning their household duties to gaze at him.[2] They are also said to forget their own homes when they are with the Lord.[3] Such behaviour is obviously seen with admiration in the *Rāmcaritmānas*.

Again, whereas the previous versions of the story had shown Rāma refusing to allow Guha to follow him in the forest,[4] Tulsī Dās describes the situation in this way:

> Then the Lord bade Guha return home; but when he heard it, he grew pale and there was anguish in his heart. With folded hands Guha humbly said, "Hear my petition, O jewel of the house of Raghu ! I shall stay with my lord and show him the way and for a few

---

1. For instance, upon learning from Rāma that he must go to the forest, his mother Kausalyā contradicts her husband by commanding her son to remain home. However, she does give her consent immediately after hearing her son's long exposition on right knowledge, which suggests that her first reaction was much more due to ignorance than to genuine love. (*A. R.*, I. 4. 12).

2. *H. L. A. R.*, I. C. 217, p. 100; C. 237, p. 109: II. 109, p. 205; C. 110, p. 206; C. 114, p. 208; VII. C. 3, p. 443.

3. *Ibid.*, I. C. 301, p. 134; VII. C. 114, p. 428.

4. *V. R.*, II. 52, vol. I. p. 291; *A. R.*, 6. 24.

> days wait upon his feet; and in whatever forest you stay, Raghurāī, I shall fashion a hut of leaves; and after that I shall obey whatever command you give me.." When he perceived his heartfelt affection, Rāma took him with him and Guha was overjoyed.[5]

We know, however, that Guha was given this permission for only a short while as Rāma asked him to return home before leaving for the hermitage of the sage Vālmīki :

> Then Raghubīr earnestly desired his friend to return home, and in obedience to Rāma's command he went his way.[6]

The element of tension is also highlighted in the scene depicting the Lord's farewell to his fellow combatants after the return to Ayodhyā. Whereas in the *Adhyātma Rāmāyaṇa* Aṅgada was mentioned only casually among those who received a gift before leaving,[7] he is heard in the *Rāmcartimānas* beseeching Rāma to allow him to stay as his servant:

> Whither shall I go if I leave your lotus feet? Consider, O king, and tell me, what can I do at home if I part from my Lord?...Shelter your humble servant.. Command me not now, O Lord, to return to my home.[8]

In this case, however, Rāma maintains his decision:

> Raghupati...raised him and clasped him to his heart, and his lotus eyes were full of tears...With many words of consolation (he) bade him farewell.[9]

Tulsī Dās prolongs the scene with obvious delight as he portrays the ever hopeful Aṅgada reluctantly taking leave of Rāma:

---

5. *H. L. A. R.*, II, C. 104, p. 203.
6. *Ibid.*, II. D. 111, p. 207.
7. *A. R.*, VI. 14. 5; Aṅgada is not mentioned in the corresponding passage of the *Vālmīki Rāmāyaṇa*.
8. *H. L. A. R.*, VII. C. 16, p. 442.
9. *Ibid.*

> Aṅgada's heart overflowed with love as again and again he turned and looked back at Rāma, repeatedly prostrating himself and hoping that even then Rāma would bid him stay. He dwelt continually with anxious longing on the way Rāma looked and spoke and walked and on his smiling embraces; but when he saw it was the Lord's will, with many a humble prayer he laid upon his heart the lotus feet and set forth.[10]

Unlike Aṅgada, Hanumān obtains from Sugrīva, with the approval of Rāma, permission to stay ten more days in Ayodhyā.[11] Both of these scenes are new, and both illustrate a certain tension between love of God and social duty.

Other devotees, however, experience a tension much more dramatic than the examples just given. Such is the case of the citizens of Ayodhyā, Lakṣmaṇa, Sītā, Vibhīṣaṇa and Bharata, who are all exalted as exemplary devotees.[12] The following analyses will show how the tension is dealt with in these typical cases, and how it is finally resolved within the framework of orthodox theism.

The Citizens of Ayodhyā

In the *Vālmiki Rāmāyaṇa*, the point was made that the people of Ayodhyā forsook their duty to follow Rāma in the forest. They resolved to leave gardens, fields and houses in order to "follow the virtuous Rāma through good or evil fortune".[13] Rāma deplored that the people had followed him "without considering their homes".[14] After Rāma's departure from Ayodhyā "merchants no longer exhibited their wares nor did those in charge of the home attend to the cooking".[15] Even the "holy reading and sacred recitations" were interrupted![16]

---

10. *Ibid.*
11. *Ibid.*, VII. C. 17, p. 442.
12. This list is not meant to be exhaustive. Others, such as Janaka and especially Daśaratha, would be other obvious examples of this tension, but as they have been dealt with previously, they will not be reconsidered in this chapter.
13. *V. R.*, II. 33, vol. 1, p. 247.
14. *Ibid.*, II. 46, vol. I, p. 276.
15. *Ibid.*, II. 48, vol. I, p. 279.
16. *Ibid.*, II. 48, vol. I, p. 280.

The *Vālmiki Rāmāyaṇa* makes it clear that in the judgment of the citizens, the decision to send Rāma into exile was contrary to the law. Thus, Daśaratha, who is said to have spoken "under the influence of some evil spirit", is blamed for sending his son to the forest, an act reprehensible in itself "even if a son be bereft of every virtue".[17] The same accusation is repeated later when the grieving people insist that "in his folly, the king, for the destruction of the world of beings, has banished the faithful and virtuous Rāma to the forest".[18] They even look askance at Rāma who seems to condone a decision contrary to the law; thus, the Brahmins ask that Rāma be brought back to Ayodhyā "in accord with the law",[19] and the people express wonder that Rāma "who ever protected us, like a father the children born of his loins, how could he leave us in order to enter the forest?"[20]

The next significant element is that the main reason behind the people's behaviour and objections is not love of God[21] but insecurity engendered by the impending chaos which will invade Ayodhyā once Rāma is gone. Several times in this account, the point is made that Rāma is the protector of Ayodhyā, nay the protector of the whole world order. Thus, the women ask, "Where has he gone, he the protector of the whole world, now banished to the forest by his Sire, goaded on by Kaikeyī?"[22] Later, the reminder is again made that "through Kaikeyī's fault, all will be brought to ruin; the whole universe, without a support or a defender, will be destroyed."[23] The insecurity of the people is explicitly voiced by the women in the following passage:

> Who can enjoy this mournful place (Ayodhyā) filled with anxious people, who are despondent and appre-

---

17. *Ibid.*, II. 33, vol. I, p. 246.
18. *Ibid.*, II. 41, vol. I, p. 266.
19. *Ibid.*, II. 45, vol. I, p. 274.
20. *Ibid.*, II, 46, vol. I, p. 276.
21. We have already seen that Rāma was still considered as a human hero when Canto II, which we are now considering, was written.
22. *Ibid.*, II. 41, vol. I, p. 266.
23. *Ibid.*, II. 48, vol. I, p. 280.

> hensive? Since, by Kaikeyī's action, the king is without guidance, what further use is life to us?[24]

A striking contrast is painted by Vālmīki between Rāma and Kaikeyī, who respectively personify *dharma* and *adharma*. Thus, Ayodhyā is described as "the kingdom of Kaikeyī", where disorder reigns supreme.[25] Kaikeyī's fault is even seen as the cause of the world disorder; it is through her fault that "all will be brought to ruin", that "the whole universe will be destroyed".[26] Several descriptions are made of the city in chaos under the rule of Kaikeyī,[27] contrasting with the picture of the forest where Rāma now dwells.[28] It is clear that by abandoning Ayodhyā the people were convinced they were escaping a world where chaos (*adharma*) reigned supreme, in order to follow Rāma in the forest where order (*dharma*) was restored because of the king's securing presence:

> Let the forest where Rāghava (Rāma) is going be our city; and the city we are abandoning become a forest.[29]

Vālmīki and Tulsī Dās differ in two important respects. Whereas Vālmīki stresses insecurity as the people's motive for abandoning Ayodhyā, Tulsī Dās will emphasize love. Whereas Vālmīki shows that in the people's judgement the abandonment of Ayodhyā was not the abandonment of social duty as such, Tulsī Dās will admit overtly that by following Rāma the people were conscious of acting against their social duty.

The *Adhyātma Rāmāyaṇa* introduces a new dimension to the story by making superior knowledge the pole around which everything revolves. Bewildered by the king's decision to banish "his dear son of truthful resolve for the sake of a woman", they express their desire to follow Rāma in the forest:

> O men, it does not befit us to live here. We shall go to the forest this very day and accompany Rāma to

24. *Ibid.*, II. 48, vol. I, p. 279.
25. *Ibid.*, II. 49, vol. I, p. 280.
26. *Ibid.*
27. For instance, *Ibid.*, II. 33, vol. I, p. 247.
28. For instance, *Ibid.*, II, 48, vol. I, p. 279.
29. *Ibid.*, II. 33, vol. I, p. 247.

the place where he wishes to go with his brother and Sītā.[30]

Upon hearing this, a sage by the name of Vāmadeva immediately dissuades his grieving hearers from following Rāma by showing that just as in his previous incarnations the Supreme Viṣṇu assumed various forms to relieve humanity in distress, so "this very person has now incarnated as Rāma—the Lord of the world (in order to) kill Rāvaṇa and other demons by the millions".[31] He adds that Viṣṇu incarnated as Rāma after having been propitiated to that effect by Daśaratha.[32] The people should not, therefore, pass judgment on Daśaratha or Kaikeyī since they are "not at all the slightest agent(s) here";[33] it is the creator who deludes the world through the influence of *māyā*.[34] He concludes by inviting the people to consider all that is happening as the result of Viṣṇu's incarnation "for helping his devotees in their devotion, for the destruction of Rāvaṇa, for accomplishing the object of his father the king".[35] Vāmadeva's argument proves convincing for we are told that "on hearing all this and knowing Rāma to be the all pervading Hari, (the people) left off the doubt which like a knot had become fastened in their hearts and meditated upon Rāma".[36]

For the *Adhyātma Rāmāyaṇa*, then, the people's desire to leave Ayodhyā was reprehensible as their sorrow was rooted in ignorance of the true nature and purpose of Rāma's exile. Throughout the story, the reader will be reminded again that what is happening really belongs to the order of illusion, for ultimately all men are of the same changeless essence, and men of superior knowledge realize that at this level nothing really happens. Here again, the tension is not between social duty and love of God, but between social duty and sorrow rooted in ignorance.

With the above in mind, we now proceed to examine Tulsī Dās' approach to the subject at hand. Upon hearing that

---

30. *A. R.*, II. 5. 4-5.
31. *Ibid.*, II. 5. 20.
32. *Ibid.*, II. 5. 21-22.
33. *Ibid.*, II. 5. 24.
34. *Ibid.*, II. 5. 28.
35. *Ibid.*, II. 5. 29.
36. *Ibid.*, II. 5. 20.

Rāma left Ayodhyā for his sylvan exile, the citizens realize that without him life will become meaningless:

> Apart from Rāma, Lakṣmaṇa and Sītā there is no happiness. Where Rāma is, is all we need. What can we do in Avadh now (that) Raghubīr (Rāma) has gone?[37]

In adding that the people set out to join Rāma in exile, Tulsī Dās is careful to point out on the one hand that this entails an abandonment of their "happy homes", and on the other hand that the motivation behind this departure was "love to the lotus feet of Rāma".[38]

The next episode shows Rāma trying to persuade his followers to return, but to no avail:

> He repeatedly instructed them in their duty (*dharma*) but they loved (*prema*) him so much that they refused to turn back.[39]

Thus, the intensity of their love for Rāma impels the people to abandon their home thereby refusing to comply to their social duty.

Such behaviour is obviously edifying in the eyes of Tulsī Dās, who seldom misses an occasion to observe that when Rāma happens to pass by a village, people all "(forsake) their household duties and (come) running out to see him".[40] That the link between devotion and abandonment of one's duty is consciously set forth is illustrated by a passage immediately following the above episode where it is stated in a long hymn of praise that "he who abandons caste and brotherhood, wealth, *duty* (*dharma*) and position, dear kinsfolk and *happy home* (sadan sudhadai) and treasures in his soul yourself (i.e. Rāma) alone —in his heart Raghurāī, make your stay".[41]

It is to be noted, however, that Rāma persistently refuses to allow the citizens to stay with him in exile. His will in this

37. *H. L. A. R.*, II. C. 84, p. 195.
38. *Ibid.*, pp. 195-196.
39. *Ibid.*, C. 85, p. 196.
40. *Ibid.*, C. 114, p. 208.
41. *Ibid.*, C. 131, p. 214. (Emphasis is mine).

case is that the devotees remain lovingly attached to him, without forsaking their social and domestic duties.

From the above three-fold analysis, it may be concluded that Tulsī Dās is the first author who clearly sets forth the difficult tension between social duty and love of God. These two themes emerge clearly as the two predominant poles in the passages of the *Rāmcaritmānas* referred to above, and their centrality will be maintained in the other character portrayals about to be analyzed. It may also be concluded that Tulsī Dās' portrayal of the citizens of Ayodhyā reveals both his sympathy for the devotional trends of his time and his approval of the orthodox insistence on duty. Although he praises the devotees for desiring to follow Rāma above all else he nevertheless makes it clear that Rāma does not approve of their negligence towards social duty. The fact remains, however, that from the devotees' point of view, social duty constitutes an impediment to one's desire to follow Rāma more closely. Thus, after being told for the last time to return to Ayodhyā, the people still complain that "wealth and home and pleasure and parents and brothers...lend not cheerful aid to our quest for Rāma's feet".[42]

Lakṣmaṇa

In the *Vālmíki Rāmāyaṇa*, Lakṣmaṇa obtained Rāma's consent after proving that there could not be a real conflict between social duty and his desire to accompany Rāma since there was in fact no duty for him to stay in Ayodhyā. In answer to Rāma, who had pleaded with him to stay behind in order to protect their respective mothers, Lakṣmaṇa argued that his presence in Ayodhyā would not be necessary since Bharata was quite capable of looking after the queens, and Kausalyā was sufficiently well guarded:

> Undoubtedly on account of thine power, O Hero, Bharata will show himself to be full of deference and consideration for Kausalyā and Sumitrā. If, having been invested with supreme authority, the wretched Bharata, in his perversity and pride, does not protect

42. *Ibid.*, D. 185, p. 236.

> them, I shall destroy that wicked and cruel being without mercy, as also all his sympathizers and the Three Worlds themselves. But then the noble Kausalyā is well able to command countless warriors like myself, she who owns thousands of villages. My reverend mother also has innumerable defenders like unto me to protect her. Therefore take me with thee, *there is no wrong in this*! Thus my purpose will be accomplished and thine interests safeguarded.[43]

Once again, the tension between love of God and social duty is not envisaged by Vālmīki. By accompanying his brother, Lakṣmaṇa was not infringing upon any duty, and therefore he could say that "there (was) no wrong in this".

The case of Lakṣmaṇa is briefly dealt with in the *Adhyātma Rāmāyaṇa*. In asking Rāma permission to accompany him to the forest, Lakṣmaṇa presents two arguments. The first deals, once more, with knowledge. "Rāma, thou has dispelled from my mind the doubt that had lurked there".[44] This is obviously a reference to Rāma's long previous discourse[45] to Lakṣmaṇa, dealing with the importance of high knowledge (*jñāna*). It seems, therefore, that Lakṣmaṇa's first reason to follow Rāma is gratitude for the knowledge received. The second argument has to do with Lakṣmaṇa's emotional incapacity to suffer separation : "Do thou be gracious unto me, otherwise I shall give up my life breaths".[46] Although loving devotion is present in this episode, there is no allusion made to Lakṣmaṇa's duty to stay at Ayodhyā.

Once more, Tulsī Dās adopts a distinctive approach. Contrary to the citizens, Lakṣmaṇa hesitates before voicing to Rāma his desire to follow him:

> What will Raghunāth tell me to do? Will he make me stay at home or will he take me with him?[47]

---

43. *V. R.*, II. 31, vol. I, pp. 241-242.
44. *A. R.*, II. 4. 51.
45. *Ibid.*, II. 4. 18.
46. *Ibid.*, II. 4. 52.
47. *H. L. A. R.*, C. 70, p. 190.

While Rāma admires his brother's readiness to renounce "life and home and all", he clearly reminds him that his duty is to stay home and be a comfort to his parents :

> Those who willingly accept the advice of their mother or father or *guru* or lord have achieved their life's purpose...Remember this, my brother, and heed my counsel; do service to the feet of your father and mother...I go to the forest, and if I took you with me, Avadh would be left quite desolate and *guru*, father, mother, subjects and kinsfolk would all have to bear the burden of intolerable pain. Stay then, and be a comfort to them all; any other course, dear brother, would be very wrong...Stay, then, and *regard this as your duty* (*nīti*).[48]

Lakṣmaṇa's response clearly sets forth the tension between "the moral precepts of the scriptures" and the way of love :

> I am your slave (*dās*) and you my master (*svāmi*); if you desert me, what can I do? Master, you have given me good advice, but I cannot take it for I am a coward. Only great men, steadfast upholders of the right (*dharma*) are to follow the moral precepts of the scriptures but I am a mere child, nurtured in my lord's affection. I know no guru, father or mother save yourself—believe me, Lord, I speak in all sincerity ! All the love (*saneha*) in the world, all claims of kinship, all affection and confidence of which the *Vedas* themselves have spoken, all these that are mine are centered in yourself alone. Teach the precepts (*dharma*) of religion to one who aims at glory, dominion and high estate; but should he be abandoned, O ocean of grace, who is devoted (*rata*) in thought and word and deed to your feet?[49]

This argument wins over Rāma's heart and he allows his devoted brother to follow him. Although it is not made clear

48. *Ibid.*, D. 70—C. 72, pp. 190-191. (Emphasis is mine).
49. *Ibid.*, D. 71—C. 72, p. 191.

why Rāma gives Lakṣmaṇa his assent whereas he refused it to the citizens of Ayodhyā, it is important to note that Lakṣmaṇa is allowed to follow Rāma in spite of his duty, that of being a comfort to the people of Ayodhyā, and because of his loving devotion to his Lord.

Sītā

In the *Vālmiki Rāmāyaṇa*, Sītā is advised not to follow her husband mainly because of the dangers of forest dwelling.[50] There is no reference to any duty incumbent upon her to stay in Ayodhyā. Thus, not only Sītā does not transgress any duty by leaving Rāma, but she herself reminds the latter of her obligation to abide by the law according to which a wife must not be separated from her husband.[51]

The *Adhyātma Rāmāyaṇa* again deals briefly with the case of Sītā. Contrary to the previous case, Rāma objects to Sītā's desire to follow him, on the grounds that life in the forest is too rugged for a woman.[52] Sītā counters with a five-fold argument : (*i*) she is Rāma's lawful and faithful wife; (*ii*) no one can assail her in the company of Rāma; (*iii*) rather than cause Rāma trouble, she will be his helpmate; (*iv*) she must conform to the Rāmāyaṇic tradition: "I have heard divers *Rāmāyaṇas* from Brahmins; where and when did Rāma go to the forest without Sītā, do thou tell me?"[53] (*v*) should Rāma refuse, she would in his presence give up her life.[54]

Here again, as in the previous cases, there is no tension between love of God and social duty. Rather, Sītā seems to convince Rāma by providing that in fact her duty was to accompany her husband, and like Lakṣmaṇa in showing her emotional incapacity to bear separation from her husband.

In the *Rāmcaritmānas* Sītā's mother-in-law, Kausalyā, is the first to voice her opposition to letting her son's delicate wife accompany him to the forest. Her twofold argument is contained within this one verse:

---

50. *V. R.*, II. 28, vol. I, pp. 234-236.
51. *V. R.*, I. 32, vol. I, p. 71.
52. *A. R.*, II. 4. 63-69.
53. *Ibid.*, II. 4, 78.
54. *Ibid.*

> Hearken, my son; Sītā is very delicate, and dear to your father and mother and all the household.[55]

Kausalyā expands at length on the above, saying on the one hand that Sītā is "frightened at the sight of a monkey in a picture" and that on the other hand if she remains at home "she will be my strong support". Having said this, the Queen leaves the whole matter in her son's hands.

In support of his mother's views, Rāma speaks to his wife in a firm tone, adding to his mother's twofold argument the severe warning that the refusal to submit to one's duty eventually leads to all sorts of troubles:

> Listen, princess, to my advice, and think no other thoughts than these. If you desire your own good and mine, pay heed to what I say and stay at home. My will (*āyasu*) is this, that you should serve my mother... There is no other duty (*dharma*) higher than this—to do reverent service to the feet of your husband's parents ...It is for my mother's sake that I leave you here. The reward of submission to the duty (*dharma*) that both the guru and scripture impose can easily be won; Gāleva and king Nahuṣa had to endure all sorts of troubles because they were obstinate...If you are stubborn, wife, because you love me so, you will be sorry in the end. Impenetrable are the woods and very fearful; dreadful the heat and cold, the water and the wind... She who is too proud to pay heed to the advice of her guru or her husband, who sincerely wish her well, shall in the end have her fill of remorse, and of a surety her good shall turn to ill.[56]

Tulsī Dās' insistence on Sītā's *duty* to stay home and serve her husband's parents contrasts with the Vālmīkian account, where Sītā was advised not to follow her husband mainly because of the dangers of forest dwelling.[57] The difference helps bring out the intention of the two authors. For Vālmīki,

---

55. *H. L. A. R.*, II. C. 58, p. 185.
56. *Ibid.*, C. 51—D. 53, pp. 186-187.
57. See note 37 above.

one must under no circumstances transgress his duty; hence Sītā transgresses no duty by following her husband. For Tulsī Dās, Sītā has a definite duty to stay home; hence, by following her husband, she transgresses her social duty.

In her answer to Rāma, Sītā emphasizes clearly her main reason for persisting in her demand; she would be unable to bear the pain of separation (*viyoga duḥkha*):

> Mother, father, sisters and dear brothers, the loved ones of the family and the circle of friends, the mother and father of her lord, the guru, relatives and helpers, fair sons and noble who bring happiness, nay, all there is of love and kinship, O my husband, is to a wife without her lord a grief that burns even more fiercely than the sun... With you, my husband, all is happiness, if only I behold your face like the pure autumn moon... You have told me, my lord, of the many hardships in the forest; but, O lord of grace (*kṛpā*), all these together are nowise to be compared with separation (*viyoga*) from a husband... If you make me stay at Avadh till your return, know well that my life will not endure ![58]

In comparison with the previous accounts, the above shows a significant difference. In the *Vālmiki Rāmāyaṇa*, Sītā's argument hinged on the obligation to abide by the law according to which a wife must not be separated from her husband. The same point headed the list of Sītā a five-fold argument presented in the *Adhyātma Rāmāyaṇa*. In the *Rāmcaritmānas* Sītā's argument emphasizes the pain of separation caused by her love for her husband. She acknowledges her duty is as her husband and her mother-in-law have spelled it out. Yet her love makes separation impossible:

> The lord of my life has given me such advice (to stay home) as is *the very best for me*; but still I think and feel in my heart that there is no sorrow (*duḥkha*) in the world like *separation* from a husband.[59]

58. *H. L. A. R.*, II. C. 65—D. 66, p. 188.
59. *Ibid.*, II. C. 64, p. 188. (Emphasis is mine).

Rāma yields to his wife's persistent demand, realizing that if he compelled her to stay, she would die. Rather than admonishing her further for her "stubbornness", he consoles her with affectionate words:

> Grieve no more, but come with me to the forest; this is no time for sorrowing; make haste and prepare for our journey to the woods.[60]

Before leaving, Rāma and Sītā pay a farewell visit to King Daśaratha. The latter pleads with Sītā to stay home on the same twofold ground that the dangers of the forest are too great and that she should stay with her parents. Again, Sīta resists, not out of respect for the *law* of non-separation from her husband, but out of *devotion* to the feet of Rāma:

> But Sītā's soul was devoted to the feet of Rāma; home pleased her not, nor did the forest frighten her. All the rest then warned Sītā with tales of the manifold troubles to be encountered in the woods. The minister's wife and the prudent wife of the *guru* lovingly and tenderly said, "It was not you whom the king banished to the forest; do what your lord's parents and the guru advise". But Sītā would have none of this cautious advice, well-meant and soft and gentle though it was.[61]

The gravity of Sītā's duty to stay with her husband's parents is further brought home by a later episode showing Daśaratha sending Sumantra after the departed trio, instructing him to beg Sītā to come back, or else he would die:

> So try every means to bring her back; if she returns, my life will be preserved; if not the end of the matter will be my death.[62]

Upon hearing his father's message from the mouth of Sumantra, Rāma tries further to convince his wife to comply

60. *Ibid.*, C. 68, p. 189.
61. *Ibid.*, C. 78—D. 78, p. 193.
62. *Ibid.*, C. 82, p. 195.

to the King's desperate request. Again Sītā refuses out of love towards Rāma :

> My lord's father is the emperor...whose influence extends throughout the fourteen worlds...Such an one have I for a father-in-law, Avadh for my home, a beloved family and a mother-in-law who is to me a mother. Yet in none of these can I dream of finding happiness apart from the dust of Raghupati's lotus-feet.[63]

From the above, it is clear that in the *Rāmcaritmānas* Sītā is, like Lakṣmaṇa, allowed to follow Rāma in spite of her "highest duty" and because of her love to the Lord. The last member of Rāma's immediate family whose case must now be examined is Bharata. However, as the latter deserves special attention because of the importance Tulsī Dās attached to his dilemma, and because of the particular way in which it highlights the rôle of Rāma's will, the case of Vibhīṣaṇa will first be considered.

Vibhīṣaṇa

The case of Vibhīṣaṇa is particularly interesting as it shows a subject prefering Rāma to his own sovereign. In the *Vālmiki Rāmāyaṇa*, Vibhīṣaṇa's reasoning hinges on a two fold argument which is neither motivated by his love for the Lord nor by a desire to bring Rāvaṇa to worship Rāma.

The first argument is that Rāma is both innocent and invincible :

> He has subdued his passions and is invincible, yet you seek to defeat him...What wrong has the illustrious Rāma ever done to the King of the Titans that he should go to Janasthāna and bear away the consort of that great One?[64]

The second argument is that Rāvaṇa is both perverse and vulnerable :

---

63. *Ibid.*, C. 98, p. 201.
64. *V.R.*, VI. 9. vol. III, p. 22.

> You (Rāvaṇa's courtiers), the friends of this monarch (Rāvaṇa) who is dominated by passion, violent by nature and whose acts are thoughtless, flatter him, as though you were his foes... It is for you unitedly to rescue that monarch from the surging waters of the ocean Rāma.[65]

It is on the basis of the above arguments that Vibhīṣaṇa opposes Rāvaṇa, thus prompting the latter to repudiate him.

In the *Adhyātma Rāmāyaṇa,* Vibhīṣaṇa's argument focuses on Rāma's might against which Rāvaṇa's resistance would be futile. He explains to his obdurate brother that Rāma's strength is that of *kāla* (death) who has become incarnated "for the purpose of removing the load of the earth.[66] Since Rāvaṇa refuses to give up Sītā, he will surely be destroyed.[67] It is in order to avoid witnessing the inevitable destruction of Rāvaṇa and the other demons that Vibhīṣaṇa, who was repudiated by his brother for his severe warnings, goes "to the lotus feet of Rāma desirous of serving him with a mind overflowing with devoiton...[68] for the purpose of emancipation (*mokṣa*)".[69] After addressing Rāma as "lover of thy devotees (*bhakti*)",[70] Vibhīṣaṇa goes on to declare the well known verse where devotion (*bhakti*) is clearly described as but a means leading to knowledge (*jñāna*). Thus, even though love of God plays a certain rôle, it is subordinated to knowledge.

We now turn to the *Rāmcaritmānas.* Having been reassured by Hanumān as to Rāma's merciful affection towards all those who sincerely want to become his servants, Vibhīṣaṇa entreats his brother Rāvaṇa, the demon sovereign of Laṅkā, to give up his evil deeds and worship Rāma :

> Again and again I touch your feet and beseech you, O ten-headed, have done with pride, delusion and conceit, and worship the King of Kosala ![71]

65. *Ibid.*, VI. 14, vol. III, p. 33.
66. *A. R.*, VI. 2. 35.
67. *Ibid.*, VI. 2. 23.
68. *Ibid.*, VI. 2. 46.
69. *Ibid.*, VI. 3. 6.
70. *Ibid.*, VI. 3. 17.
71. *H. L. A. R.*, V. D. 39, p. 357.

Rāvaṇa retorts by accusing Vibhīṣaṇa of praising the enemy, but Vibhīṣaṇa insists that the demon king should return Sītā to Rāma. Again, Rāvaṇa accuses him of taking the enemy's part, and repudiates him by striking him violently. Vibhīṣaṇa justifies his brother's violence but condemns his resistance to Rāma :

> You have done well to strike me for you are as my father; but still, O King, it were well for you that you should worship Rāma.[72]

Having exhausted all means of converting his brother, Vibhīṣaṇa complies with the latter's command to leave Laṅkā, and seeks refuge with Rāma :

> Rāma is true to his purpose, the mighty Lord, and your court is doomed to death ! Now I go to seek refuge with Raghubīr; let no one blame me.[73]

In spite of his entourage's suspicion, Rāma welcomes the demon devotee, praising him for gathering up "all objects of natural affection—mother, father, brother, son and wife, wealth, home, friends and family—like strands, and making of them one strong rope to bind his soul to my (Rāma's) feet".[74]

Vibhīṣaṇa's expulsion, prompted by his love for Rāma, is not basically different from the point already made, namely that in certain cases one's ardent love of God justifies the abandoning of one's social situation in order to follow the Lord more closely. Tulsī Dās concludes by praising Rāma who "accepted Vibhīṣaṇa as his votary and made him his own, and all the monkeys were delighted with the Lord's loving-kindness".[75] From the above, it is clear that contrary to Vālmīki and the author of the *Adhyātma Rāmāyaṇa* Tulsī Dās' intention is to show that Vibhīṣaṇa's separation was due above all to the intensity of his love for Rāma.

---

72. *Ibid.*, C. 41, p. 357.
73. *Ibid.*, V. D. 41, p. 357.
74. *Ibid.*, V. C. 48, p. 360.
75. *Ibid.*, V. C. 50, p. 361.

Bharata

For *Vālmiki*, Bharata's refusal of the throne is not an act of disobedience to his social duty. On the contrary since no one but the eldest son can be made a king, Bharata considers it his duty to refuse the throne and bring back his brother from the forest:

> Early on the fourteenth day, those whose duty it was to proclaim the (new) king, coming together addressed Bharata, saying: "Our Venerable Master, Daśaratha, has ascended to heaven, after banishing thine elder brother, Rāma, to the forest with the valiant Lakṣmaṇa. From now on do thou be our king, lest some unanticipated hostile attack find the empire without defence..." Then, Bharata, faithful to his duty, having circumambulated the sacred urn, keeping it on his right, said to them all: "It has ever been the tradition in our family, that the throne *should belong to the eldest* son : therefore, you, who are righteous men, cannot proclaim me king.[76]

Thus, in the Vālmīkian account, Bharata's first reason for refusing to replace Rāma is that it would make of him a usurper of the crown. Moreover, the king's decision to send Rāma into exile is questionable as it is due to a loss of judgment[77] and to the enslavement of passion.[78]

The *Adhyātma Rāmāyaṇa* imitates the *Vālmiki Rāmāyaṇa* in showing that for Bharata nothing, not even his father's command, justifies replacing the older son on the throne :

> What have I to do with the kingdom, O Muni? Rāma is our Lord and king. We are verily his servants. Tomorrow morning we shall go to bring Rāma back forthwith.[79]

Upon meeting Rāma in the forest, Bharata begs him in the

76. *V. R.*, II. 79, vol. I, pp. 354-355. (Emphasis is mine)
77. *Ibid.*, II. 106, vol. I, p. 410.
78. *Ibid.*, II. 11, vol. I, p. 185.
79. *A. R.*, II. 8. 5-6.

name of social and domestic duty, to rule the kingdom of Ayodhyā:

> It is the duty of the Kṣatriya to protect the people. Having celebrated diverse sacrifices and begotten sons for the continuation of the race and placed thy son on the throne, thou shalt go to the forest.[80]

Moreover, Bharata argues that he is not bound by his father's command, for "if overpowered with love and of a foolish disposition, conquered by a woman and bereft of intellect the father says anything, it should not be taken as truth".[81] Rāma retorts that his father was only being true to his word; therefore, his command had to be obeyed. Bharata then vows to live in the forest and serve Rāma during his fourteen year exile.[82]

Vasiṣṭha then enters the scene and explains to Bharata that both he (Bharata) and Rāma should follow their father's order, which is but an element in the plan to kill Rāvaṇa.[83] The argument at last proves convincing and Bharata gladly returns to Ayodhyā to serve as regent. Thus, instead of conforming to the personal will of God, Bharata complies with a plan to kill the demons. Instead of returning to Ayodhyā prompted by his love of God, he does so after obtaining a deeper knowledge of the situation. It is because ignorance has been discarded that he is now able to overcome the dilemma.

Bharata's dilemma plays a central rôle in the *Rāmcaritmānas*. It is dealt with at length in the second half of the Ayodhyā-kāṇḍa.

Immediately after the death of his desperate father, Kaikeyī's son is sent for and told of the scheme to make him his father's successor on the throne of Ayodhyā. Contrary to his mother's expectations, Bharata refuses and resolves to convince Rāma to return as king of Ayodhyā.

After performing the elaborate cremation rites for his father, Bharata is summoned by the sage Vasiṣṭha along with ministers

---

80. *Ibid.*, II. 8. 23-24.
81. *Ibid.*, II. 8. 33.
82. *Ibid.*, II. 8. 39.
83. *Ibid.*, II. 8. 43-47.

and nobles, to discuss the problem of the royal succession. He is told solemnly, in front of all those present and with their approval, that he should act in obedience to the king's command :

> Act in obedience to the king's command (*rājāyasu*); the king has given you the throne and you must honour your father's word (*vacanu*)... The king valued his word, but not his life; honour, then, my son, your father's word; obey the king's command, for in obedience is your highest good... It is a Vedic rule—that he receives the royal dignities on whom his father confers them.[84]

After hearing Kausalyā's approval of Vasiṣṭha's declaration, Bharata replies by first acknowledging his duty to obey:

> The advice of a *guru*, a father, a mother, a master or a friend should be cheerfully followed, as for the best; and to ponder whether it be right or wrong *is to fail in duty* (*dharma*) and incur a load of guilt.[85]

Nonetheless, because he feels he is the cause of his brother's exile, because he knows his good lies in the service of Rāma, and because he knows that Rāma is more righteous than he is, he determines to leave the following morning to seek the rightful heir and ask him to return to his capital:

> My good lies in the *service of Rāma*, but my mother's crooked dealings have robbed me of this good; yet reflection has shown me that herein and nowhere else can I find happiness...I tell you truly...*a monarch must be righteous*...and I am the villainous *cause of all this trouble* and yet I sit here in my right senses to listen to all this talk.[86]

Bharata's argument meets with the approval of the assembly, whose appraisal, voiced by the great sage Bharadvāja, is based

84. *H. L. A. R.*, II. C. 175, p. 222.
85. *Ibid.*, II. C. 177, pp. 232-233. (Emphasis is mine)
86. *Ibid.*, II. C. 178—C. 179, p. 233. (Emphasis is mine)

on the principle that love of Rāma is the superior motivation. Action dictated by tradition is good. Action dictated by love of Rāma is better :

> Had you reigned, you would not have been at fault, and Rāma would have been well content to hear of it. Now, Bharata, you have acted very rightly...for devotion to Rāma's feet is the source of all good fortune in the world.[87]

This passage brings out clearly the central issue of Bharata's predicament, which does not consist in a conflict between right and wrong. Rather, Bharata must choose between a good (social duty) and a superior good (love of God). It is a question of priority.

After having reached Rāma's hermitage in the forest, Bharata is shown in anxiety over the result of his journey. From this point on, the will (*āyasu*) of Rāma will be emphasized in a special way. Thus, Bharata thinks that Rāma will certainly return if the *guru* bids him, "but then the sage will only bid Rāma do what he knows to be his will".[88]

The following morning, the sage Vasiṣṭha reminds Bharata in front of all the Brahmins, nobles, ministers and councillors, that "Brahmā, Hari, Hara, the moon, the sun and the guardians of the quarters, illusion, life, and fate and time in their entirety—the *will of Rāma rules them all.*"[89] Accordingly, he advises Bharata to keep in mind Rāma's will and pleasure when deciding upon a plan to bring about Rāma's coronation, warning him that "no one can possibly win to success who withstands Rāma".[90]

The following episode shows Bharata and Vasiṣṭha, together with the whole company, in the presence of Rāma. Both Rāma and Vasiṣṭha refuse each other's invitation to take a decision concerning the throne of Ayodhyā. Upon Vasiṣṭha's invitation, Bharata first apologizes to Rāma for being through the fault of Kaikeyī the cause of his exile. Rāma reassures his

87. *Ibid.*, II. D. 207, p. 245.
88. *Ibid.*, II. C. 253, p. 264.
89. *Ibid.*, II. C. 254, p. 264. (Emphasis is mine)
90. *Ibid.*, II. C. 256, p. 265.

brother, attributing the fault to *kāla* and not to Kaikeyī, still less to her innocent son. It is significant that the whole situation should be attributed to *kāla*, which is itself subordinated to Rāma's will.[91]

Thus rehabilitated and realizing that in obedience to Rāma's infinite will lies his highest good,[92] Bharata is now ready to submit his request to the Lord :

> It is to the interest of all that my Lord should return (to Ayodhyā), but to yield to your will is a thousand times better...Listen, divine Lord, to this my one petition, and then do as you think right. I have prepared and brought what is needed for your coronation; if you think proper, Lord, make use of it...O Lord of compassion, do whatever pleases you...By my Lord's feet I swear and affirm in all sincerity, that is the only plan that can bring blessing to the world. If my lord gladly and freely will give each one of us his commands, all will dutifully obey them and all this trouble and misunderstanding will be at an end.[93]

The arrival of King Janaka and his followers further delays Rāma's answer and brings more hesitation. Asked to give a decision over the whole matter, the King of Mithilā refuses; whereupon Bharata repeats his entreaty to Rāma that he make his will known. In his request, he admits his folly in annulling Rāma's word and his father's by assembling a host to seek Rāma, but sings the praises of the Lord for his pardon:

> Whether it was from grief or affection or childishness that I came hither despite your commands, you in your mercy have reckoned me your friend and taken it all in good part.[94]

Yielding to his brother's insistent request, Rāma finally agrees to make his will known. Without condemning Bharata

91. *Ibid.*, II. C. 254, p. 264.
92. *Ibid.*, II. C. 266, p. 269.
93. *Ibid.*, II. C. 268—D. 269, p. 270.
94. *Ibid.*, II. C. 200, p. 283.

for having, against his will, followed him to the forest, Rāma nevertheless maintains his decision that his father's command be respected:

> Obedience to the command of parents, guru or master upholds all righteousness, as Śeṣa upholds the world. Obey, then, this command, and cause me to obey it too, and so, dear brother, be the guardian of the Solar Race. Only obedience leads the aspirant to perfect success.[95]

The above illustrates clearly a fundamental aspect of Tulsī Dās' views on the relation between social duty and love of God. Fidelity to one's social duty is conducive to salvation insofar as it is an expression of Rāma's will which he reveals to his devotees. Before carrying out his father's order, Bharata has made sure that by doing so he would be serving the Lord. Only when communion with Rāma is restored, by the latter's rehabilitating grace, will he be able to accept his duty as provisional regent:

> Bharata was greatly comforted, for the kindness of his master had put to flight his pain and sense of guilt. His face was cheerful, his soul no more disconsolate; he seemed like a dumb man to whom Sarasvatī had granted the gift of speech. Again, doing loving obeisance, he folded his lotus hands and said, "Lord, I am as happy as if I were to journey with you; I have reaped the reward of my birth into this world. Now, gracious Lord, *whatever be your command*, that will I reverently and dutifully obey.[96]

Thus, we may say that whereas in the *Vālmiki Rāmāyaṇa* the conflict between written duty and unwritten duty (i.e. the king's will) was resolved in favour of the latter, in the *Rāmcaritmānas* the parallel problem revolves around two different poles; love of God and social duty, priority being given to the former. By means of a delicate substitution, Tulsī Dās has

95. *Ibid.*, II. C. 306, p. 286.
96. *Ibid.*, II. C. 307, p. 286. (Emphasis is mine)

been able to introduce love of God as the dominant theme of an Epic which was intended to promote duty, without however diminishing the dramatic intensity of the original story.

From the above it follows that for Tulsī Dās devotees are expected, in general, to fulfill their normal social and domestic duties. To that extent, we may say that love of God and social duty go hand in hand, and that Tulsī Dās has, as Macfie observved, linked morality and religion :

> He has made religious enthusiasm the inspiration of right living...Devotion to Rāma must produce good men.[97]

However, there are cases when love of God releases one from social duties. In other words, if in most cases love of God should be expressed in the fulfilment of one's social duty, in some other exceptional cases it could equally entail the immediate forsaking of such duty as the better way of expressing that same love of God. In both cases, the ultimate criterion of decision can only be Rāma's will.

In the *Vālmiki Rāmāyaṇa*, Bharata was faced with the dilemma of having to decide whether he should conform to his father's morally doubtful command, or also abide by the written law according to which the eldest son is the rightful heir. In the *Adhyātma Rāmāyaṇa*, the dilemma is solved by right knowledge ; in the *Rāmcaritmānas*, it is solved by loving submission to the will of Rāma. Tulsī Dās has summed it up admirably by describing Bharata as "the pattern of devotion (*saneha*), who would never even think of thwarting Rāma's will (*rājai*)".[98]

By loving Rāma in conformity with his will, the devotee rests assured that he is following the better way. Rāma, who is the quintessence of love and righteousness (the antithesis of Rāvaṇa), cannot command what is wrong. Unlike Kṛṣṇa, who is above all a teacher, Rāma is first and foremost a leader who has given convincing evidence of his moral integrity in the very exercise of his leadership. Because the devotee knows that Rāma's will is the expression of God's love and righteousness, he gladly conforms to his command in devotion and obedience.

97. Macfie, J. M. *The Rāmāyan of Tulsīdās,* pp. 186-187.
98. *H. L. A. R.*, II. C. 289—D. 289, p. 279.

Thus, Rāma's will becomes not only the ultimate criterion of decision but also the supreme principle of integration by which the tension between love of God and social duty is dissolved.

From the devotee's standpoint, however, Rāma's will remains mysterious, as the *Rāmcaritmānas* keeps reminding its listeners. Although inward detachment from worldly concerns is required of all those who seek salvation, the will of Rāma, like that of Kṛṣṇa in the *Bhagavad Gītā,* is that the devotee achieve this inward detachment without ceasing to perform his social and domestic duties. Such is the case of the citizens of Ayodhyā, Bharata and Hanumān. But it is also Rāma's will that concessions be made to certain devotees who out of sincere love and devotion ask deliverance from even the external observance of social and domestic duties in order to follow him more closely. Such is the case of Sītā, Lakṣmaṇa and Vibhīṣana.

The forsaking of one's ordinary social and domestic duties is not, therefore, a matter of individual initiative, let alone of selfish caprice; it is a decision the ultimate criterion of which can only be the will of God. Nor is the abandonment of one's ordinary duties to be interpreted as the abrogation of duty as such. For the devotee is now entrusted with a duty of another level, to serve the Lord through praise and worship.

Conclusion to Part III

The systematic comparison of the *Rāmcaritmānas* with the *Vālmīki Rāmāyaṇa* and the *Adhyātma Rāmāyaṇa* warrants the conclusion that on the question of the relation between love of God and social duty, Tulsī Dās consciously introduced new dimensions to the Rāmāyaṇic tradition of North India. While both the *Vālmīki Rāmāyaṇa* and the *Adhyātma Rāmāyaṇa* maintained the "middle stream", neither had considered love of God as the predominent "message" of the Rāma story. Neither had emphasized the tension between love of God and social duty. Neither had justified the desire of certain devotees to forsake social duty out of love for the Lord.

It also follows from the above analysis that the *Rāmcaritmānas* agrees with the *Bhagavad Gītā* in prefering loving devotion as the easiest way to God, in considering one's appointed duties as a way of conforming to God's will, and in proposing the obligation to fulfil one's social duties as the general rule. However, contrary to the *Bhagavad Gitā*, the *Rāmcaritmānas* provides justification for the exceptional devotees who, like Tulsī Dās himself, considered spending their whole time in worship and praise of the Lord as a special calling.

On the other hand, Tulsī Dās' closeness to the Purāṇic views on these same issues can now be affirmed on the basis of several elements common to both the *Bhāgavata Purāṇa* and the *Rāmcaritmānas.* Both consider love of God as the preeminent path leading to salvation. Both hold the view that the mere pursuit of social duty without love of God is meaningless. Both held that the intensity of one's devotion does not necessarily entail the abolition of one's social and domestic duties. Both consider the will of the Lord as the ultimate criterion of man's actions, with the consequence that one's social duty is to be observed not as an end in itself, but because it is the mysterious will of God. Both consider with admiration certain devotees who, moved by an intense devotion to the Lord, neglect their duty to follow Him. There can be little doubt that in his *rifacimento* of the *Rāmāyaṇa*, Tulsī Dās had in mind the *Bhāgavata Purāṇa*, and that the influence of the latter is reflected in his attempt to integrate love of God and social duty. It may be affirmed, therefore, that Tulsī Dās revived the middle stream by adopting a position better attuned to the temperament of his milieu, a position distinct not only from that of the *Vālmīki Rāmāyaṇa* but also from that of the *Bhagavad Gitā*, both of which in other times and for different purposes had also reaffirmed the middle stream of orthodox theism. The subordination of social duty to love of God had become a part of the Kṛṣṇaite doctrine with the spread of the *Bhāgavata Purāṇa*, and this doctrine had gained acceptance in North India, particularly under the influence of Vallabhācarya and Sūr Dās. Although there is no documentary evidence to prove it, it seems likely that the same doctrine had by the sixteenth century become accepted among Rāma devotees.

It has also been shown, however, that the emergence of love of God as the preeminent salvific path does not entail, in the *Rāmcaritmānas*, any inherent incompatibility with the obligation to perform one's social duties. In fact, most of the subjects of Ayodhyā are asked to perform their social duty at the cost of enduring physical separation from Rāma. Such emphasis on śāstric values, at a time when the influence of antinomian theism pervaded contemporary cultic trends, can be interpreted as the reaffirmation of the middle stream of orthodox theism. In a context where a growing number of devotees tended to oppose genuine love of God to the traditional paths expounded "in the *Vedas* and the *Purāṇas*", Tulsī Dās maintains that respect for the traditional is certification thst one's love of God is real and not illusory.

Thus, while he disagreed with the exclusivistic views of the "extreme" positions, namely Vedic orthodoxy and antinomian theism, Tulsī Dās' marked sympathy for the devotional trends of his time favoured a rapproachement with his antinomian hearers, and his insistence on the fulfilment of social and domestic duties favoured a similar rapproachement with his orthodox listeners. In this respect, one could, with few alterations, say of Tulsī Dās what R. S. D. Sen said of Vālmīki himself :

> The old traditions and tales may get a new and up-to-date interpretation at the hands of the epic master, or otherwise undergo some change or modification in his poem as far as details are concerned, but it is the old story told again with greater eloquence, force and refinement than ever being interpreted in the light of contemporary thought. The more the poet forgets himself and loses himself in the life of the nation, the wider will be the circle of his admirers and the more lasting his performance.[99]

Until the advent of Tulsī Dās, it seems that no complete version of the Rāmāyaṇa had attempted to apply to the Rāmāyaṇic tradition his approach to the problem of relating love of God and social duty. The fact that he was able to give enduring expression to such a change of approach without alienating himself from the admirers of the old Epic bears witness to his special aptitude for acclaiming renovation without destroying tradition, for promoting change without sacrificing continuity.

---

99. Sen, R. S. D. *Bengali Rāmāyaṇas*, p. 2.

CONCLUSION

The above study has sought to demonstrate that in rewriting the *Rāmāyaṇa* Tulsī Dās had foremost in his mind the important theme of the interaction of love of God and social duty. On the assumption that an awareness of the poet's heritage as a Hindu and the immediate context in which he lived is necessary for a proper understanding of his views, an effort was made to descry within the variegated and complex framework of the tradition a basis for establishing conventional types that might prove helpful in situating his distinctive position. It has been argued that the tradition offered sufficient evidence for the existence of three typical streams with differing emphases. Whereas the "central" stream sought to maintain a balance between the two "poles", namely love of God and social duty, the two "extreme" tendencies tended to emphasize either one or the other of these poles. It has been shown that while all three streams were still very much alive in medieval North India, the antinomian emphasis on love of God, with the accompanying tendency to minimize the important place traditionally assigned to prescribed social and domestic duties, was a rising trend whose influence was especially noticeable on the masses.

Again on the assumption that religious trends do not live in complete isolation from the socio-political context in which they develop, an attempt was made to describe that context, dominated by Akbar's vision of universality, as another possible source of menace which combined with the antinomian to undermine the tradition. After showing that orthodox milieux responded in a typical way to the situation by intensified commentarial activity on traditional regulations, it has been argued that Tulsī Dās chose to reaffirm the middle stream of orthodox theism by reviving the *Rāmāyaṇa*, which had nourished his personal piety since early infancy.

On the basis of a comparative study with the *Vālmiki Rāmāyaṇa* and the *Adhyātma Rāmāyaṇa*, accepted as Tulsī Dās' two most influential Rāmāyaṇic sources, it has been shown that while all three versions maintained the middle position, the predominance accorded to love of God in the *Rāmcaritmānas* constituted a distinctive feature of the latter. As a consequence, it was seen that the *Rāmcaritmānas* is closer not only to the spirit of the *Bhagavad Gītā* and the *Bhāgavata Purāṇa*, but also to the growing devotional trends of medieval North India, especially among the uneducated masses whom Tulsī Dās seemed to have particularly in mind when writing his *magnum opus*.

Finally, it was also shown that Tulsī Dās, like the *Gītā* and the *Bhāgavata Purāṇa* but unlike his Rāmāyaṇic sources, explicitly dealt with the tension between love of God and social duty, which was felt as a malaise shared by a rising number of contemporary devotees; that he resolved the tension by proposing the will of God as the ultimate criterion of decision and the supreme principle of integration; that by proposing the will of God as the ultimate criterion of decision he was able both to emphasize the obligation for most devotees to fulfill their social duties as prescribed by tradition and to justify the claim that in certain cases social duties might be forsaken by those who, like Tulsī Dās himself, considered spending their entire life in praise and worship of God as a special calling; that by proposing the will of God as the supreme principle of integration he suggested a way of dissolving the tension between love of God and social duty.

It is hoped that the present research will help to throw additional light on the relevance of the *Rāmcaritmānas* as an important 'event'', both religious and sociological, in the history of the Hindu tradition, particularly in its quest for a better integration of devotion and duty.

It is also hoped that this work will be a contribution to research in the field of comparative religion. The interaction of love of God and social duty is of vital importance to other religious traditions besides Hinduism. For instance, early Christianity had to take dramatic decisions *vis-à-vis* its Jewish or Roman entourage on the basis of its understanding of the relation between love of God and social duty. Likewise, as early as the third century after the death of Muhammad, tensions had developed between the *sufīs* and the guardians of Muslim orthodoxy, which led to the martyrdom of Hallāj (922 A.D.), accused of having denied the value of the pilgrimage at Mekka in virtue of his doctrine that love of God was an interior experience.[1] The examination of how in such traditions the central position was challenged and reaffirmed would bring into perspective the significance and distinctiveness of the tradition itself, and would provide an interesting basis of comparison between the different traditions.

The Hindu reader—particularly if he is a Rāma devotee—who looks upon the *Rāmcaritmānas* as the timeless expression of the essence of the tradition, may look askance at the concern of the present study for the distinctiveness and sociological relevance of Tulsī Dās' *magnum opus*. It is hoped that he will nevertheless not remain indifferent to the point of view of a Western "outsider", whose approach both in intent and methodology is perhaps different, but whose appreciation for the Hindu tradition has deepened as a result of his contacts with Tulsī Dās.

It has been recently held that the crisis which confronts Western man today is the result of his excessive fragmentation of law and religion.[2] Among Tulsī Dās' contemporary listeners, many had good reasons to pronounce a similar diagnosis on the society in which they lived. The *Rāmcaritmānas* came as a timely reminder that while mysticism must not be stifled as a special calling, a religious tradition also faces disintegration when social duty and love of God are divorced rather than properly integrated.

1. Gardet, L. *L'Islam*, pp. 230-234.
2. Berman, H. J., *op. cit.*, p. 183.

BIBLIOGRAPHY

I. Primary Works

(*Adbhuta Rāmāyaṇa*) In original Sanskrit. Bombay : Sri Venkatesvara Press, n.d.

Adhyātma Rāmāyaṇa

1. *Adhyātma Rāmāyaṇa.* Original Sanskrit with Hindi translation. Gorakhpur: Gitapress, 1932.
2. *The Adhyātma Rāmāyaṇa.* Translated by Rai Bahadur Lala Baij Nath. Allāhābād: Panini Office, 1913. Sacred Books of the Hindus: Extra volume 1.

(*Ālvār Hymns*) Hooper, J. S. M. *Hymns of the Āḷvārs*, with English translation. Calcutta: Association Press, 1929.

Bhagavad Gitā

1. Deutsch, E. *Bhagavad Gitā.* English translation with introduction. New York: Holt, Rinehart and Winston, 1968.
2. Edgerton, F. *The Bhagavad Gitā Translated and Interpreted.* New York: Harper and Row, 1964.
3. Zaehner, R. C. *The Bhagavad Gitā.* Original text with translation and commentary. London: Oxford University Press, 1969. First published by the Clarendon Press, 1969.
4. Sastry, A. M. *The Bhagavad Gitā, with the Commentary of Śri Śaṅkara.* Original text with translation. Madras: V. Ramaswamy Sastrulu & Sons, 1961. First published in 1897.

Bhāgavata Purāṇa

1. *Bhāgavata Purāṇa.* Translated into French by E. Burnouf. Paris: Imprimerie royale, 1840.
2. *Śrimad Bhāgavata Mahāpurāṇa.* Original text with translation by G. L. Goswami. 2 vols. Gorakhpur: Gita Press, 1971.

(*Harivaṁśa*) *Harivamsha.* Translated by M. N. Dutt. Calcutta: H.C. Dass Elysium Press.

(*Kabir*) *One Hundred Poems of Kabir.* Translated by R. Tagore. London: Macmillan, 1962.

(*Liṅgāyats*) Ramanujan, A. K. *Speaking of Śiva.* Translation of selected hymns of the Liṅgāyats with introduction. Baltimore: Penguin Books, 1973.

(*Mahābhārata*) *The Mahabharata of Krishna—Dwaipayana Vyasa.* Translated by P. C. Roy. Second edition. Calcutta: Oriental Publishing Co. n.d.

(*Manu Smṛti*) *The Laws of Manu.* Translated by G. Bühler New York: Dover Publications Inc., 1969. First published in 1886.

(*Mirā Bāi*) Pandey, S. M. & Zide, M. *Poems from Mirabai.* An unpublished anthology, Chicago: University of Chicago, 1964.

(*Sūr Dās*) Pandey, S. M. & Zide, M. *The Poems of Sūrdās.* An unpublished anthology. Chicago University of Chicago, 1964.

Tulsī Dās

1. (*Kavitāvalī*) Allchin, F. R. *Kavitāvalī.* Translation with introduction. New York: Barnes & Co., 1964.
2. Allchin, F. R. *Tulsī Dās Petition to Rām*, London: George Allen & Unwin Ltd., 1966.
3. (*Rāmcaritmānas*) *Sri Ramcharitamanas.* Original Hindi with translation. Gorakhpur: Gita Press, 1972. First published in 1968.
4. Atkins, A. G. *The Ramayana of Tulsidas.* Original text and translation. New Delhi: Hindustan Times, 1954.
5. Hill, W. D. P. *The Holy Lake of the Acts of Rāma.* English translation with introduction. Bombay: Oxford University Press, 1971. First published in 1952.
6. Growse, F. S. *The Rāmāyaṇa of Tulsī Dās.* English translation. Allahabad: Ram Narain Lal Beni Prasad, 1966. First published in 1877.
7. Vaudeville, C. *Le lac spiritual.* Translation into French of the *Ayodhyā Kāṇḍa* of the *Rāmcaritmānas.*

(*Upaniṣads*) Deussen, P. *Sechzig Upanishad's Des Veda.* Translation into German. Darmastadt: Wissenschaftliche Buchgesellschaft, 1963.

Vālmīki

1. *The Ramayana of Valmiki.* Translated by H. P. Shastri. 3 vols. London: Shantisadan, 1953-1959.
2. *Le Rāmāyaṇa de Vālmīki.* Translated into French by A. A. Roussel. Paris: Bibliotheque orientale, 1903.
3. *Das Rāmāyaṇa*, by H. Jacobi. Bonn: F. Cohen, 1893.

(*Vedānta Sūtra*) *The Vedānta-Sūtras.* Translated by G. Thibaut. Delhi: Motilal Banarsidass, 1967. First published in 1920. *The Sacred Books of the East.* Edited by M. Muller, vol. XXXIV.

(*Viṣṇu Purāṇa*) Translated by H. H. Wilson. Calcutta: Punthi Pustak, 1972.

(*Yoga Vāsiṣṭha Rāmāyaṇa*) *The Yoga-Vasistha Maharamayan.* Translated by V. L. Mitra. Calcutta: Bonnerjee and Co., 1891.

II. Secondary Works

Allan, J. and others. *The Cambridge Shorter History of India.* Delhi: S. Chand and Co., 1969. First published in 1934.

Babineau, E. "The Religious views of Tulsī Dās". M. A. dissertation, McMaster University, 1972.

Bagchi, P. C. "Studies on the *Adhyātma Rāmāyaṇa*", *Calcutta Sanskrit Series*, XI. Calcutta: Metropolitan Printing and Publishing House, 1935. vol. I, pp. 1-78.

Barth, A. "The Religions of India", *Chowkhamba Sanskrit Studies*, vol. XXV. Varanasi: Chowkhamba Sanskrit Series Office, 1963.

Basham, A. L. *The Wonder that was India.* London: Sidgwick and Jackson, 1954.

Berman, H. J. *The Interaction of Law and Religion.* London: S. C. M. Press Ltd., 1974.

Bhandarkar, R. G. *Vaiṣṇavism, Śaivism and Minor Religious Systems.* Strassburg: K. J. Trübner, 1913.

Bharadwaj, K. D. *Philosophy of Rāmānuja.* New Delhi: Sir Shankar Lall Charitable Trust Society, 1958.

Bharadwaj, R. "The Philosophy of Tulsī Dās". Ph. D. dissertation, University of Agra, 1954.

Bulcke, C. "The Genesis of the *Vālmiki Rāmāyaṇa* Recensions", *Journal of the Oriental Institute*, 1955.

Bulkey, K. *Rām Kathā.* Calcutta: Hindī Parisad Prakāsan, 1972. First published in 1950.

Carpenter, J. N. *The Theology of Tulsī Dās.* Edinburgh: 1930.

Carpenter, J. E. *The Theism in Mediaeval India.* London: Williams & N. 1921.

Chandra, K. R. *A Critical Study of Paumacariyaṁ.* Bihar: Research Institute of Prakrit, Jainology, Ahimsa, 1970.

Chatterjee, S. & Datta, D. *An Introduction to Indian Philosophy*, Calcutta, Calcutta University Press, 1968. First published in 1939.

Dasgupta, S. N. *Hindu Mysticism.* New York: Frederick Ungar Publishing Co., 1959. First published in 1927.

——— *A History of Indian Philosophy.* 5 vols. London: Cambridge University Press, 1966-1969. First published in 1922-1955.

Devaraja, N. K. *Hinduism and Christianity.* New York: Asia Publishing House, 1969.

Dhavamony, M. *Love of God According to Śaiva Siddhānta.* Oxford: Clarendon Press, 1971.

Farquhar, J. N, "The Historical Position of Rāmānanda", *Journal of the Asiatic Society*, LII, 1920.

——— "The Historical Position of Rāmānanda", *Journal of the Royal Asiatic Society*, LIV, 1922.

——— *An Outline of the Religious Literature of India.* Delhi: Motilal Banarsidass, 1967. First published in 1920.

Gardet, L. *L'Islam.* Paris: Desclée et Brouwer, 1967.

Ghosh, J. C. *Bengali Literature.* London: Oxford University Press, 1948.

Gonda, J. *Les religions de l'Inde.* 2 vols. Paris: Payot, 1962-1965.

Grierson, G. "Notes on Tulsī Dās", *Indian Antiquary*, XXII, 1893.

——— "On the Adbhuta Rāmāyaṇa", *Bulletin of the School of Oriental Studies*, 1926.

——— "Il Rāmcaritamānasa e il Rāmāyana by L. P. Tessitori", *Royal Asiatic Society of Great Britain and Ireland*, 1912.

Gupta, M. P. *Gosvāmi Tulsi Dās.* Allahabad: Udayana Publications, 1946.

Handoo, C. K. *Tulasī Dāsa, Poet, Saint and Philosopher of the Sixteenth Century.* New Delhi: Orient Longmans, 1964.

Hiriyanna, M. *Outlines of Indian Philosophy.* London: G. Allen and Unwin, 1970. First published in 1932.

Hopkins, E. W. *The Religions of India.* New Delhi: Munshiram Manoharlal, 1970. First published in 1885.

Hopkins, T. J. "The Social Teaching of the Bhāgavata Purāṇa", *Krishna : Myths, Rites and Attitudes.* Edited by M. Singer. Chicago: University of Chicago Press, 1966.

Jaiswal, S. *The Origin and Development of Vaiṣṇavism.* Delhi: Munshiram Manoharlal, 1967.

Jindal, K. B. *A History of Hindi Literature.* Allahabad: Kikad Mahal, 1955.

Kane, P. V. *History of Dharmaśāstra.* 5 vols. Poona: Bhandarkar Oriental Research Institute, 1930-1962.

Keay, F. E. *A History of Hindi Literature.* Calcutta: Y. M. C. A. Publishing House, 1960, First published in 1920.

Keith, A. B. *The Karma Mīmāṁsā.* London: Oxford University Press, 1921.

Khan, B. *The Concept of Dharma in Vālmiki Rāmāyaṇa.* Delhi: Munshiram Manoharlal, 1965.

Laoust, H. *Les Chismes dans l' Islam*, Paris: Payot 1965.

Lingat, R. *The Classical Law of India.* Translated from the French by J. D. M. Derrett. Berkeley: University of California Press, Ltd., 1973.

Macfie, J. M. *The Rāmāyaṇ of Tulsī Dās.* Edinburgh: T. & T. Clark, 1930.

Macnicol, N. *Indian Theism.* Oxford: Humphrey Milford, 1915.

Majumdar, R. C. & others. *An Advanced History of India.* New York: Macmillan and Co. Ltd., 1967. First published in 1946.

Majumdar, R. C., gen. ed. *The History and Culture of the Indian People.* 10 vols. Bombay: Bharatiya Vidya Bhavan, 1966. First published in 1957.

McLeod, W. H. *Guru Nānak and the Sikh Religion.* Oxford: Clarendon Press, 1968.

Misra, A. P. *The Development and Place of Bhakti in Śaṅkara Vedānta.* Allahabad: Allahabad University Press, 1967

Misra, J. *The Religious Poetry of Sūr Dās.* Patna: United Press, 1934.

Morgan, K., ed. *The Religion of the Hindus.* New York: Royal Press Co., 1953.

Naidu, S. S. R. *A Comparative Study of Kamba Ramayanam and Tulsi Ramayan.* Madras: The Manorama Press, 1971.

——————— "Kulashekara Alwar and Rashkhan", *Annals of Oriental Research* XIV 1958.

Narain, K. *An Outline of Madhva Philosophy.* Allahabad: Udayana Publications, 1962.

Rajagopalachari, C. *The Ideal Brother: Bharata.* Kanpur: National Book Depot, 1973.

Ram, S. "The Originality of the Ramayan of Tulsi Dasa", *Journal of the Royal Asiatic Society,* 1914.

Ranade, R. D. *Pathway to God in Hindi Literature.* Bombay: Bharatiya Vidya Bhavan, 1959.

——————— *Pathway to God in Marāthī Literature.* Bombay: Bharatiya Vidya Bhavan, 1961.

Rao, T. A. G. *Sir Subrahmanya Ayyar Lectures on the History of Śrī Vaiṣṇavas.* Madras: Superintendent, Government Press, 1923.

Regmi, A. S. S. *Prasannarāghava of Mahākavi Śrī Jayadeva.* Varanasi: Chowkhamba Vidyabhawan, 1963.

Rukmani, T. S. *A Critical Study of the Bhāgavata Purāṇa.* Varanasi: Chowkhamba Sanskrit Series Office, 1970.

Sakumār, M. E. *Mānas: Bālkāṇḍa Ke Srot.* Varanasi: Mayapati Press, 1957.

Sen, K. "The Medieval Mystics of North India", *The Cultural Heritage of India,* vol. 4. Edited by H. Bhattacharyya. Calcutta: Ramakrishna Institute of Culture, 1953.

Sen, R. S. D. *The Bengali Rāmāyaṇas.* Calcutta: University of Calcutta Press, 1920.

Shāstri, R. M. "The Authorship of the Adhyātmarāmāyaṇa", Ganganath Jha Research Institute, I. 1943.

Shastri, S. *Index Verborum to the Tulasī Rāmāyaṇa,* Lahore: Gita Press, 1937.

Sukla, R. C. *Gosvāmi Tulsī Dās.* Prayag: Indian Press, 1935.

Tara Chand. *Influence of Islam on Indian Culture.* Allahabad: Indian Press Private Ltd., 1963.

Tessitori, L. P. "Il Rāmacaritmānasa e il Rāmāyaṇa", Giornale della Societa Asiatica Italiana, 1911-1912.

Thakur, S. C. *Christian and Hindu Ethics.* London: George Allen & Unwin Ltd., 1969.

Trimingham, J. S. *The Sufi Orders in Islam.* London: Oxford University Press, 1971.

Tripathi, R. M. Tulsīdās aur unkī Kavitā, 2 Vols. Allahabad Hindi mandir, 1937.

Varadachari, K. C. *Ālvārs of South India.* Bombay: Bharatiya Vidya Bhavan. 1966.

Vaudeville, C. *Etude sur les sources et la composition du Rāmāyaṇa de Tulsī Dās*, Paris: Librarie d'Amerique et d'Orient, 1955.

———— "Kabīr and Interior Religion", *History of Religions,* 1964.

———— "Le problème de la composition du Rāmāyaṇa Hindi de Tulsī Dās", *Actes du XXIe Congrès des Orientalistes.* Paris: Librairie d'Amérique et d'Orient, 1935.

Westcott, G. H. *Kabīr and Kabīr Panth.* Calcutta: Susil Gupta, 1953.

Whaling, F. "The Growth of the Religous Significance of Rama in North-India". Ph. D. dissertation, Harvard University, 1973.

White, C. S. J. "Sufism in Medieval Hindi Literature", *History of Religions,* 1965.

Winternitz, M. *A History of Indian Literature.* 3 vols. Trans. Mrs. S. Ketkar. Calcutta: University of Calcutta Press, 1963.

Yocum, G. E. "Shrines, Shamanism, and Love Poetry: Elements of Popular Tamil Bhakti", *Journal of the American Academy of Religions,* 1973.

Zaehner, R. C. *Hindu and Muslim Mysticism.* New York : Schocken Books 1969. First published in 1960.

———— *Hinduism.* New York: Oxford University Press, 1966. First published in 1962.

INDEX